THE DOW THEORY

THE DOW THEORY

AN EXPLANATION OF ITS DEVELOPMENT
AND
AN ATTEMPT TO DEFINE ITS USEFULNESS
AS
AN AID IN SPECULATION

BY

ROBERT RHEA

FRASER PUBLISHING COMPANY
BURLINGTON, VERMONT

Originally published in 1932
by Barron's

Library of Congress Catalog Card Number: 93-72199
ISBN: 0-87034-110-3

Printed in the United States of America

FOREWORD

What has come to be spoken of as the Dow Theory is in effect the combined market wisdom of the late Charles H. Dow and William Peter Hamilton.

Dow was one of the founders of Dow, Jones & Co. who, beside conducting a nationwide financial news service, published *The Wall Street Journal*, of which he was the first editor.

Hamilton for twenty years until his death in 1929 brilliantly edited this newspaper.

Hamilton in his early years as a reporter had been closely associated with Dow.

It is hard to realize that little over thirty years ago, Dow was presenting a radically novel idea, when he showed that beneath the fluctuations in individual stocks there was present at all times a trend of the market as a whole. Until then people who thought about such matters at all generally assumed that fluctuations in the prices of stocks were individual and unrelated, dependent entirely on the circumstances of the particular company and the current attitude of those speculators who chose to trade in each particular stock.

Hamilton developed what he called the "implications" of Dow's theory. To Hamilton the stock market was a barometer of business, a barometer which also frequently forecast its own probable future trend. He developed a remarkable skill in reading this barometer, publishing his readings with his reasons therefor from time to time in *The Wall Street Journal* as editorials entitled "The Price Movement."

Dow's only expression of his theory of the market was in a number of editorials written in the period 1900–1902.

In 1922 Hamilton published *The Stock Market Barometer:*

a Study of its Forecast Value Based on Charles H. Dow's Theory of the Price Movement. This book and his numerous editorials are the source material for his theories.

Mr. Rhea after a careful study of Dow's and Hamilton's writings (there were 252 editorials to be analyzed) has performed a valuable service in presenting the Dow Theory in a form to serve the individual investor or speculator.

HUGH BANCROFT

Boston, May 21, 1932

PREFACE

I have no qualifications to justify my writing a book on the Dow theory except a firm conviction that it is the only reasonably sure method of forecasting stock market movements.

When a man is confined to bed for a great number of years as I have been, he has an opportunity seldom afforded others for study and private research, and unless he avails himself of some such privilege and considers it as offsetting the pleasures enjoyed by more fortunate men, he is apt to lose interest in life.

For more than ten years my business affairs have been conducted from my bed and my only recreation has been the study of business economics—particularly the trends of business and of the stock market; and either the Dow theory or just plain luck caused me to buy a few stocks at the proper time in 1921 and prevented my owning any during the final stages of the 1929 uprush. Moreover, either the Dow theory or luck caused me to carry a short account of small proportions during the two years after the crash. Thus my study has paid dividends, and if I can explain the theory as I try to practice it, others may be helped. I hope so, anyhow.

For the use of myself and a group of friends, all serious market students, I undertook the production of a set of charts of the Dow-Jones daily stock averages, with daily stock sales also shown. The production costs in small quantities proved to be excessive, with the result that a considerable number were printed and offered for sale. A satisfactory demand developed at once, with a few remarks on the introductory sheet concerning the Dow theory and the writings of the late William Peter Hamilton, editor of *The Wall Street Journal*, bringing in an unexpected by-product in the shape of more than five hundred letters of inquiry. So this book is being written as a means of offering those correspondents, many of whom I now call friends, the benefit of my study of the theory.

Critics will, no doubt, find many flaws in the phrasing and arrangement of the subject matter. Many will perhaps disagree with the conclusions drawn and definitions chosen, but it is possible that some of those reading this book with a sympathetic understanding of my limitations as a writer may find things in it that will prove helpful in their trading. It is for them that this study is written.

I wish to express here my appreciation to Mr. Hugh Bancroft for writing the foreword and for granting permission to use the Dow-Jones daily stock averages and material appearing editorially in those great financial publications which he heads, *The Wall Street Journal* and *Barron's*.

ROBERT RHEA

Colorado Springs, Colorado
March 10, 1932

CONTENTS

CHAPTER   PAGE

FOREWORD BY MR. HUGH BANCROFT vii

I   THE EVOLUTION OF A THEORY 1

II   THE DOW THEORY WHICH HAMILTON INTERPRETED . . 10

III   MANIPULATION 16

IV   THE AVERAGES DISCOUNT EVERYTHING 19

V   THE THEORY IS NOT INFALLIBLE 26

VI   DOW'S THREE MOVEMENTS 32

VII   PRIMARY MOVEMENTS 35

VIII   PRIMARY BEAR MARKETS 37

IX   PRIMARY BULL MARKETS 44

X   SECONDARY REACTIONS 52

XI   DAILY FLUCTUATIONS 67

XII   BOTH AVERAGES MUST CONFIRM 68

XIII   DETERMINING THE TREND 75

XIV   LINES 79

XV   THE RELATION OF VOLUME TO PRICE MOVEMENTS . . . 86

XVI   DOUBLE TOPS AND DOUBLE BOTTOMS 93

XVII   INDIVIDUAL STOCKS 96

XVIII   SPECULATION 98

XIX   STOCK MARKET PHILOSOPHY 105

APPENDIX 115
THE EDITORIALS OF WILLIAM PETER HAMILTON

CHAPTER I

THE EVOLUTION OF A THEORY

Charles H. Dow, founder of the country's greatest financial news agency—Dow, Jones & Company—was one of the owners of *The Wall Street Journal*, which he edited until his death in 1902. During the last few years of his life he wrote a few editorials dealing with stock speculation which are the only personal record we have of his observations of recurring characteristics of the stock market. These observations were based upon the movement of daily average prices of railroad and industrial stocks included in the Dow-Jones averages.[1]

Mr. Dow did not designate his stock market observations as the Dow theory. That was done by his friend S. A. Nelson, who wrote *The A B C of Stock Speculation* in 1902. It was he who first attempted to explain Dow's methods in a practical manner.

Many successful men today believe the implications of the daily movement of the Dow-Jones rail and industrial averages to be the most dependable indicator of both price and business trends yet devised, and they usually refer to inferences drawn from the movement of the averages as "the Dow theory."

Until 1897 only one stock average had been kept by Dow, Jones & Co., but at the beginning of that year separate averages were started for railroad and industrial stocks. During the time Dow wrote, he had at the most only a five-year record of both averages to examine, and it is indeed remarkable that he was able, in so short a time, to establish the fundamentals of such a useful theory of price movements based on the dual averages. It is true that some

[1] The Dow-Jones public utility average was not started until late in 1929. It was carried back to the beginning of that year.

of his conclusions later proved to be erroneous, but the fundamentals have proved sound when tested against market movements for 28 years after his death.

William Peter Hamilton, who served under Dow, carried on the study and interpretation of the theory through occasional editorial forecasts. His observations and predictions generally proved to be accurate, with the result that they soon became one of the most popular features of *The Wall Street Journal* until his death in December, 1929.

In 1922 Hamilton wrote *The Stock Market Barometer*,[2] a book in which he explained the Dow theory in more detail than was possible within the limitations of editorial comment. This book, which achieved a genuine success, is now out of print. It provoked a veritable storm of controversy, repercussions of which may yet be occasionally noticed in financial columns. One of the primary reasons for this controversy is the general unwillingness of those who claim ability to forecast stock market trends by means of elaborate statistical research to concede the usefulness of the Dow theory. These critics are usually entirely ignorant of the principles underlying this valuable and workable theory.

The development of the automobile and of the Dow theory since 1902 have certain similarities. To the automobile of 1902, our engineers later added improved motive power, demountable rims, electric lights, self-starters, and other needed refinements which eventually gave us a reliable and convenient means of transportation. In a similar manner, Hamilton tested and improved the Dow theory between 1902 and 1929. As the record of the averages unfolded with the years, he gave us a well-defined and exceptionally reliable method of forecasting the trends of both stock prices and business activity.

It is no great job to put together a mass of figures derived from past business records and to make an index which is supposed to

---

[2] English economists were among the first to give fitting recognition to the value of *The Stock Market Barometer* as a valuable contribution to the subject of stock market speculation, as may be gathered from the election of Hamilton to fellowship in the Royal Statistical Society in 1923.

forecast trends reliably. The trouble with all such methods is that they deal with the past and, of necessity, must, to a great extent, be based on the assumption that history will repeat itself. Then, too, before the value of such an index can be accepted, it must be tested for a great many years against actual developments. Dow's theory has survived just such a test.

The Dow theory provides a method of forecasting that is self-adjusting, and its effectiveness has been proved, year by year, for more than three decades. The proof lies in Hamilton's successful application of the theory through those years, the accuracy of whose forecasts made editorially in *The Wall Street Journal* cannot be questioned. It is a pity that his modesty never permitted him to evidence the soundness of his application of Dow's theory by republishing as a group his numerous clearly-reasoned forecasts.

This book represents an effort to reduce the Dow theory to a manual for those wishing to use it as an aid in speculation, only a relatively small part of the subject matter represents original work or the ideas of the author. Everything written by Hamilton concerning the implications of the averages was collected and studied carefully. However, insofar as possible his phrasing is used, so that this may properly be considered as a scrap book of pertinent comment from his pen classified and arranged for the convenience of students of the averages. Unless otherwise indicated, all quotations are from Hamilton's writing in *The Wall Street Journal* or *Barron's*. The somewhat voluminous appendix presents the full text of every editorial dealing with the price movement appearing from 1903 through 1929. Any reader questioning the writer's interpretations of Hamilton's comment, therefore, may read the text of the original comment and draw his own conclusions.

Students of the theory can attain a certain proficiency in forecasting the movements of the averages by careful study of each article quoted in the appendix. However, before attempting such a study, one should procure the tabulated prices of the Dow-

Jones averages.[3] In addition, it is essential that the student be provided with properly-drawn charts of the daily price movements of the railroad and industrial stock averages, the usefulness of which is enhanced if the volume of trading is also shown.[4] Hamilton repeatedly made use of market activity when summing up evidence and arriving at conclusions. Parenthetically, it may be added that the student who draws his own charts is afforded an excellent opportunity to study price movement as the picture unfolds.

Students wishing to derive the greatest benefit from material presented in the appendix should first read carefully the entire collection of writings. This will disclose the fact that during the first 10 years Hamilton had not developed the lucidity of expression that characterized his later work. He always stated his case briefly and concisely, perhaps too much so in the earlier years. In later years, he apparently realized that students of the Dow theory desired more detailed explanations. In any event, his deductions were more fully and clearly reasoned during the last 20 years of his editorship. For this reason, the student may find it desirable to begin his examination of the forecasts with the year 1910 and work forward, afterwards going through the earlier material if he so desires. When one has obtained a fair working knowledge of the theory, he may make a more detailed study which can be converted into speculative profits.

Years ago we were given a problem in arithmetic and, after the answer had been determined, were allowed to verify the accuracy of our calculations by looking up the answer at the back of the book. This method is sound when learning to master the implications of the averages. It is suggested that a date be chosen from the forecasts contained in the appendix for the beginning of the study, that the corresponding date be located on the charts, and that the charted data following that date be covered so that

---

[3] *The Dow-Jones Averages and The Barron's Averages;* Barron's Book Department, Boston.

[4] RHEA—*Dow-Jones Daily Stock Averages and Sales;* Barron's Book Department, Boston.

the exposed portion of the chart will represent the picture which might have been before Hamilton on the day the forecast was made. Then the chart should be studied and a forecast, with the reasons for it, jotted down. This can later be compared with Hamilton's comment and the effectiveness of both forecasts be visualized.

The usefulness of the Dow theory improves with age. Certainly a more comprehensive study of the subject is possible with a 35-year record before us than when Dow worked with the figures of only a few years, while those who use it 20 years from now will have a greater advantage than we now enjoy. Dow always refrained from making definite forecasts, his caution probably being due to the fact that he had but little proof of the soundness of his theory. As the years passed by, Hamilton's precision in its use constantly improved, although he did make a bad mistake in 1926, as will be explained later. However, this mistake really rounds out the general usefulness of the theory, in that proof was thereby provided that it is not infallible, a fact often stressed by Hamilton during the years when he was scoring a bull's eye with every forecast.

Dow's theory, fundamentally simple and wholly empirical, was entirely based on his study of the Dow-Jones averages which he originated. At no time did he attempt to define his theory as such, being content to present his observations in a series of editorials in *The Wall Street Journal* during 1900–1902 on the subject of stock speculation. Using those articles as a basis, Hamilton later proceeded to apply Dow's observations in a practical manner by making forecasts of stock market movements, with the result that after a few years his editorial writings were utilized both as a reliable guide for future market trends and as a text which enabled many of his readers to become proficient in the art of understanding the implications of the averages according to the Dow theory.

Because Dow wrote so little on the subject and Hamilton so much, and because Dow never dared use his observations to the extent of making a definite editorial forecast of stock market trends, whereas Hamilton did have the courage to attempt it, no examination of Dow's work is attempted here. It should always be remembered, however, that the fundamentals of the theory upon which Hamilton worked were developed by his predecessor, a fact he never allowed his readers to forget. Such a phrase as, "On the late Charles H. Dow's well-known method of reading the stock market movement from the Dow-Jones average—" frequently prefaced Hamilton's forecasts.

One should also remember that *The Wall Street Journal* has never descended to the level of becoming a tipster's sheet, that Hamilton was a great editor rather than a professional "Investment Counselor," and that he made no attempt to write a forecast every time he saw a clear implication of future trend in the averages. Moreover, his active mind was, of course, often on other timely subjects, with the result that he had neither the time nor the inclination to follow the movements of the averages with unvarying attention. Moreover, we have certain knowledge that at times he became disgusted at the use made of his forecasts by unscrupulous advisory services, with the result that for long periods he refused to write his opinion on the inferences to be drawn from the price movement.

In order that students may understand how completely Hamilton believed in the effectiveness of the averages as a forecasting medium, although recognizing the obvious limitations of the theory, a number of selections from his editorials over a 25-year period are quoted below:

"Study of the averages is based on 'Dow's theory,' propounded by the late Charles H. Dow, the founder of this newspaper. The books which published that theory seem to be out of print; but briefly it was this: Simultaneously in any broad stock market there are—acting, reacting and interacting—three definite movements. That on the surface is the daily fluctuation; the second is a briefer movement typified by the reaction in a bull market or the sharp recovery in a bear market which has been oversold; the third and main movement is that which decides the trend over a period of many months, or the main true movement of the market.

"It is with these facts well in mind that the student approaches analysis of the averages, premising that broad conclusions are valueless on the daily fluctuation and deceptive on the secondary movement, but possible and helpful on the main movement of the market, and of real barometrical value to general business. It may be said as a matter of record that studies in the price movement, with these facts well in view, published in these columns from time to time and especially in the years before the war, were far oftener right than wrong, and were wrong for the most part when they departed from Dow's sound and scientific rule." (Aug. 8, 1919)

"A sympathetic reader asks if the method of estimating the trend of the stock market by analysis of previous movements as shown in the industrial and railroad price averages is not empirical? Of course it is, but not entirely so, and the method is far removed from quackery. Any conclusion reached from a number of recorded instances is open to that charge. It depends on the scientific accuracy of the method of indication.

"It admits highly human and obvious limitations. But such as it is, it can honestly claim that it has a quality of forecast which no other business record yet devised has even closely approached." (*The Stock Market Barometer*)

"A number of students demand from . . . Dow's theory of the triple market movement, a degree of mathematical and even pictorial accuracy which it neither possesses nor needs." (Oct. 18, 1922)

"They can, of course, find plenty of movements, especially secondary ones, which they think the barometer failed to forecast. What of it? An instrument of any such accuracy as they demand would be a human impossibility, and indeed, I do not think that any of us in the present stage of man's moral development, could be trusted with such a certainty. One way to bring about a world smash would be for some thoroughly well-intentioned altruist to take the management of the planet out of the hands of its Creator.

"The stock market barometer is not perfect, or to put it more correctly, the adolescent science of reading it is far from having attained perfection.

"The data of the Weather Bureau are of the highest value, but they do not pretend to predict a dry summer or a mild winter. You and I know from personal experience that the weather in New York is likely to be cold in January and hot in July.

"The law that governs the movement of the stock market, . . . would be equally true of the London Stock Exchange, the Paris Bourse, or even the Berlin Boerse. But we may go further. The principles underlying that law would be true if those Stock Exchanges and ours were wiped out of existence. They would come into operation again, automatically and inevitably, with the re-establishment of a free market in securities in any great Capital. So far as I know, there has not been a record corresponding to the Dow-Jones averages kept by any of the London financial publications. But the stock market there would have the same quality of forecast which the New York market has if similar data were available.

"The theory makes little of cycles or systems, interesting and even well-grounded inferences or common fads. It uses them all so far as they are useful, together with every other scrap of information it is possible to collect. The market movement reflects all the real knowledge available.

". . . the pragmatic basis for the theory, a working hypothesis if nothing more, lies in human nature itself. Prosperity will drive men to excess, and repentance for the consequence of those excesses will produce a corresponding depression. Following the dark hour of absolute panic, labor will be thankful for what it can get and will save slowly out of smaller wages, while capital will be content with small profits and quick returns.

"When, in the United States Senate, the late Senator Spooner, reading an editorial of *The Wall Street Journal*, said, 'Listen to the bloodless verdict of the market place,' he saw the merciless accuracy of that verdict; because it is, and necessarily must be, based upon all the evidence, even when given by unconscious and unwilling witnesses." (*The Stock Market Barometer*)

CHAPTER II

THE DOW THEORY WHICH HAMILTON INTERPRETED

To a stock trader, a knowledge of the past movements of the Dow-Jones averages is as necessary as a record of the tides is to a ship's captain, but the record of the averages over 35 years is difficult to study until reduced to a graphic picture. Changing the simile slightly, a trader's charts of the daily movements of the averages are as useful to him as are navigation charts to a mariner. But the mariner, also, finds a barometer a necessary part of the equipment of a safe navigator. A barometer able to forecast fair, foul, and unchanged market weather was given the trader by Charles H. Dow and William Peter Hamilton. This barometer is called the Dow theory, and an ability to read it correctly is as vital to a trader as the understanding of his barometer is to the ship's captain.

The closing average prices of the Dow-Jones industrial and railroad stocks, together with the daily total of transactions in the New York Stock Exchange, are the only material needed by students desiring to utilize the Dow theory as an aid in forecasting the trend of stock prices and business.

In this chapter, the writer's definitions of terminology and of the theory will be given, classified as to subject matter in a manner that has proved helpful. As neither Dow nor Hamilton ever attempted an exact definition, it is perhaps presumptuous to do so now. The writer has undertaken the task only after more than 10 years of actual trading based upon the implications of the averages, a study of the writings of both Dow and Hamilton extending over many years, and an exchange of opinions and experiences with students of the theory in many parts of the country, many of whom are successful traders. In addition to this, literally hundreds of charts were drawn for the purpose of studying the movements of the averages. Every statement made by Hamilton concerning the price movement was tested against the charted averages. In fact, for more than 10 years a consistent effort has been made to sift out and arrange the data in order to define the Dow theory, not as Dow left it to us at the time of his death in 1902, but as the idea developed from Hamilton's application and refinement of that theory.

Since exceptions can be found to every part of the defined theory, there is no better way in which the student can become familiar with the subject than to study the charted averages and locate the exceptions, the times when he might have been misled in his market operations by assuming the theory to be infallible. Such study, over a reasonable period of time, is certain to develop his ability in the art of reading the averages, and to a trader such ability means financial gain, although mistakes will be made, because reading the averages is an empirical science. It somewhat resembles surgery, and a good surgeon is sometimes wrong in his diagnosis.

Perhaps the greatest danger in the application of the theory to speculation in stocks lies in the fact that the neophyte, having beginner's luck, may arrive at correct conclusions several times and then, thinking that he has discovered a sure method of beating the market, read his signals wrong. Or, what is even worse, he may be right at the wrong time. In either of these events, the Dow theory is usually blamed, when the fault lies with the trader's impatience.

Each portion of the theory and its terminology, as here defined, will be discussed in detail in subsequent chapters. If the subject matter proves perplexing, the reader should realize that the Dow theory, like algebra, is not readily understood after a mere casual reading of a text book on the subject.

The successful use of the theory as an aid in stock speculation must be predicated upon the acceptance, without any reservations whatsoever, of a few hypotheses, viz:

Manipulation:—*Manipulation is possible in the day to day movement of the averages, and secondary reactions are subject to such an influence to a more limited degree, but the primary trend can never be manipulated.*

The Averages Discount Everything:—*The fluctuations of the daily closing prices of the Dow-Jones rail and industrial averages afford a composite index of all the hopes, disappointments, and knowledge of everyone who knows anything of financial matters, and for that reason the effects of coming events (excluding acts of God) are always properly anticipated in their movement. The averages quickly appraise such calamities as fires and earthquakes.*

The Theory Is Not Infallible:—*The Dow theory is not an infallible system for beating the market. Its successful use as an aid in speculation requires serious study, and the summing up of evidence must be impartial. The wish must never be allowed to father the thought.*

If these essential elements, around which the theory has been built up, cannot be accepted as axioms, then further study of the subject will prove to be confusing, if not actually misleading.

Reducing the theory to definite *theorems* proved to be a difficult task, but this was done in 1925. Subsequent study, together with application of these theorems to trading operations, has not indicated the advisability of altering them now.

Dow's Three Movements:—*There are three movements of the averages, all of which may be in progress at one and the same time. The first, and most important, is the primary trend: the broad upward or downward movements known as bull or bear markets, which may be of several years duration. The second, and most deceptive movement, is the secondary reaction: an important decline in a primary bull market or a rally in a primary bear* *market. These reactions usually last from three weeks to as many months. The third, and usually unimportant, movement is the daily fluctuation.*

Primary Movements:—*The primary movement is the broad basic trend generally known as a bull or bear market extending over periods which have varied from less than a year to several years. The correct determination of the direction of this movement is the most important factor in successful speculation. There is no known method of forecasting the extent or duration of a primary movement.*

Primary Bear Markets:—*A primary bear market is the long downward movement interrupted by important rallies. It is caused by various economic ills and does not terminate until stock prices have thoroughly discounted the worst that is apt to occur. There are three principal phases of a bear market: the first represents the abandonment of the hopes upon which stocks were purchased at inflated prices; the second reflects selling due to decreased business and earnings, and the third is caused by distress selling of sound securities, regardless of their value, by those who must find a cash market for at least a portion of their assets.*

Primary Bull Markets:—*A primary bull market is a broad upward movement, interrupted by secondary reactions, and averaging longer than two years. During this time, stock prices advance because of a demand created by both investment and speculative buying caused by improving business conditions and increased speculative activity. There are three phases of a bull period: the first is represented by reviving confidence in the future of business; the second is the response of stock prices to the known improvement in corporation earnings, and the third is the period when speculation is rampant and inflation apparent—a period when stocks are advanced on hopes and expectations.*

Secondary Reactions:—*For the purpose of this discussion, a secondary reaction is considered to be an important decline in a* *bull market or advance in a bear market, usually lasting from three weeks to as many months, during which intervals the price movement generally retraces from 33 per cent to 66 per cent of the primary price change since the termination of the last preceding secondary reaction. These reactions are frequently erroneously assumed to represent a change of primary trend, because obviously the first stage of a bull market must always coincide with a movement which might have proved to have been merely a secondary reaction in a bear market, the contra being true after the peak has been attained in a bull market.*

Daily Fluctuations:—*Inferences drawn from one day's movement of the averages are almost certain to be misleading and are of but little value except when "lines" are being formed. The day to day movement must be recorded and studied, however, because a series of charted daily movements always eventually develops into a pattern easily recognized as having a forecasting value.*

Both Averages Must Confirm:—*The movements of both the railroad and industrial stock averages should always be considered together. The movement of one price average must be confirmed by the other before reliable inferences may be drawn. Conclusions based upon the movement of one average, unconfirmed by the other, are almost certain to prove misleading.*

Determining the Trend:—*Successive rallies penetrating preceding high points, with ensuing declines terminating above preceding low points, offer a bullish indication. Conversely, failure of the rallies to penetrate previous high points, with ensuing declines carrying below former low points, is bearish. Inferences so drawn are useful in appraising secondary reactions and are of major importance in forecasting the resumption, continuation, or change of the primary trend. For the purpose of this discussion, a rally or a decline is defined as one or more daily movements resulting in a net reversal of direction exceeding three per cent of the price of either average. Such movements have but little au-*

thority unless confirmed in direction by both averages, but the confirmation need not occur on the same day.

Lines:—*A "line" is a price movement extending two to three weeks or longer, during which period the price variation of both averages move within a range of approximately five per cent. Such a movement indicates either accumulation or distribution. Simultaneous advances above the limits of the "line" indicate accumulation and predict higher prices; conversely, simultaneous declines below the "line" imply distribution and lower prices are sure to follow. Conclusions drawn from the movement of one average, not confirmed by the other, generally prove to be incorrect.*

The Relation of Volume to Price Movements:—*A market which has been overbought becomes dull on rallies and develops activity on declines; conversely, when a market is oversold, the tendency is to become dull on declines and active on rallies. Bull markets terminate in a period of excessive activity and begin with comparatively light transactions.*

Double Tops and Double Bottoms:—*"Double tops" and "double bottoms" are of but little value in forecasting the price movement and have proved to be deceptive more often than not.*

Individual Stocks:—*All active and well distributed stocks of great American corporations generally rally and decline with the averages, but any individual stock may reflect conditions not applicable to the average price of any diversified list of stocks.*

CHAPTER III

MANIPULATION

Manipulation is possible in the day to day movement of the averages, and secondary reactions are subject to such an influence to a more limited degree, but the primary trend can never be manipulated.

Hamilton frequently discussed the subject of stock market manipulation. There are many who will disagree with his belief that manipulation is a negligible factor in primary movements, but it should always be remembered that he had, as a background for his opinions, a most intimate acquaintance with the veterans of Wall Street, and the advantage of having spent his life in accumulating facts pertaining to financial matters.

The following comment, taken at random from his many editorials, affords convincing proof that his views on the subject of manipulation did not vary:

"A limited number of stocks may be manipulated at one time, and may give an entirely false view of the situation. It is impossible, however, to manipulate the whole list so that the average price of 20 active stocks will show changes sufficiently important to draw market deductions from them." (Nov. 28, 1908)

"Anybody will admit that while manipulation is possible in the day-to-day market movement, and the short swing is subject to such an influence in a more limited degree, the great market movement must be beyond the manipulation of the combined financial interests of the world. (Feb. 26, 1909)

". . . the market itself is bigger than all the 'pools' and 'insiders' put together." (May 8, 1922)

"One of the greatest of misconceptions, that which has militated

16

most against the usefulness of the stock market barometer, is the belief that manipulation can falsify stock market movements otherwise authoritative and instructive. The writer claims no more authority than may come from twenty-two years of stark intimacy with Wall Street, preceded by practical acquaintance with the London Stock Exchange, the Paris Bourse and even that wildly speculative market in gold shares, 'Between the Chains,' in Johannesburg in 1895. But in all that experience, for what it may be worth, it is impossible to recall a single instance of a major market movement which depended for its impetus, or even for its genesis, upon manipulation. These discussions have been made in vain if they have failed to show that all the primary bull markets and every primary bear market have been vindicated, in the course of their development and before their close, by the facts of general business, however much over-speculation or over-liquidation may have tended to excess, as they always do, in the last stage of the primary swing." (*The Stock Market Barometer*)

". . . no power, not the U. S. Treasury and the Federal Reserve System combined, could usefully manipulate forty active stocks or deflect their record to any but a negligible extent." (April 27, 1923)

The average amateur trader believes the stock market is guided in its trends by a certain mysterious "power," this belief being the one factor, next to impatience, most responsible for his losses. He reads tipster sheets avidly; he scans the newspapers industriously for news likely, in his opinion, to change the trend of the market. He does not seem to realize that by the time news of real importance is printed, its effect, so far as the basic trend of the market is concerned, has long ago been discounted.

It is true that a flurry in the price of wheat or cotton may influence the day to day movement of stock prices. Moreover, sometimes newspaper headlines contain news which is construed as bullish or bearish by market dabblers, who collectively rush in to buy or sell, thus influencing or "manipulating" the market for a short period. The professional speculator is always ready to help the movement along by "placing his line" while the little fellow timidly "lays out" a few shares; then, when the little fellow decides to increase his commitments, the professional begins to unload and the reaction ends, and the primary movement is again resumed. It is doubtful if many of these reactions would ever be caused by newspaper headlines alone unless the market was either overbought or oversold at the time—the "technical situation" so dear to the hearts of financial news reporters.

Those who believe the primary trend can be manipulated could, no doubt, study the subject for a few days and be convinced that such a thing is impossible. For instance, on September 1, 1929, the total market value of all stocks listed on the New York Stock Exchange was reported to have amounted to more than $89,000,-000,000. Imagine the money which would have been involved in depressing such a mass of values even 10 per cent!

CHAPTER IV

THE AVERAGES DISCOUNT EVERYTHING

The fluctuations of the daily closing prices of the Dow-Jones rail and industrial averages afford a composite index of all the hopes, disappointments, and knowledge of everyone who knows anything of financial matters, and for that reason the effects of coming events (excluding acts of God) are always properly discounted in their movement. The averages quickly appraise such calamities as fires and earthquakes.

Whenever a group of market students get together, some one of them nearly always starts a debate as to whether stock prices, by their action, discount events not foreseen by the individual speculator. Surely all students who have an understanding of the Dow theory *know* this to be a fact; it is the basic principle underlying the successful application of the theory to trading and investment, and those who do not concede it to be true would be wise if they did not attempt to make use of the theory.

But little comment from the writer is needed, because the ideas of both Dow and Hamilton on this subject can be presented in these clearly reasoned excerpts from editorials written over a 30-year period.

"It cannot too often be said that the stock market reflects absolutely all everybody knows about the business of the country. The corporations which sell the farmer implements, motor trucks and fertilizers know his condition better than he knows it himself. There are corporations listed in the Stock Exchange, complying with its stringent listing requirements, dealing in practically everything the country makes and consumes—the coal, the coke, the iron ore, the pig iron, the steel billet, and manufactured

19

watch spring—and all their knowledge is infallibly reflected in the price of securities. All the banks know about the exchange of those commodities and the financing of their production and marketing is reflected in stock prices adjusted to the value of each contribution to knowledge small or large." (Oct. 4, 1921)

". . . the average . . . discount . . . activity and dullness, good news and bad, crop forecasts and political possibilities, and the net result is, in fact, the average. It is this which makes them so valuable for study, and makes it possible to get light on the future market movement not obtainable in any other way." (May 2, 1912)

"The superficial observer is constantly startled to find that the stock market fails to respond to sudden and important developments; while it seems to be guided by impulses too obscure to be traceable. Consciously or unconsciously, the movement of prices reflects not the past but the future. When coming events cast their shadows before, the shadow falls on the New York Stock Exchange." (March 27, 1911)

"The passionless barometer is disinterested because every sale and purchase which goes to make up its findings, is interested. Its verdict is the balance of all the desires, compulsions and hopes of those who buy and sell stocks. The whole business of the country must necessarily be reflected correctly in the meeting of all these minds, not as an irresponsible debating society but as a listening jury whose members, together, bring more than the counsel or the judge can ever tell them in finding what has been called 'the bloodless verdict of the marketplace.' " (March 29, 1926)

"The market does not trade upon what everybody knows, but upon what those with the best information can foresee. There is an explanation for every stock market movement somewhere in the future, and the much talked of manipulation is a trifling factor." (Jan. 20, 1913)

Here is an extract from an editorial written by Dow in 1901:

"The market is not like a balloon plunging hither and thither in the wind. As a whole, it represents a serious, well-considered effort on the part of farsighted and well-informed men to adjust prices to such values as exist or which are expected to exist in the not too remote future. The thought with great operators is not whether a price can be advanced, but whether the value of property which they propose to buy will lead investors and speculators six months hence to take stock at figures from ten to twenty points above present prices." (July 20, 1901)

"Everything that everybody knows about anything with even a remote bearing on finance finds its way into Wall Street, in the form of information; the stock market itself, in its fluctuations, represents the sifted value of all this knowledge." (May 29, 1929)

"It cannot be too often repeated that the stock market, while adjusting itself to the unexpected, as in the secondary reactions, is based not upon surrounding conditions but upon what may be expected as far ahead as the combined intelligence of the market can see." (Sept. 25, 1922)

". . . Speculation anticipates the developments of business . . ." (*The Stock Market Barometer*)

In the spring of 1927, after a bull market had been running nearly six years, this comment appeared: ". . . The averages are saying that business is likely to maintain its volume and character for as many months ahead as the most efficient trade telescopes can see." (April 23, 1927)

When stocks were very near the bottom of the 1921 lows, but after the actual lows had been reached, the following explanation was given as to why the averages did not decline on current bad news:

"When the market is taken by surprise there is a panic, and history records how seldom it is taken by surprise. Today all the bear factors are known, serious as they admittedly are. But the stock market is not trading on what is common knowledge today but upon the sum of expert knowledge applied to conditions as they can be foreseen many months ahead." (Oct. 4, 1921)

". . . eventually every decline of the past was fully explained

by subsequent developments in the businesses of the country."
(March 8, 1926)

"It is good experience that a change of direction, or an interruption of the major movement, has usually other explanations,
to supplement at least the one which appeals to the popular
fancy." (Aug. 15, 1927)

"It is the constant phrase of the street that a movement is over
'when the news is out.' Stockholders and intelligent speculators
operate not on what everybody knows, but on what they alone
know or intelligently anticipate. We have often had the spectacle
of a general decline in the market, only followed six months afterwards by a contraction in business, or a general advance in the
market anticipating by an equal time improving industrial conditions not then obvious." (June 29, 1906)

". . . Speculation in stocks itself creates exactly the confidence which stimulates an expansion of general business. This
is really only another way of saying that the stock market is a
barometer, acting not upon the news of the day, but upon what
the combined intelligence of the business world can anticipate."
(May 22, 1922)

One of the greatest financiers in America once said to Hamilton: "If I had 50 per cent of all the knowledge which is reflected
in the movement of stocks, I am confident that I would be far
better equipped than any other man in Wall Street."

"Of course no tree ever grows to the sky, but it is nevertheless
true that the market discounts everything but the completely unexpected. It does not profess to be able to foresee the San Francisco earthquake, or an incident like the Northern Pacific corner,
and opinions differ as to whether the Great War was foreseen,
and to some extent discounted, in the long bear market before its
actual outbreak." (July 15, 1927)

". . . assuming that Wall Street is the reservoir of all that
everybody knows about everything connected with business. The
assumption is fully justified and that is why the stock market
averages reflect so much more than any individual can possibly

know or the wealthiest combination can manipulate." (Oct. 4, 1927)

It is imperative that every student of the Dow theory be absolutely convinced that the averages do forecast coming events and correctly evaluate those happenings. The value of this portion of the theory is of tremendous importance to the speculator while trying to swim with the tide.

A typical recent example proving the usefulness of this part of the theory is the long and drastic decline during 1931, when the averages lost a greater percentage of their value than in any other year. During that period, the market was discounting and evaluating the seriousness of foreign troubles, especially the abandonment of the gold standard by Great Britain, bank failures, railroad receiverships, and the evident need of higher taxation made necessary by an anticipated treasury deficit of substantial proportions. This decline was halted in June by a typical secondary reaction caused by the usual combination of short covering and unwise investment buying, both of which were stimulated by public acceptance of a press optimism, politically sponsored and splendidly advertised, based upon the Hoover moratorium.

Another interruption of the primary bear trend occurred in October. The reason generally accepted as being responsible for this secondary movement was the imposition of a rule on the New York Stock Exchange placing certain restrictions on short selling which caused the short interest to cover. Simultaneously, a very capably managed pool gave wheat a spectacular upward whirl. The press of the country generally heralded this purely speculative movement as being the long expected turning point in declining commodity prices, so fish in great number took the bait in the usual manner and the usual secondary movement was completed in the usual time. Then the bear market resumed its inexorable march to lower ground. The secondary trend was due and would have occurred even had the advance in wheat not occurred. If the excuse of commodity betterment had not been found, then something else just as satisfactory would have been proclaimed as being responsible. "The averages are remorseless. They represent all everybody knows or foresees about conditions."

A few more quotations on the important subject of the ability of the averages to discount the future are offered, even though the repetition becomes tedious to the reader.

"It is always taken in the periodical discussions of the average price movement appearing in this place that the average discounts everything—volume, general conditions, dividends, interest rates, politics—and just because it is an average it is the impartial summing up of every possible market influence." (March 7, 1912)

"It is assumed that the average eliminates every individual consideration; politics, money, crops—everything but the chapter of accidents, and ultimately that . . ." (April 5, 1912)

"When a large manufacturer sees bad times ahead he sells securities to put himself in a strong financial position and he is only one of thousands. The stock market declines long before the emergency develops which he and others foresaw." (July 15, 1924)

"The market reflects a multitude of facts, each of which only a few people . . . know about his own business." (July 15, 1924)

"The stock market barometer takes account of dear money and pig iron furnace operations, together with crop prospects, grain prices, bank clearings, merchants' collections, political prospects, foreign trade, savings bank figures, wages, volume of railroad freight and a hundred and one other things. The average price of active stocks is the result of all this, impartially reflected in a market which no interest is big enough to influence." (July 15, 1924)

"The market foresaw the World War, as the action of the barometer in the early part of 1914 clearly showed." (March 16, 1925)

"We prefer in these studies to ignore the volume of general business, the state of trade, the condition of crops, the political outlook, and the other possibilities which are influences in the daily movement, but not often seriously apparent in the short swings, to say nothing of the main broad movement of the market. Analysis of the averages over a long period of years shows that the averages discount all these things and are more trustworthy as a guide if transitory influences are ignored." (July 14, 1911)

CHAPTER V

THE THEORY IS NOT INFALLIBLE

The Dow theory is not an infallible system for beating the market. Its successful use as an aid in speculation requires serious study, and the summing up of evidence must be impartial. The wish must never be allowed to father the thought.

The broad generalization necessary in outlining the operation of the Dow theory leaves much to be desired; nevertheless, the theory lends itself to definition with much more ease than other empirical sciences. Can a surgeon write a few simple rules which would enable a banker to remove an appendix from a broker? No—for the reason that surgery is an empirical science, developed as a result of the study of the case histories of thousands of more or less successful operations—truly a "cut and try" method. Landing an airplane successfully is also an empirical science. A skillful and intelligent pilot could easily write a few simple directions on the subject which another pilot would understand, but should our banker essay a landing by the rules, he would probably ride away from his wreck in an ambulance. Why? Perhaps, because the pilot did not properly qualify the landing rules as to which wing should be put down in the event of a cross wind landing. But the banker could write a simple rule for determining the yield on a bond which would enable the doctor, pilot, or broker to figure the answer correctly, because arithmetic is an exact science, and in an exact science there is only one answer—the correct one. The Dow theory is an empirical science. It is not infallible, but it is very useful when handled intelligently, and its intelligent use requires only careful and consistent study.

In his book, Hamilton wrote: "The stock market barometer is

not perfect, or, to put it more correctly, the adolescent science of reading it is far from having attained perfection."

Students of the averages are prone to allow the wish to become father to the thought. They buy after a long advance and then blame the theory if they run into a big secondary reaction which depletes their margins. Such operators think they are following the implications of the averages because they own a chart, usually of only the industrial average, with many mythical resistance points carefully marked. The theory is not to blame for their losses, because it implies buying in bull markets only when severe declines have occurred and when the market has displayed a tendency to go dead on declines or to become active on rallies.

Then some students insist upon attempting to apply the theory to day to day trading. They generally lose money.

There is another kind of trader who insists on mixing up carloadings, money rates, etc., with the Dow theory, probably getting the idea from some of our important statistical organizations whose records are so pathetic. These traders have about the same luck as the professional forecasters—lots of luck, but most of it bad. If these traders understood the theory, they would accept as a fundamental the fact that the averages properly discount and evaluate all statistical knowledge.

The question is frequently asked, "What percentage of trades, timed in accordance with a reasonably competent interpretation of the Dow theory, will be profitable?" It is the writer's belief that any trader endowed with ordinary market sense and plenty of patience who has studied and used the averages as a guide through the complete cycle of a bull and bear market should be able to make at least seven profitable turns out of every 10 efforts —and each profitable trade should net a gain in excess of the loss on a trade improperly timed. Many men have consistently bettered this record, but they seldom make more than four or five trades a year. They do not watch the tape but play for the important movements and are not concerned with a few points loss or gain.

Those of us who claim an understanding of the price movement know that the Dow theory, while not infallible, is to be trusted far more than the judgment of the best trader. Those who trade on the theory know that losses are generally occasioned by trusting the theory too little and not because it is relied upon too much.

Suppose a trade timed by inferences drawn from the averages and the trade begins to show a heavy loss. Then either the signals have been misunderstood, or one of the few movements when the theory has gone wrong is occurring. In such a situation, the loss should be taken and the trader should stay out of the market until the signals are easy to read, when he should try again.

Speculators, particularly the kind who might more properly be called gamblers, insist on trying to read into the movement of the averages a particularity of detail which does not and cannot exist.

Any thinking man will readily realize that if the Dow theory were infallible, or if even one or two men could always interpret its implications correctly, there would probably soon be no speculation in stocks.

In 1926 Hamilton made a serious error in reading the implications of the averages, calling a secondary reaction in a bull market a bear market. Students of the theory should study the charted prices for the year following the fall of 1925 as being a typical case of where incorrect conclusions could easily have been formed. To the writer, it has always seemed that Hamilton had decided a bear market was due and allowed his belief to influence his reading of the charts—a case of trusting his judgment too much and his theory too little.

A bull market had started in the late summer of 1923 and had progressed in the usual manner all through 1924. From the latter part of March, 1925, until Feb. 26, 1926, an impressive advance, with scarcely an interruption, had occurred. The extent and duration of that long advance alone warranted a secondary reaction of unusual proportions. A glance at the charted averages for the years from 1897 to 1926 would have shown that the bull market then in progress had, in duration, lasted about as long as others; in addition, it would have been found that the industrial average was at a new all-time high and that money was tight. It can be realized how even a devout believer in the Dow theory might try to make his reading of the averages conform to his belief that the bull market should be at an end.

It is of interest to attempt to follow Hamilton's reasoning which led him eventually to call a secondary reaction a bear market. On Oct. 5, 1925, he pointed out that the yield on the 20 industrials [5] was below 4%, a point "where people are buying on hopes and potentialities rather than on demonstrated value." He also stated: "On any reading of the averages based upon sound principles it is clear that the major bull market is still in force, but will bear watching." Anyone reading the complete editorial would conclude that Hamilton was bearish on the market but could find at the time nothing in the averages to support his belief. He closed the editorial with the following statement: "This is a time when the old theory of double tops might prove useful, as, for instance, any close approach to the high points of September 19 or September 23, followed by a reaction in both averages." This was a strange statement considering Hamilton had stated that the theory of "double tops" and "double bottoms" had not proved useful.

On Nov. 9, 1925, Hamilton concluded an editorial with these words: "So far as any inference from the Dow-Jones stock averages is concerned the major bull market in stocks is still ruling, with some secondary reaction due, but no bear market in sight," but elsewhere in the same article he stated, "Sometime, and probably next year, we shall experience a marked shortage of capital for investment and speculation, and the stock market will know it first. It will develop a major downward movement, when the whole country is bubbling with prosperity and ever expanding hope."

[5] The list of industrial stocks was not increased to the present total of 30 until October, 1928.

Thus, it becomes obvious that he had personally decided on a bear market, and it is not unreasonable to assume that he was on the alert to find the averages confirming his predictions.

On Nov. 19, 1925, after a sharp reaction had occurred, Hamilton again cautioned his readers to watch out for a double top as a probable indication that the major upward movement had terminated, but on Dec. 17, 1925, he wrote a clearly reasoned summary of the price movement based entirely on his interpretation of the Dow theory, in which he said: "The major bull movement in operation since October, 1923, is still in force with a typical secondary reaction in the industrial stocks uncompleted." However, he warned that the averages would bear watching, which indicates that he thought prices too high, regardless of the theory.

On January 26 attention was invited to the "double top" made by the industrials which was not confirmed by the rails. Dozens of times Hamilton had warned his readers that conclusions drawn from the action of one average, not confirmed by the other, were almost sure to prove misleading.

On Feb. 15, 1926, "double tops" were again referred to and he reasoned that failure to penetrate those tops, together with a subsequent further decline, would probably indicate a bear market. On March 5, when the industrials had declined only about 12 points and the rails 7 from their respective highs, he announced that ". . . the end of the bull movement was plainly shown (on Feb. 15) as it has been in such studies for the past twenty-five years."

On March 8 he called attention to his having called the turn near the top by means of "The significant 'double top,' " and he stated that "what seems sufficiently clear is that the major tendency of the market for an indefinite time to come will be downward."

On April 12, more than two weeks after the low point of the secondary reaction, which had been erroneously termed a bear market, Hamilton continued to point out his earlier forecasts, ending an article with the statement that the averages were

". . . certainly not taking back the inferences which were drawn in these columns when the price movement was studied seven weeks ago."

A glance at the charted price movement will show that this last bearish forecast was written about the time when prices were ready for the long advance which terminated in 1929. A mistake of the sort discussed above can be disastrous to a speculator, and doubtless many who followed Hamilton's forecasts lost heavily on the market at that time. In summarizing the reasons which led to the error, it is obvious that Hamilton trusted the averages too little and his own judgment too much. By means of the "double top" idea, he fitted the averages to his belief. This was the only time he ever definitely used that idea, and it led to his downfall. Another point he either ignored or did not want to see was the fact that the industrials had advanced 47.08 points and the rails 20.14 points without a really important secondary movement occurring. The Dow theory under Hamilton's interpretation considers a reaction of from 40% to 60% of the ground gained in a long advance to be a normal happening. In this case, the reaction amounted to 26.88 points for the industrials and 10.71 points for the rails—55% and 53%, respectively. Hamilton's "bear market" was, in fact, nothing more or less than a perfectly normal secondary reaction, and under a conscientious application of the Dow theory it would never have been called anything else.

CHAPTER VI

DOW'S THREE MOVEMENTS

There are three movements of the averages, all of which may be in progress at one and the same time. The first, and most important, is the primary trend: the broad upward or downward movements known as bull or bear markets, which may be of several years' duration. The second, and most deceptive movement, is the secondary reaction: an important decline in a primary bull market or a rally in a primary bear market. These reactions usually last from three weeks to as many months. The third, and usually unimportant, movement is the daily fluctuation.

Every driver of an automobile can remember the confusion of mind, hands, and feet upon the occasion of his first driving lesson, with someone beside him insisting that the road be watched, or that the foot be taken off the accelerator and the brakes applied, all at one and the same time. But with experience, the use of the accelerator and brake becomes automatic, as does the habit of watching the road. Perhaps a like confusion exists when a student first attempts to understand Dow's three price movements, but in time their recognition becomes almost an automatic mental or visual process. Temporary reversals of market trends—secondary reactions—are recognized as serving the same purpose marketwise as the brakes on an automobile: they act as a means of checking excess velocity. The use of the accelerator, which may be used to retard as well as advance a car, may be compared with the daily movement, which on some days is working with the primary or secondary movement, and on other days, against it.

Each of the three movements will be discussed in later chapters, but because a thorough understanding of each is so important, it is perhaps advisable to quote from Hamilton's writings over a period of years:

"We should know our theory by heart. It is that the stock market has three movements—its broad swing upward or downward, extending from a year to three years; its secondary reactions or rallies, as the case may be, lasting from a few days to many weeks; and the daily fluctuation. These movements are simultaneous, much as the advancing tide shows wave recessions, although each succeeding roller comes further up the beach. Perhaps it might be permissible to say that the secondary movement suspends for a time the great primary swing, although a natural law is still in force even when we counteract it." (*The Stock Market Barometer*)

At another time, the three movements were explained as follows:

"These are the broad market movements; upwards or downwards, which may continue for years and are seldom shorter than a year at the least; then there is the short market swing, which may take anywhere from one month to three months. These two movements are in operation together and, obviously, may contradict each other. They are still further complicated by the daily movement, which is the third current to be considered by the navigator in these difficult waters." (Feb. 26, 1909)

Twenty-five years ago the phrasing was—"There are three movements in the market which are in progress at one and the same time. These are—first, the day to day movement resulting mainly from the operation of the traders, which may be called the tertiary movement; second, the movement usually extending from 20 to 60 days, reflecting the ebb and flow of speculative sentiment which is called the secondary movement; and, third, the main movement, usually extending for a period of years, caused by the adjustment of prices to underlying values, usually called the primary movement." (Sept. 17, 1904)

In 1914 this somewhat shorter explanation was written: "It may be explained again that the 'theory' of Charles H. Dow, confirmed by many years of observation, was that the market had three simultaneous movements. The first of these is the great primary movement lasting for a year or more. The second is the occasional rally in a bear market, or the break in a bull market. The third represents the daily fluctuations." (April 16, 1914)

CHAPTER VII

PRIMARY MOVEMENTS

The primary movement is the broad basic trend generally known as a bull or bear market extending over periods which have varied from less than a year to several years. The correct determination of the direction of this movement is the most important factor in successful speculation. There is no known method of forecasting the extent or duration of a primary movement.

There is no way in which the duration of a primary movement may be determined but ". . . the length and extent of major swings adds a great deal to the prediction value of the barometer. There is no rule to indicate exactly how many points constitutes a major swing, any more than there is a rule to define the extent of business expansion or depression which the movement predicts." (March 10, 1924) Critics of the Dow theory sometimes complain that, to be useful, it should forecast in advance just where the market will go and the time it will require to get there. It seems proper to submit here the wish that the weather bureau could tell us the day, hour, and depth of snowstorms or the exact duration of hot spells, but weather forecasting, like the Dow theory, is wholly empirical and has not yet been perfected to that extent. Moreover, it probably never will be. However, we have become accustomed to accepting weather forecasts, recognizing the limitations surrounding them, and being very thankful that the science of forecasting gives us warning of approaching storms or other changes. Our attitude should be the same toward the Dow theory.

Novices in the art of reading the implications of the averages are prone to mistake extensive secondary reactions in primary movements as indicating a change of primary trend. Correct interpretation at such times is often difficult, even for the expert, but careful study will generally enable the student to detect the change. If he is in doubt, he should stand on the side lines until the pattern of the daily averages affords an opportunity for clearer interpretation. Hamilton was frequently perplexed, and no better explanation of the reasonable doubts which sometimes exist in every trader's mind is needed than his statement that "It must always be remembered, however, that there is a main current in the stock market, with innumerable cross currents, eddies, and backwaters, any one of which may be mistaken for a day, a week, or even a longer period for the main stream. The market is a barometer. There is no movement in it which has not a meaning. That meaning is sometimes not disclosed until long after the movement takes place, and is still oftener never known at all; but it may truly be said that every movement is reasonable if only the knowledge of its source is complete." (June 29, 1906)

CHAPTER VIII

PRIMARY BEAR MARKETS

A primary bear market is the long downward movement interrupted by important rallies. It is caused by various economic ills and does not terminate until stock prices have thoroughly discounted the worst that is apt to occur. There are three principal phases of a bear market: the first represents the abandonment of the hopes upon which stocks were purchased at inflated prices; the second reflects selling due to decreased business and earnings, and the third is caused by distress selling of sound securities, regardless of their value, by those who must find a cash market for at least a portion of their assets.

In 1921, Hamilton stated that the average duration of bull swings for the preceding 25 years was 25 months, whereas the duration of the bear markets was 17 months. In other words, bear markets run about 70% of the average time required for bull markets.

Bear markets seem to be divided into three phases: the first being the abandonment of hopes upon which the final uprush of the preceding bull market was predicted; the second, the reflection of decreased earning power and reduction of dividends, and the third representing distress liquidation of securities which must be sold to meet living expenses. Each of these phases seems to be divided by a secondary reaction which is often erroneously assumed to be the beginning of a bull market. Such secondary movements seldom prove perplexing to those who understand the Dow theory.

Business on the New York Stock Exchange, as reflected by total daily stock sales, is far lighter in bear markets than in bull periods. The flattening of the volume curve is one of the indications of the possible termination of a bear market.

Hamilton often said the old maxim of Wall Street, "Never sell a dull market," was bad advice in a major bear market. He noticed that the time to sell in a bear market was when the volume dries up after a sharp rally and that activity on declines indicated continuance of the bear trend. He often expressed his belief as follows: "One of the platitudes most constantly quoted in Wall Street is to the effect that one should never sell a dull market short. That advice is probably right oftener than it is wrong, but it is always wrong in an extended bear swing. In such a swing the tendency is to become dull on rallies and active on declines." (May 21, 1909)

Several things well worth remembering are contained in the following excerpt from an editorial appearing in 1921:—"On Dow's old theory . . . the secondary rallies in a bear market are sudden and rapid, conspicuously so in the recovery after an actual panic break. The test is not at the bottom but in what the market does after a rally in a condition . . . where stocks could easily become sold out or oversold. Sentiment is always super-bearish at the bottom, and the professionals begin to 'copper' public sentiment when the elevator boy talks of his 'short position.'

"A secondary rally in a bear market, as the averages for many years past show with curious uniformity, is followed by the making of a line which thoroughly tests the public absorption power. On a serious break . . . there is always heavy buying in support, to protect weak accounts too large to be liquidated, and this stock is fed out on a recovery. It is largely offset by the covering of shorts and bargain buying, but if the absorption power is still lacking there is a further and slower decline, usually establishing new low points." (June 23, 1921)

"Long experience, which can be verified from the averages, teaches that in a broad bull movement, of a kind that lasts over a year or more, the advance looks slow compared to the sharpness of the occasional reactions. In the same way, in a bear market, sharp recoveries are in order." (March 19, 1910)

At this point, it is of interest to understand the fundamental principles operating during a declining or advancing market.

In bear markets good stocks will suffer with the bad ones, because people sell at some price that for which there is an assured market in order to protect what they cannot sell at any price. During periods of acute depression, people who never speculate are compelled to take sound investment stocks out of their safety deposit boxes and sell them for anything they will bring because, regardless of the loss entailed, such stocks will bring cash, and cash is needed for living expenses. These people created a "rainy day" fund and "it rained." Possibly they would have preferred to have sold their homes or other assets, but could find no cash market. Maybe they had previously borrowed on life insurance, thus forcing an insurance company to sell some of its securities at depreciated prices for whatever they would bring in order to procure funds for making the policy loan. Perhaps the same people had depleted their bank balances, thereby forcing the bank to liquidate securities in order to maintain cash reserves. Thus a vicious circle is formed, forcing sound securities on the market at a time when there are not enough buyers to go around. In other words, the law of supply and demand is working, and when the supply is greater than the demand prices must decline. The reader of the investment recommendations of many of our prominent advisory services may properly wonder why the economists employed by those concerns apparently ignore or fail to understand this important phase of a bear swing.

What causes the termination of a long decline in stock prices? Here is an excellent explanation of the whole cycle—the genesis of both bull and bear markets—as given in *The Stock Market Barometer*:

"Presently we wake up to find that our income is in excess of our expenditure, that money is cheap, that the spirit of adventure is in the air. We proceed from dull or quiet business times to real

activity. This gradually develops into extended speculation, with
high money rates, inflated wages and other familiar symptoms.
After a period of years of good times the strain of the chain is
on its weakest link. There is a collapse . . . a depression foreshadowed in the stock market and in the price of commodities,
followed by extensive unemployment, often an actual increase in
savings-bank deposits, but a complete absence of money available
for adventure."

Hamilton tells us not to try to use the Dow theory to pick the
day when the lows of a bear market are to be made: "No knowledge of the stock market barometer will enable any of us to call
the absolute turn from a bear market to a bull market."

On September 18, 1921, when the averages had advanced less
than five points above their bear market lows, Hamilton wrote the
following in an article for *Barron's:*

"There is a pertinent instance and test in the action of the
current market. I have been challenged to offer proof of the prediction value of the stock market barometer. With the demor-
alized condition of European finance, the disaster to the cotton
crop, the uncertainties produced by deflation, the unprincipled
opportunism of our lawmakers and tax-imposers, all the after-
math of war inflation—unemployment, uneconomic wages in coal
mining and railroading—with all these things overhanging the
business of the country at the present moment, the stock market
has acted as if there were better things in sight. It has been saying that the bear market which set in at the end of October and
the beginning of November, 1919, saw its low point on June 20,
1921, at 64.90 for the twenty industrials and 65.52 for the
twenty railroad stocks."

Then a few days later this comment from his pen appeared in
The Wall Street Journal:

"More than one correspondent has written to this paper to call
attention to unsatisfactory conditions and to ask, therefore, why
it should be said in the study of the price movement, through the
averages, published September 21, that the stock market seems

to be setting the stage for a long upward swing in prices. All sorts of reasons are given for a pessimistic view—bankruptcy in Germany, railroad rates and wages, tariff and tax uncertainty, and the obtuseness of Congress in considering such matters with common sense. The answer is that the stock market has considered all these things, with sources of information far more exhaustive than any of these critics can possibly possess." (Sept. 21, 1921)

These forecasts were responsible for this writer's buying a few stocks and bonds at that time, an investment which later provided funds for the building of a home and the making of a business investment. Earnings of the latter have meant the difference between comparative luxury and being a ward of the Veterans' Bureau in a government hospital. These forecasts inspired the years of study of the averages that followed—a search for something at the rainbow's end which proved to be a fascinating and generally profitable pastime.

A letter to Hamilton in the late fall of 1921 requesting reasons for his inferences brought a reply explaining that dull volume, sideways movement, the market's indifference to bad news, and failure to rally were all indications that the worst was over and that he felt his statements to be warranted by the character of the daily movement of the averages.

The diagram shown on the next page was prepared while a study of characteristic actions of the averages at the bottom of bear markets was being made. The terminations of nine bear markets were arranged one above another and the daily movement was plotted to ratio scale so that the low points of each average in each period could properly be taken as being 100; thus, price advances would automatically be transposed to show the percentage of price range above the low point.

This arrangement was then considered in relation to the volume of trading during these periods. It was found that the terminating valley of seven of these nine bear markets contained a period of from 60 to 90 days when each average moved in a line within a range of about three per cent of a mean price, although this move-

DOW-JONES DAILY STOCK AVERAGES
SIX MONTHS VALLEY OF NINE BEAR MARKETS.
Ratio Scale--Lowest Points Taken To Equal 100 Percent
Heavy Line, Industrials; Light, Rails.

A Photographic Reduction of a Tracing Made From
"GRAPHIC CHARTS: DOW-JONES DAILY STOCK AVERAGES AND SALES"

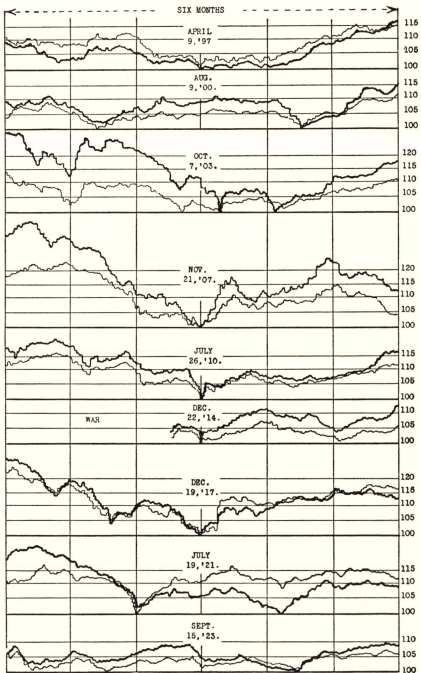

SIX MONTHS

APRIL
9,'97

AUG.
9,'00.

OCT.
7,'03.

NOV.
21,'07.

JULY
26,'10.

DEC.
22,'14.

WAR

DEC.
19,'17.

JULY
19,'21.

SEPT.
15,'23.

ment did not necessarily occur simultaneously in both averages. In the other two periods, the range was approximately five per cent.

In six of these valleys, the volume of trading diminished steadily for several months prior to the dates on which the low points were made, whereas in the other three periods the assumption of extremely dull trading as an indicator would have been misleading.

Much has been written about double bottoms at the end of bear markets. It is true that such a phenomenon sometimes occurs, but one is almost certain to go wrong if this be taken as an indicator. Those who point to the frequency of double bottoms fail to consider that many double bottoms appear during bear markets at points that were not the bottom. A check of all the double bottoms appearing during the primary bear movements will show that there are several bottoms which were *not* the end of the primary movement for each one that did occur at the low point. A much more useful application of the movement of the averages at such a time is to consider a low of one average, not confirmed by the other, as indicating a possible change of trend of secondary importance, if not of primary significance.

It seems to be much easier to forecast price movements in bear periods than when the primary trend is upwards. At least, it is certainly easier to pick the bottom than the top of a market.

The student of the averages who can pick the bottom within 10% of the low price is indeed fortunate, but before the price has advanced 20%, the indications of the trend change should be obvious to anyone accustomed to using the Dow theory.

CHAPTER IX

PRIMARY BULL MARKETS

A primary bull market is a broad upward movement, inter-rupted by secondary reactions, and averaging longer than two years. During this time, stock prices advance because of a de-mand created by both investment and speculative buying caused by improving business conditions and increased speculative activ-ity. There are three phases of a bull period: the first is repre-sented by reviving confidence in the future of business; the sec-ond is the response of stock prices to the known improvement in corporation earnings, and the third is the period when specula-tion is rampant and inflation apparent—a period when stocks are advanced on hopes and expectations.

As has been stated before, the Dow theory is merely a common-sense method of drawing useful inferences as to future market movements from the recorded daily price fluctuations of the Dow-Jones railroad and industrial stock averages. There is no place in the life of an adventurer in speculative finance where an under-standing of the theory can be as useful as when a major bear swing is ending and a big bull market is in the making.

Hamilton seemed to be able to pick the bottoms easily, and he repeatedly stated that it was much easier to do than to determine the peak after the upswing. There can be little doubt that his wisdom in financial matters was a factor in his success, but others less skilled have been able successfully to apply the theory at the right time without any especial knowledge other than reasonable understanding of the implications of the averages.

In writing about bull and bear markets, one must bear in mind that the first stage of a primary bull market is indistinguishable

from the last secondary reaction in a bear market until a period
of time has elapsed. Likewise, the first stage of a primary bear
market must first be classified as a probable secondary reaction in
a major bull swing. Consequently, any discussion of the ending
of a bear market must cover the beginning of the ensuing primary bull movement. In the preceding chapter, typical endings
of bear periods were discussed and it is only necessary again to
point out that at the end of the bear period the market seems to
be immune to further bad news and pessimism. It also appears
to have lost its ability to bounce back after severe declines and has
every appearance of having reached a state of equilibrium where
speculative activities are at low ebb, where offerings do little to
depress prices, but where there appears to be no demand sufficient to lift quotations. The market is a dragging affair with but
little public participation. Pessimism is rampant, dividends are
being passed, some important companies are usually in financial
difficulties, and a certain amount of political unrest is generally
apparent. Because of all these things, stocks make a "line." Then,
when this "line" is definitely broken on the upside, the daily fluctuations of the railroad and industrial averages show a definite
tendency to work to slightly higher ground on each rally, with
the ensuing declines failing to go through the last immediate low.
It is then, and not before, that a speculative position on the long
side is clearly indicated. This period is one requiring patience,
but when a sizable reaction has occurred after a considerable advance, with the reaction failing to break through the bear market
lows and the next series of rallies going through the high point
of the last major reaction of the preceding bear market, then
stocks may be purchased with reasonable safety.

Some readers might ask why the secondary rally in the spring
of 1930 did not indicate the termination of a bear market and the
beginning of a new bull period. One answer is that any student of
the averages knows that bull markets do not begin with violent
rallies. Moreover, a reaction recovering from 25 per cent or even
100 per cent of the ground lost is not without precedent in the

early stages of a primary bear movement. Much has been written concerning the beginning of a bull market. The following excerpt is from a long editorial discussing the development of a bull market from a very low price base: "The preceding bear market had driven securities far below their acknowledged worth, for the good reason that the Stock Exchange presented a market for them at some price where the market for other things had disappeared altogether. It is part of the barometrical effect of the stock market that it must necessarily be the first to feel the pressure of general liquidation.

"In the first stage of a bull market, then, there is a return to known values. In the second stage, and often the longest stage, there is an adjustment to these values as they become more stable with improving general business, and it is this period which most frequently sees the longest and most deceptive secondary reactions in a major bull market. The third is the stage where general confidence is discounting not merely present values but future possibilities." (June 25, 1923)

Here is a paragraph declaring that patience is needed during the long slow climb upwards and that courage is required to ride through the sharp secondary reactions of a healthy bull market: "Long experience, which can be verified from the averages, teaches that in a broad bull movement, of a kind that lasts over a year or more, the advance looks slow compared to the sharpness of the occasional reactions. In the same way, in a bear market, sharp recoveries are in order." (March 19, 1910)

The business of those in Wall Street who own "wise money" is to buy stocks for less than they are worth, or for less than they will be worth within a reasonable length of time, and eventually to sell them at a higher market level. If these owners of "wise money" have the intelligence and skill to use it in this way, they are doing just what a merchant does in purchasing quantities of sheeting and other cotton goods when the prices of that staple are low and the mills are making price concessions because of dull business. The merchant expects to sell his purchases at a later time on a rising market. When the intelligent element in Wall Street considers stocks selling well below the line of intrinsic worth, prospects and earning power considered, quiet accumulation starts. Gradually the public realizes that stocks are not getting lower and becomes conscious of the fact that pessimism or necessity had forced stocks too low. The public then begins to buy, the floating supply of good stocks diminishes, prices advance, and a bull market has been established. Hamilton warns us, however, that the reversal of primary movement is never sudden, for "The conditions which make for a big upward or a big downward movement of the primary class practically never change themselves overnight, however encouraging the first recovery may seem." (July 29, 1910)

This discussion of the Dow theory is intended to define its usefulness to traders rather than to describe its application as a business forecasting device. The writer does not presume to attempt to improve on Hamilton's splendid book, *The Stock Market Barometer*, which was written with the thought of interpreting the movements of the averages as a barometer of business, but those who are able to learn the theory as applied to speculation will, at the same time, recognize its usefulness as a reliable indicator of business trends.

Hamilton admitted the difficulties usually encountered in picking the top. He wrote: ". . . It is much harder to call the turn at the top than at the bottom. After a long bear market the discrepancy between the average price and what may be assumed as the line of values on real earnings, dividend yield and the value of money, is easily apparent. But after a long advance, many stocks are selling well within proved value. Any may have possibilities by no means discounted. The market, moreover, perhaps because of the complexity of the situation and more truly because of the stability of the general prosperity predicted by the barometer, may hold within a relatively small distance from the top for an indefinite time. It might indeed be said that there are instances of nearly a year with a range not far from the top, before an aggressive bear market has been established." (Feb. 15, 1926)

At another time, he wrote: ". . . The task of calling the exact top to a major movement is beyond the scope of any barometer. It is additionally difficult where there has been no inflated speculation." (June 13, 1923) By this, he meant that if there had been no inflated speculation even a competent student of the averages might easily believe a downward movement, later proving to have been the first decline of a primary bear market, was nothing more than a secondary reaction in a bull market.

Hamilton was fond of using the axioms of Wall Street to make his points clear. In a discussion of the averages at a time when a peak was near, he wrote: "Experienced traders in Wall Street say that when the elevator boy and the shoeblack are asking for bull tips on the market it is time to sell and go fishing." Near the end of many bull markets he often warned his readers that "The tree does not grow to the sky."

In the spring of 1929, before the final uprush, Hamilton admitted that the implication of the averages left no doubt as to the primary trend still being upward, but he evidently wanted his readers to pocket their profits and get out of the market. Here was his warning: ". . . The student should ask himself if stocks are not selling well above the line of values, if people are not buying upon hope which may be at least deferred long enough to make both the heart and the pocketbook sick." (April 5, 1929)

Not many days before the high point in 1909, 20 years earlier, was attained, this plea for caution appeared:—"It must never be forgotten that however great the prosperity of the country, advances in prices do not go on forever, and that a movement at least partly inflated which establishes record high prices is apt to show something out of the common in the inevitable reaction when a top-heavy market breaks." (Aug. 24, 1909)

Hamilton many times expressed the conviction that ". . . the market will ultimately turn (downward) when business is still good, but not far from a turn." (April 6, 1922) Economists pointed out that business turned down before stock prices in the bull market which terminated in 1929. Perhaps it is true, but in that case the bull market had generated more pressure in its boiler than the boiler of any other market had ever carried. Whether or not it proved dependable in forecasting the turn of *business* in 1929, no one can question the fact that it did give a positive proof in October of that year that the tide of *stock prices* had turned. Any student of the theory sufficiently skilled in its use to have learned to trade successfully on secondary reactions would have unloaded his stocks in September. Many of them did. Without exception, those who did not have since wished that they had trusted the Dow theory more and their own judgment less.

Of all the bull markets recorded by the Dow-Jones averages since 1897, never were the averages as easy to read as at the turn after the peak of 1929 was attained.

All the usual indications of inflation were present. Volume of trading was excessive and brokers' loans were making new peaks regularly—in fact, call money rates were so high that many corporations were finding it profitable to liquidate inventories and lend their cash equivalent to Wall Street at fantastic returns. Pool activities were being conducted on a disgraceful scale, brokerage offices were hanging out S. R. O. signs, and leading stocks were yielding less than the best grade of bonds. Worthless equities were being sky-rocketed without regard for intrinsic worth or earning power. The whole country appeared insane on the subject of stock speculation. Veteran traders look back at those months and wonder how they could have become so inoculated with the "new era" views as to have been caught in the inevitable crash. Bankers whose good sense might have saved the situation had speculators listened to them were shouted down as destructionists, while other bankers, whose names will go down in history as "racketeers," were praised as supermen.

Through all this excitement, the Dow theory did not falter. During the spring of 1929, the averages were saying that the supply of stocks equaled the demand—that important interests were handing out stocks in huge amounts and that other interests were absorbing them. Then the averages proclaimed the buying to be more powerful than the selling—new highs were made by both averages and the market bounded joyously on its upward path. The Dow theory was saying that the steam in the boiler was sufficient to carry prices upward again.

Between May 12 and June 5, a movement occurred which would have resembled a significant downward movement but for the fact that the tendency of volume was to increase on advances and quiet down on declines, and this fact, under the Dow theory, proclaimed the movement to be nothing more than secondary reaction in a bull market.

The peak of the bull market was reached Sept. 3, 1929. Between that day and October 4, a decline occurred which seemingly was only another reaction in a bull market. However, when the ensuing rally started on October 5 the volume of trading diminished, and in eight trading days any student of the Dow theory could look at his charts and know that the steam pressure in the market boiler was insufficient to lift prices further because the volume had continued to diminish as prices advanced. Chartists noticed at the time that the recovery had carried only to the lower limits of what could be called a reaction in a bear market. Thus the Dow theory student had a clear signal to unload his speculative line at about the 350 level of the industrial averages—less than 10 per cent below the peak! Then those who did not do so then were given a stronger warning each day as the volume of trading increased with declining prices, and when the lows of October 4 were finally broken during the week ending October 20, the verdict of a bear market was unquestioned by those who were able to read the averages.

The last forecast of a primary change from Hamilton's pen was a definite pronouncement of the beginning of the great bear market which started in September, 1929. As the pattern of the averages unfolded day by day, the ominous forecast was apparent to him. In a study of the price movement appearing in *Barron's* Sept. 23, 1929, the formation of a line in the averages was commented upon. On Oct. 21, 1929, *Barron's* called attention to the significance of a series of rallies and declines which afforded a bearish implication. On Oct. 25, 1929, an editorial, now famous, entitled "A Turn in the Tide" appeared in *The Wall Street Journal* in which the decline since September was definitely proclaimed to be the first stage of a primary bear market. Hamilton died suddenly a few weeks later, and it is fitting that his last forecast of a primary change should have been one of his best.

CHAPTER X

SECONDARY REACTIONS

For the purpose of this discussion, a secondary reaction is considered to be an important decline in a bull market or advance in a bear market, usually lasting from three weeks to as many months, during which interval the price movement generally retraces from 33 per cent to 66 per cent of the primary price change since the termination of the last preceding secondary reaction. These reactions are frequently erroneously assumed to represent a change of primary trend, because obviously the first stage of a bull market must always coincide with a movement which might have proved to have been merely a secondary reaction in a bear market, the contra being true after the peak has been attained in a bull market.

Secondary reactions are as necessary to the stock market as safety valves to steam boilers. They constitute the greatest hazard faced by the margin trader and also perhaps afford the greatest opportunity for gain to the student of the averages who can recognize a reaction as such and not confuse it with a reversal of primary trend. Hamilton said: "One of the safeguards of a bull market is the secondary reaction. It is the most effective check on excessive speculation."

When a secondary reaction is in the making, the question is often asked, "How far will it go?" Under the implications of the averages, one is reasonably safe in saying that important secondary movements generally retrace from one-third to two-thirds or more of the ground lost since the termination of the last major interruption of the market. This generalization can be tremendously useful, but those who try to place exact limits on secondary reactions are doomed to failure just as surely as would be the weather man who forecasted a snowfall of exactly three and one-half inches within a specified time. The latter is generally right about the snow and the approximate date on which it will occur, but he cannot successfully name the hour of the storm or the depth of the snowfall. The student of the Dow theory is in a similar position.

There are many causes contributing to these reactions, the most important of which is an oversold condition in a bear market or a top-heavy long account in a bull market. Such a situation tends to increase as the primary trend progresses and is commonly referred to as the "technical condition" of the market. Secondary reactions are usually blamed on some specific piece of news, but the real cause is a weakness in the market itself which makes it susceptible to this development.

As a healthy bull market makes headway, the public participates more freely. Such purchases are generally made on hopes of selling out when prices are higher, but a day comes when there are not enough buyers to go around for all the stock that is offered. Professional traders, ever on the alert for such situations, then proceed to saturate the market with short sales, while the little fellow becomes panicky and sells his stock, thereby helping along the reversal of trend. The combined effect of these sales is a sharp decline, during which time the advance of a number of weeks is frequently retraced in as many days. Such violent declines uncover weak long positions and bring out marginal selling. As a result, stocks are depressed to a level at which astute traders begin their accumulation for the next advance.

In a bear market, the opposite is true. Steady liquidation of securities by those who prefer or need cash reduces quotations day after day, with professionals, realizing there is more room on the bottom than on the top, hastening the decline with short sales. Eventually the market is forced to a lower level than is warranted by conditions. The short interest is perhaps too extended, with wise traders sensing the fact that liquidation has, for the time at least, run its course. They begin to accumulate stocks for the inevitable rally which, as an examination of the averages will show, occurs periodically. On July 29, 1910, when such a condition existed, Hamilton wrote: "On its normal movement in such a rally as seems now to have set in, about 40 per cent of the last break should be rapidly recovered. Should the market become dull after such a rally most professionals would sell stocks, on the theory that enough buying power had not been generated to warrant the assumption of a real bull swing."

The newspapers usually herald such a situation as "running in the shorts." Shorts hurry to cover their commitments and frequently go long for a short turn, which, added to unwise investment buying, results in a sharp upturn for the whole market. Such rallies carry along until buying power begins to diminish, at which time those who bought for the turn take their profits. The old law of supply and demand continues its inexorable march and prices decline again until levels are reached where the demand will again exceed the supply. In panic or semi-panic declines, some stock is generally taken over by banks and others to support the market, with such holdings being fed out very carefully on the advance. At such a time, May 21, 1909, Hamilton's written comment was: "Various meanings are ascribed to reductions in the volume of trading. One of the platitudes most constantly quoted in Wall Street is to the effect that one should never sell a dull market short. That advice is probably right oftener than it is wrong, but it is always wrong in an extended bear swing. In such a swing the tendency is to become dull on rallies and active on declines."

Secondary reactions are always confusing and Hamilton's perplexities were often expressed thus: "Secondary reactions in a bull market are hard to guess and even the indications are sometimes deceptive." Frequently, they bear many of the earmarks of a reversal of primary trend, such as a change from a bull market to a bear market. It is this same confusion in the minds

of traders which makes the secondaries such valuable insurance
for the market as a whole. On Sept. 11, 1924, in commenting on
secondary reactions, Hamilton stated: "More than twenty years'
experience in discussions of this kind has taught that the secondary reaction in the market, superficial in itself, is not governed
by the same laws as those which obtain in the major bull movement of which they are a characteristic part. The reaction in a
bull market resembles only in direction and not in kind the true
primary bear movement." In a bull market, when too much
pressure has been generated on the upside, a secondary occurs
in much the same manner as the safety valve of a steam boiler
pops and relieves the pressure before the factor of safety of the
boiler has been exceeded. On Nov. 3, 1922, Hamilton commented
on this in the following words: "There is a philosophy about the
secondary reaction in a bull market which should not be overlooked in studying a system which is scientific, with no elements
of empiricism or quackery. It has been remarked here before
that such secondary reactions are started by developments which
could by no possibility have been foreseen. These have their obvious effect upon an over-extended bull account. The market,
therefore, proceeds to perform its most valuable service, that of
insurance. It recedes to a safer level until it is entirely clear as to
the nature of the unfavorable symptom which it cannot yet
diagnose with certainty. Indeed, it may almost be said that a
bear argument understood is a bear argument discounted."

Quiet, weak spots in bear markets are generally good ones to
short, as they generally develop into serious declines. However,
after a market has drastically declined, following such a manifestation, and then goes into a semi-panic collapse, it is wise to
cover short positions and even perhaps make commitments for
long account. On the other hand, when a quiet but firm market
develops activity and strength on the upside, it may be bought
with the intention of closing out such commitments either while
strength and activity is still increasing or when the market re-

fuses to advance further on an increasing volume of transactions. However, the speculator who goes short in a *bull* market is merely guessing at secondary reactions and the odds are heavily against his cashing profits on such sales. It would be far better for him, after taking profits on a rally, to stand on the side lines during the decline and await the inevitable dull period after a recession in a bull market before again making commitments. Dullness after a reaction affords the amateur a chance to "go along" on an even basis with the most experienced professional.

Secondary reactions have certain characteristics which one can recognize and identify, but there are other secondary market characteristics which even expert traders cannot anticipate. There is general recognition that it is practically impossible to determine with any degree of accuracy the beginning of a secondary reaction. Any daily movement counter to the primary trend may be the beginning of a secondary reaction. Frequently, when stocks have gone into a panic or semi-panic collapse, the beginning of the reaction can be determined by the steadily increasing volume of trading, but the climax of such activity may be reached on the last day of the primary movement or on the first or second day of the secondary reaction. One definite characteristic of secondary reactions is that the movement counter to the primary trend is always much faster than that which occurred during the preceding primary movement. Hamilton noticed that "in a primary bear market the rallies are apt to be violent and erratic, and always occupy less time than the decline which they partially recover. In a bull market the reverse is the case." Often the primary movement of several weeks is retracted in a few days. Students of the averages can, by examining their charts over the years, see a similarity in such action which should enable them to determine with reasonable accuracy the difference between a secondary and primary movement. At the peak of a bull market, when the averages turn down, violent declines are generally conspicuously absent; on the other hand, any rally from the bottom of a bear market which subsequently proves to be the beginning of a new bull market is generally characterized by slow advances and frequent minor recessions, with a decrease in the volume of trading noticeable on the declines.

The beginnings of secondary reactions are frequently heralded by an action of the averages over several days wherein the rails and industrials cease confirming each other in direction, but this characteristic cannot be taken as a rule, for it is also noticeable at the peak of most bull markets and at the bottom of bear markets.

In commenting on secondary reactions in an editorial written Dec. 30, 1921, Hamilton wrote: "One of Wall Street's old maxims was, 'Never sell a dull market.' Rallies in a bear market are sharp, but experienced traders wisely put out their shorts again when the market becomes dull after a recovery. Exactly the converse is true in a bull market, where traders buy stocks if the market becomes dull following a reaction."

Important secondary reactions usually plot a pattern wherein the counter movement is accomplished in either two or three stages, with the industrials and rails, of course, usually confirming each other in these movements. To illustrate, the following rallies and declines, representing secondary movements of the averages, are described:

A typical example of a normal secondary reaction in a bull market was after a long advance prior to May 14, 1928; on that date the industrial averages were 220.88, following a high for the rails on May 9 at 147.05. Between the 9th and 14th, the two averages did not confirm. By May 22, the industrials had declined to 211.73 and the rails to 142.02, followed by a rally to June 2, when the industrials went to 220.96 but the rails stopped at 144.33. On June 12, the industrials were priced at 202.65, with the rails at 134.78. These declines were followed by a two day rally to June 14, when the industrials sold at 210.76 and the rails at 138.10. The market then sold off through June 18 to 201.96 for industrials and 133.51 for the rails, but the volume curve had been dropping steadily and, at the low point, was slightly above a million shares, whereas transactions of two to four million shares had been normal for many months. This decline had terminated within the usual secondary limits.

A characteristic secondary reaction in a bear market occurred in June and July, 1931. A long decline from February 24 had carried the industrials from 194.36 to 121.70 on June 2 and the rails from 111.58 to 66.85 on June 3. As the low point was approached, the volume of trading steadily increased. The industrials rallied to 134.73 on June 4 and the rails to 76.17 on the following day; then, on June 6, the industrials declined to 129.91 and the rails to 73.72, followed by a rally to 137.03 and 79.65, respectively, on June 13. By June 19, the prices were 130.31 and 74.71, after which the final rally of the reaction occurred which carried the industrials to 156.93 and the rails to 88.31 on June 27, the high point of the reaction. The volume curve shows that the trading diminished for several days before the peak was reached. This reaction lasted about four weeks, during which the industrials recovered 45 per cent and the rails 48 per cent of the primary decline occurring subsequent to February 24, the date on which the preceding reaction had reached its high point.

It is a uniform characteristic of secondary reactions in bull markets that the extreme low point of the reaction is generally accompanied by fairly heavy volume. Then the market usually advances for a day or two on uniform or slightly declining volume, followed by a further decline which fails to penetrate the recent lows, and if the volume diminishes perceptibly on this decline, it is reasonable to assume that the secondary reaction has run its course and that the primary bull trend is apt to be resumed, provided the secondary reaction can be assumed to have run its normal course, which should be somewhere between 33 per cent and 66 per cent of the total primary advance attained since the last preceding important secondary reaction.

An analysis of the extent of secondary reactions will be presented in terms of percentage later in this chapter.

It is important to stress the fact that every trader should at all times consider the volume of trading when examining secondary movements. The relation of volume is not nearly as uniform in its implications as are certain other characteristics, but such consideration is certainly valuable when attempting to determine the point in a reaction where stocks may be safely brought in a bull market or should be sold when the primary trend is downward.

Whenever prices have pushed through into new low ground in bear markets or to new highs in bull markets, it is usually safe to assume the primary direction will be maintained for a considerable time; but every trader should remember that from such new peaks or valleys secondary reactions may occur with amazing rapidity. It will be shown later that the extent of the secondary movement, which must inevitably occur, can be reasonably well defined, as can its duration, although the three weeks to three months usually required for its completion constitute an anxious period for the margin trader. It is during such periods that much is heard of "double bottoms" and "double tops." As long as prices move between the limits defined by the primary limit on one side and the probable extent of the secondary movement on the other, the trader is generally in "no man's land." It is during these periods that "lines" are most apt to appear.

A secondary movement is comparatively easy to describe, but does not lend itself to precise definition. Sometimes it begins or ends with "lines"—and sometimes not. If the primary movement which preceded it was very slow, the secondary reaction may be sharp, with a reasonably well-defined "line" a fairly uniform characteristic of every secondary movement extending more than eight weeks.

Over a period of years, Hamilton had a great deal to say about the duration and extent of secondary movements. Those who care to study his entire editorial writings will find many articles commenting upon typical secondary characteristics, with the following excerpts typical of his thought on the subject.

Some years ago he noted that a secondary reaction "tends to overrun itself, and there is usually a recovery which, as history over the past quarter of a century shows, frequently runs to as much as 60 per cent of the decline. During this recovery strong interests, who supported the market to help out the weak holders, distribute the stock they were compelled to purchase. The future course of the market turns on its ability to absorb this stock. After this almost automatic recovery, following a semi-panic break, the market usually sells off again, slowly, day by day, and not uncommonly approaches the old low level which the first fever of selling had established. It is not true that such breaks necessarily mark the end of major movements, although they have occurred at such times." (April 4, 1926)

"After a real stock market panic, as distinguished from a severe decline, the average price has always shown a regular movement in which approximately 40 to 60 per cent of the decline is recovered, and subsequently lost as the stock bought to protect on the panic comes out." (Dec. 25, 1907)

"It has been found that a market after a severe break, followed successively by a rally of 40 per cent or better, a slower subsequent reaction and minor fluctuations either way, acts like a pendulum running down until it reaches equilibrium. This is not unusually a condition following a panic break in the market." (Sept. 20, 1910)

"Tested over a number of years, the averages show that the decline after a long advance is usually about half recovered, and that the market then backs and fills between the old low and that point until a new impulse develops." (April 16, 1906)

Such comments as the above were the inspiration for much research work by the writer into secondary movements which proved beyond doubt that Hamilton was correct in his observations. This study was made with the full consciousness of the fact that anyone would fail in attempting to place an exact mathematical interpretation on that portion of the Dow theory pertaining to the duration and extent of secondary reactions. The Dow theory, as has been said before, is empirical and cannot be defined by mathematical computations. However, just as the records of the

Weather Bureau over a great many years are useful in making weather forecasts, so the tabulated observation of the duration and extent of secondary market reactions prove of some use in studying future market developments.

Probably no two students would agree on any rule for selecting and tabulating the important secondary reactions which have occurred during the 35-year history of the fluctuations of the railroad and industrial stock averages as recorded by Dow, Jones & Co. This writer has attempted secondary classifications in a great many ways, each of which required many weeks of tedious work, but no method produced entirely satisfactory results. One test eliminated all reactions as negligible which did not extend more than 15 days, with the result that many really important movements were eliminated and insignificant ones were retained. Then the time element was disregarded, with all reactions resulting in a movement of less than 5 per cent of the price of the averages eliminated. Then the percentage was raised to 7½ and again to 10, but each of these methods always resulted in the eliminating of really important movements although many insignificant minor movements remained. Eventually a method of selection was developed—one too complicated to describe here—which seemed to eliminate the minor movements and to leave undisturbed the important movements. The rallies and declines for 35 years were then tabulated, as shown in Table 1; from the dates and prices there shown, there were arranged Tables 2 and 3, showing the details of primary and secondary movements in bull and bear markets. These data were then consolidated and averaged, with the following results:

In bear markets, primary movements had an average duration of 95.6 days, whereas the secondary movements averaged 66.5 days, or 69.6 per cent of the time consumed in the preceding primary movement. In bull markets, the primary movements averaged 103.5 days and the secondaries, 42.2 days, or 40.8 per cent of the primary time interval.

Hamilton frequently stated that secondary reactions tend to

run from three weeks to as many months. In testing this rule, it was found that 65.5 per cent of the reactions in bear markets terminated between 20 and 100 days, the average being 47.3 days, with 45 per cent of all reactions reaching the extreme point of the counter movement in from 25 to 55 days. Corresponding figures for bull markets disclosed that a smaller percentage, 60.5 per cent, of the secondaries terminated in the 20 to 100 day brackets and that these averaged 42.8 days duration, with 44.2 per cent of the total reactions having a duration of from 25 to 55 days.

Hamilton frequently stated his belief that secondary reactions generally retraced from 40 to 60 per cent of the price change of the preceding primary movement. In checking this belief, it was found that *all* secondaries in bear markets averaged a retracement of 55.8 per cent of the preceding primary decline, with 72.5 per cent of all such secondaries rallying not less than one-third or more than two-thirds of the preceding primary decline. All rallies recovered an average of 49.5 per cent of the last preceding primary movement.

Corresponding figures for bull markets are as follows: *All* secondary declines averaged 58.9 per cent of the preceding primary rally, but only 50.0 per cent of these declines terminated after retracing from one-third to two-thirds of the preceding advance. Of the secondary movements so terminating, the retracement averaged 54.9 per cent.

There seems to be enough similarity in the characteristics of secondary reactions in both bear and bull markets to warrant considering them as a whole, rather than considering them as having distinctly different characteristics in bear and bull markets. Considered in this manner, it was found that all primary movements averaged 100.1 calendar days before being interrupted by an important secondary reaction. All secondary trends averaged 52.2 days duration, with average retracement 57.6 per cent of the immediately preceding primary movement.

If we could say that the great majority of secondary reactions terminated around the 57 per cent recovery point, speculation would be easy. Unfortunately, careful analysis shows that 7.1 per cent of all reactions terminate after retracing between 10 per cent to 25 per cent of the preceding primary movement; 25.4 per cent terminate after retracing between 25 per cent to 40 per cent; 18.8 per cent after retracing between 40 per cent to 55 per cent; 26.7 per cent after retracing between 55 per cent to 70 per cent; 8.5 per cent after retracing from 70 per cent to 85 per cent, with 14 per cent of all secondary movements extending beyond 85 per cent retracement.

When considering secondary reactions, the time element is often useful, for 73 per cent of all secondary reactions terminate in less than 55 calendar days. It was found that 60 per cent of these reactions terminated between 25 and 55 days.

TABLE 1

IMPORTANT PRIMARY AND SECONDARY PRICE MOVEMENTS: DOW-JONES INDUSTRIAL STOCK AVERAGES

	Date	Price	Date	Price	Date	Price	Date	Price	Date	Price	Date	Price
Declined	Apr. 19, '97	38.49	Dec. 15, '02	59.57	Nov. 29, '09	95.89	Apr. 11, '18	75.58	June 12, '22	90.73	June 18, '28	201.96
Rallied	Sept. 10, '97	55.82	Feb. 16, '03	67.70	Dec. 29, '09	99.28	May 15, '18	84.04	Sept. 11, '22	102.05	Sept. 7, '28	241.72
Declined	Nov. 8, '97	45.65	Aug. 8, '03	47.38	Feb. 8, '10	85.03	June 1, '18	77.93	Sept. 30, '22	96.30	Sept. 27, '28	236.87
Rallied	Feb. 5, '98	50.23	Aug. 17, '03	53.88	Mch. 8, '10	94.56	Sept. 3, '18	83.84	Oct. 14, '22	103.43	Nov. 28, '28	295.62
Declined	Mch. 25, '98	42.00	Oct. 15, '03	42.25	July 26, '10	73.62	Sept. 11, '18	80.46	Nov. 27, '22	92.03	Dec. 8, '28	257.33
Rallied	June 2, '98	53.36	Jan. 27, '04	50.50	Oct. 18, '10	86.02	Oct. 18, '18	89.07	Mch. 20, '23	105.38	Feb. 5, '29	322.06
Declined	June 15, '98	50.87	Mch. 12, '04	46.41	Dec. 6, '10	79.68	Feb. 8, '19	79.15	May 21, '23	92.77	Mch. 25, '29	297.50
Rallied	Aug. 26, '98	60.97	Dec. 5, '04	73.23	June 19, '11	87.06	July 14, '19	112.23	May 29, '23	97.66	May 4, '29	327.08
Declined	Oct. 19, '98	51.56	Dec. 12, '04	65.77	Sept. 25, '11	72.94	Aug. 20, '19	98.46	July 31, '23	86.91	May 27, '29	293.42
Rallied	Apr. 25, '99	77.28	Apr. 14, '05	83.75	Apr. 26, '12	90.93	Nov. 3, '19	119.62	Aug. 29, '23	93.70	Sept. 3, '29	381.17
Declined	May 31, '99	67.51	May 22, '05	71.37	July 12, '12	87.97	Nov. 29, '19	103.60	Oct. 27, '23	85.76	Nov. 13, '29	198.69
Rallied	Sept. 5, '99	77.61	Jan. 19, '06	103.00	Sept. 30, '12	94.15	Jan. 3, '20	109.88	Feb. 6, '24	101.31	Apr. 17, '30	294.07
Declined	Dec. 18, '99	58.27	July 13, '06	85.18	Mch. 20, '13	78.25	Feb. 25, '20	89.98	May 20, '24	88.33	June 24, '30	211.84
Rallied	Feb. 5, '00	68.36	Oct. 9, '06	96.75	Apr. 4, '13	83.19	Apr. 8, '20	105.65	Aug. 20, '24	105.57	Sept. 10, '30	245.09
Declined	June 23, '00	53.68	Mch. 25, '07	75.39	June 11, '13	72.11	May 19, '20	87.36	Oct. 14, '24	99.18	Dec. 16, '30	157.51
Rallied	Aug. 15, '00	58.90	May 3, '07	85.02	Feb. 3, '14	83.19	July 8, '20	94.51	Jan. 22, '25	123.60	Feb. 24, '31	194.36
Declined	Sept. 24, '00	52.96	Aug. 21, '07	69.26	* Dec. 24, '14	53.17	Aug. 10, '20	83.20	Mch. 30, '25	115.00	June 2, '31	121.70
Rallied	Nov. 20, '00	69.07	Sept. 6, '07	73.89	Jan. 23, '15	58.52	Sept. 17, '20	89.95	Feb. 13, '26	162.08	June 27, '31	156.93
Declined	Dec. 8, '00	63.98	Nov. 22, '07	53.08	Feb. 24, '15	54.22	Dec. 21, '20	66.75	Mch. 30, '26	135.20	Oct. 5, '31	86.48
Rallied	Dec. 27, '00	71.04	Jan. 14, '08	65.84	Apr. 30, '15	71.78	May 5, '21	80.03	Aug. 14, '26	166.64	Nov. 9, '31	116.79
Declined	Jan. 19, '01	64.77	Feb. 10, '08	58.80	May 14, '15	60.38	June 20, '21	64.90	Oct. 19, '26	145.66		
Rallied	May 1, '01	75.93	May 18, '08	75.12	Oct. 22, '15	96.46	Aug. 2, '21	69.95	May 31, '27	172.96		
Declined	May 9, '01	67.38	June 23, '08	71.70	Apr. 22, '16	84.96	Aug. 24, '21	63.90	June 27, '27	165.73		
Rallied	June 17, '01	78.26	Aug. 10, '08	85.40	Nov. 21, '16	110.15	Sept. 10, '21	71.92	Oct. 3, '27	199.78		
Declined	Aug. 6, '01	69.05	Sept. 22, '08	77.07	Feb. 2, '17	87.01	Oct. 17, '21	69.46	Oct. 22, '27	179.78		
Rallied	Aug. 26, '01	73.83	Nov. 13, '08	88.38	June 9, '17	99.08	Dec. 15, '21	81.50	Jan. 3, '28	203.35		
Declined	Dec. 12, '01	61.61	Feb. 23, '09	79.91	Dec. 19, '17	65.95	Jan. 10, '22	78.59	Feb. 20, '28	191.33		
Rallied	Apr. 24, '02	68.44	Aug. 14, '09	99.26	Feb. 19, '18	82.08	May 29, '22	96.41	June 2, '28	220.96		

* Adjusted for change in averages from 12 to 20 stocks which artificially reduced the price of the industrial average 19.84 points.

TABLE 2

BULL MARKETS: DOW-JONES INDUSTRIAL STOCKS

PRIMARY SWINGS				SECONDARY REACTIONS			
From	To	Days	Points Change	Date Completed	Days	Points Reacted	Percentage of Primary Retraced
Apr. 19, '97	Sept. 10, '97	144	17.33	Nov. 8, '97	59	10.17	58.6
Nov. 8, '97	Feb. 5, '98	89	4.58	Mch. 25, '98	48	8.23	179.5
Mch. 25, '98	June 2, '98	69	11.36	June 15, '98	13	2.49	21.9
June 15, '98	Aug. 26, '98	72	10.10	Oct. 19, '98	54	9.41	93.2
Oct. 19, '98	Apr. 25, '99	188	25.72	May 31, '99	36	9.77	38.0
May 31, '99	Sept. 5, '99	97	10.10				
Sept. 24, '00	Nov. 20, '00	57	16.11	Dec. 8, '00	18	5.09	31.5
Dec. 8, '00	Dec. 27, '00	19	7.06	Jan. 19, '01	23	6.27	88.8
Jan. 19, '01	May 1, '01	102	11.16	May 9, '01	8	8.56	76.5
May 9, '01	June 17, '01	39	10.88				
Oct. 15, '03	June 27, '04	104	8.25	Mch. 12, '04	44	4.09	49.6
Mch. 12, '04	Dec. 5, '04	268	26.82	Dec. 12, '04	7	7.46	27.8
Dec. 12, '04	Apr. 14, '05	123	17.98	May 22, '05	38	12.38	69.0
May 22, '05	Jan. 19, '06	242	31.63				
Nov. 22, '07	Jan. 14, '08	53	12.76	Feb. 10, '08	27	7.04	55.4
Feb. 10, '08	May 18, '08	97	16.32	June 23, '08	36	3.42	20.9
June 23, '08	Aug. 10, '08	48	13.70	Sept. 22, '08	43	8.33	60.8
Sept. 22, '08	Nov. 13, '08	52	11.31	Feb. 23, '09	102	8.47	74.9
Feb. 23, '09	Aug. 14, '09	172	19.35				
Sept. 25, '11	Apr. 26, '12	213	17.99	July 12, '12	77	2.96	16.5
July 12, '12	Sept. 30, '12	80	6.18				
Dec. 24, '14	Jan. 23, '15	30	5.35	Feb. 24, '15	32	4.30	80.4
Feb. 24, '15	Apr. 30, '15	65	17.56	May 14, '15	14	11.40	64.9
May 14, '15	Oct. 22, '15	161	36.08	Apr. 22, '16	182	11.50	31.8
Apr. 22, '16	Nov. 21, '16	213	25.19				
Dec. 19, '17	Feb. 19, '18	62	16.13	Apr. 11, '18	51	6.50	40.3
Apr. 11, '18	May 15, '18	34	8.46	June 1, '18	17	6.11	72.3
June 1, '18	Sept. 3, '18	94	5.91	Sept. 11, '18	8	3.38	57.2
Sept. 11, '18	Oct. 18, '18	37	8.61	Feb. 8, '19	113	9.92	115.1
Feb. 8, '19	July 14, '19	156	33.08	Aug. 20, '19	37	13.77	41.6
Aug. 20, '19	Nov. 3, '19	75	21.16				
Aug. 24, '21	Sept. 10, '21	17	8.02	Oct. 17, '21	37	2.46	30.7
Oct. 17, '21	Dec. 15, '21	59	12.04	Jan. 10, '22	26	2.91	24.2
Jan. 10, '22	May 29, '22	139	17.82	June 12, '22	14	5.68	31.8
June 12, '22	Sept. 11, '22	91	11.32	Sept. 30, '22	19	5.75	50.7
Sept. 30, '22	Oct. 14, '22	14	7.13	Nov. 27, '22	44	11.40	160.0
Nov. 27, '22	Mch. 20, '23	113	13.35				
Oct. 27, '23	Feb. 6, '24	102	15.55	May 20, '24	103	12.98	83.4
May 20, '24	Aug. 20, '24	92	17.24	Oct. 14, '24	55	6.39	37.1
Oct. 14, '24	Jan. 22, '25	100	24.42	Mch. 30, '25	67	8.60	35.2
Mch. 30, '25	Feb. 13, '26	320	47.08	Mch. 30, '26	45	26.88	56.3
Mch. 30, '26	Aug. 14, '26	137	31.44	Oct. 19, '26	66	20.98	66.6
Oct. 19, '26	May 31, '27	224	27.30	June 27, '27	27	7.23	26.4
Jan. 27, '27	Oct. 3, '27	98	34.05	Oct. 22, '27	19	20.00	58.6
Oct. 22, '27	Jan. 3, '28	73	23.57	Feb. 20, '28	48	12.02	51.2
Feb. 20, '28	June 2, '28	102	29.63	June 18, '28	16	19.00	64.1
June 18, '28	Sept. 7, '28	81	39.76	Sept. 27, '28	20	4.85	12.4
Sept. 27, '28	Nov. 28, '28	62	58.75	Dec. 8, '28	10	38.29	65.4
Dec. 8, '28	Feb. 5, '29	59	64.73	Mch. 25, '29	48	24.56	37.9
Mch. 25, '29	May 4, '29	40	29.58	May 27, '29	23	33.66	114.0
May 27, '29	Sept. 3, '29	99	87.75				

TABLE 3

BEAR MARKETS: DOW-JONES INDUSTRIAL STOCKS

| | | | | | | | Percentage of |
| Primary Swings | | | | Secondary Reactions | | | |
From	To	Days	Points Change	Date Completed	Days	Points Reacted	Primary Retraced
Sept. 5, '99	Dec. 18, '99	104	19.34	Feb. 5, '00	49	10.09	51.7
Feb. 5, '00	June 23, '00	138	14.68	Aug. 15, '00	53	5.22	35.6
Aug. 15, '00	Sept. 24, '00	40	5.94				
June 17, '01	Aug. 6, '01	50	9.21	Aug. 26, '01	20	4.78	51.9
Aug. 26, '01	Dec. 12, '01	108	12.22	Apr. 24, '02	133	6.83	55.9
Apr. 24, '02	Dec. 15, '02	235	8.77	Feb. 16, '03	63	8.13	92.7
Feb. 16, '03	Aug. 8, '03	173	20.32	Aug. 17, '03	9	6.50	31.5
Aug. 17, '03	Oct. 15, '03	59	11.63				
Jan. 19, '06	July 13, '06	175	17.82	Oct. 9, '06	88	11.57	64.9
Oct. 9, '06	Mch. 25, '07	167	21.36	May 3, '07	39	9.63	45.2
May 3, '07	Aug. 21, '07	110	15.77	Sept. 6, '07	16	4.64	29.5
Sept. 6, '07	Nov. 22, '07	77	20.81				
Aug. 14, '09	Nov. 29, '09	107	3.37	Dec. 29, '09	30	3.39	100.6
Dec. 29, '09	Feb. 10, '10	41	14.25	Mch. 8, '10	28	9.53	66.9
Mch. 8, '10	July 26, '10	140	20.94	Oct. 18, '10	84	12.40	58.5
Oct. 18, '10	Dec. 6, '10	49	6.34	June 19, '11	195	7.38	116.5
June 19, '11	Sept. 25, '11	98	14.12				
Sept. 30, '12	Mch. 20, '13	171	15.90	Apr. 4, '13	15	4.94	31.1
Apr. 4, '13	June 11, '13	68	11.08	Feb. 3, '14	237	11.08	100.0
* Feb. 3, '14	Dec. 24, '14	324	10.80				
Nov. 21, '16	Feb. 2, '17	73	23.14	June 9, '17	127	12.07	52.2
June 19, '17	Dec. 19, '17	135	33.13				
Nov. 3, '19	Nov. 29, '19	26	16.02	Jan. 3, '20	35	6.28	39.2
Jan. 3, '20	Feb. 25, '20	53	19.90	Apr. 8, '20	42	15.67	78.7
Apr. 8, '20	May 19, '20	41	18.29	July 8, '20	50	7.15	39.1
July 8, '20	Aug. 10, '20	33	11.31	Sept. 17, '20	38	6.75	59.6
Sept. 17, '20	Dec. 21, '20	95	23.20	May 5, '21	135	13.28	56.6
May 5, '21	June 20, '21	46	15.13	Aug. 2, '21	43	5.05	33.4
Aug. 2, '21	Aug. 24, '21	22	6.05				
Mch. 20, '23	May 21, '23	62	12.61	May 29, '23	8	4.89	38.8
May 29, '23	July 31, '23	63	10.75	Aug. 29, '23	29	6.79	63.2
Aug. 29, '23	Oct. 27, '23	59	7.94				
Sept. 3, '29	Nov. 13, '29	71	182.48	Apr. 17, '30	155	95.38	52.3
Apr. 17, '30	June 24, '30	68	82.23	Sept. 10, '30	78	33.25	40.4
Sept. 10, '30	Dec. 16, '30	97	87.58	Feb. 24, '31	70	36.85	42.1
Feb. 24, '31	June 2, '31	98	72.66	June 27, '31	25	35.23	48.5
June 27, '31	Oct. 5, '31	100	70.45	Nov. 9, '31	35	30.31	43.0
Nov. 9, '31	Jan. 5, '32	57	45.55				

* Adjusted for change in averages from 12 to 20 stocks which artificially reduced the price of the industrial average 19.84 points.

CHAPTER XI

DAILY FLUCTUATIONS

Inferences drawn from one day's movement of the averages are almost certain to be misleading and are of but little value except when "lines" are being formed. The day to day movement must be recorded and studied, however, because a series of charted daily movements always eventually develops into a pattern easily recognized as having a forecasting value.

While the averages and sales for any one day have but little significance, the prices for that day should never be ignored, because the whole pattern of price structure can only be studied and understood as the daily fluctuations arrange themselves into a charted pattern having definite forecasting value. One piece of steel does not make a bridge, but every engineer knows that it is a definite part of the complete structure.

When a "line" has been forming for a considerable time, the day to day movement is significant and may have a direct bearing upon the application of the Dow theory, but this will be discussed in a later chapter. With the exception of such a situation, however, inferences drawn from the day to day movement are almost certain to be misleading. The trader attempting to draw such inferences is merely guessing and is not properly using the Dow theory, although he generally blames the Dow theory for his failure. Hamilton frequently declared that "The stock market is not logical in its movements from day to day." (July 29, 1929) However, those who persist in using the daily movement, and there are many who do, may get some encouragement from this line from Hamilton's pen: "There is a certain encouragement about the daily fluctuation occasionally." (Aug. 30, 1910) Nevertheless, he tells us that the Dow theory generally disregards the one-day price movement.

CHAPTER XII

BOTH AVERAGES MUST CONFIRM

The movement of both the railroad and industrial stock averages should always be considered together. The movement of one price average must be confirmed by the other before reliable inferences may be drawn. Conclusions based upon the movement of one average, unconfirmed by the other, are almost certain to prove misleading.

The most useful part of the Dow theory, and the part that must never be forgotten for even a day, is the fact that no price movement is worthy of consideration unless the movement is confirmed by both averages. Many who claim an understanding of the theory consider only the movement of the industrial stock average if they happen to be trading in industrials. Some even chart only the one average and profess to be able to interpret the movements correctly. It is true that there are times when such conclusions seem justified, but over any extended period such procedure inevitably results in disaster.

There are students who think the utility average should have more interpretative significance than the rails because the trading is more active in the former group. There is no intention to enter into any debate upon the subject, but the question might be pertinently asked—why not use a copper stock average, or the average of a group of motor stocks? The best answer to those who raise the question regarding the advisability of using the utility average is to point out that tests have proved the Dow theory would not be nearly as effective when applied to relative movements of the industrials and utility averages.[6] The Dow theory deals ex-

[6] A practical reason for not using the public utility average is the interlocking relationship of various leading units is such that the whole average might be influenced by conditions directly applicable to only one or two stocks.

clusively with the movement of the railroad and industrial stock averages, and any other method would not be Dow's theory as expounded by Hamilton.

It is difficult to understand why Dow did not endeavor to explain why the two averages must confirm. His theory was based upon observations that they always *did* confirm if the movement later proved to be genuine. When Hamilton wrote his book, *The Stock Market Barometer*, he also neglected to attempt any explanation as to why the rails must always confirm the industrials, which suggests that it is perhaps presumptuous to offer a few reasons which appear simple and logical today.

However, let us consider a cycle of business improvement—after a period of depression. Factories are still idle; unemployment and hard times are everywhere apparent. Inventories are low, purchasing power is depleted, dividends have been drastically reduced; but people are still eating and wearing out clothes, more children are being born, machinery is rusting, while labor cost has been materially cut. Eventually, a day comes when the sales manager of a steel company reviews his field reports and finds, although no orders are in hand, that the erection of a considerable number of bridges and apartment houses, all requiring steel, is being considered for some future time. The sales manager goes to the chief executive and discusses the situation. The chief executive then asks the superintendent about how long it will take to get the mills going when business revives. The superintendent insists he has to reline a blast furnace before much business develops. The chief executive asks his board for authority to reline the blast furnace and the repairs are started. Brick, lime, and sand are shipped in by rail and men are employed to reline the furnace. The traffic manager of the railroad tells his executive of this freight movement to the steel company and suggests that an improved future outlook is indicated if the steel company is spending money. The railroad executive then discusses the situation with his superintendent. They decide to service up ore cars to prepare for hauling ore to the blast furnace, which means buying a little paint and providing a little employment for workers. Wages paid for the repairs on the blast furnace and ore cars mean a little more purchasing power for a few people, who then buy some shoes, etc., thereby further depleting the retailers' shelves. This means, in the case of shoes, ordering a new stock from the factory, which causes the factory to require more leather and the tanner, in turn, to need more hides. Then a little steel is bought for bridges and apartment houses; the furnace is put in blast and ore starts moving. Perhaps a similar development is taking place in other lines of business.

Now the steel company has not earned a dime insofar as its published statement is concerned, and it may even be that orders received in the afore-mentioned example are so small as to be overlooked in an unfilled tonnage report. Nevertheless, the railroad has received cash for the carrying of bricks and ore, while the increased activity is almost instantly reflected in carloadings and in railroad earnings. If this line of reasoning is sound, then it is logical to say that railroad stocks should move with industrials, if not before them. Purchases of raw products must be delivered to factories by means of transportation, which still means the railroads to a very considerable extent, despite the increasing competition which these carriers are experiencing.

A complete understanding of the necessity of waiting for confirmation by both averages is absolutely necessary if the Dow theory is to be used advantageously. Because of the importance of this point, it seems best to quote rather extensively from Hamilton on the subject, even if repetition does become somewhat tedious. The following excerpts are taken from editorials written over a period of years:

". . . Dow's theory . . . stipulates for a confirmation of one average by the other. This constantly occurs at the inception of a primary movement, but is anything but consistently present when the market turns for a secondary swing. This is the plain reason for the consistent conservatism of 'The Stock Market

Barometer,' which makes good its title by claiming too little rather than too much." (April 6, 1926)

"In like secondary movements the industrial group (taken separately from the railroads) may recover much more sharply than the railroads, or the railroads may lead, and it need hardly be said that the twenty active railroad stocks and the twenty industrials, moving together, will not advance point for point with each other even in the primary movement." (*The Stock Market Barometer*)

"Dow always ignored a movement of one average which was not confirmed by the other, and experience since his death has shown the wisdom of that method of checking the reading of the averages. His theory was that a downward movement of secondary, and perhaps ultimately primary importance was established when the new lows for both averages were under the low points of the preceding reaction." (June 25, 1928)

"It is no light matter to manipulate both averages, and the indications of one without the other are generally disregarded." (July 30, 1928)

"It seems a clear inference, in a movement where the averages do not confirm each other, that uncertainty still continues as concerns the business outlook . . ." (May 24, 1924)

"In the discussions of the price movement based on Dow's theory of the averages that have appeared from time to time, it has been repeatedly noted that inferences drawn from the action of either one of the averages, while often significant, may easily be deceptive, but that the inferences become of the highest prediction value when the two averages confirm each other.

"So it was that two weeks ago when the railroad average alone had just gone to new high ground, it was possible to say that this was a strongly bullish indication, which, if followed up, as it now has been, by a similar action on the part of the industrial averages, would amount to a positive indication of the continuance of the upward trend." (July 24, 1922)

". . . the average indications are invariably deceptive when they do not corroborate each other." (Nov. 3, 1922)

"There is one fairly safe rule about reading the averages, even if it is a negative one. This is that half an indication is not necessarily better than no indication at all. The two averages must confirm each other . . ." (Aug. 27, 1928)

"It has been the safe experience that these averages must confirm each other, and that has been the reason why two dissimilar groups of twenty stocks each have been chosen for purposes of record instead of a miscellaneous group of forty stocks." (May 25, 1925)

"A new low or a new high made by the one but not confirmed by the other is almost invariably deceptive. The reason is not far to seek. One group of securities acts upon the other; and if the market for railroad stocks is sold out it cannot lift the whole list with it if there is a superabundant supply of the industrials." (June 4, 1913)

"These independent movements, on previous experience, are usually deceptive, but when both averages advance or decline together the indication of a uniform market movement is good." (Sept. 8, 1913)

". . . when one breaks through an old low level without the other, or when one establishes a new high for the short swing, unsupported, the inference is almost invariably deceptive." (Feb. 10, 1915)

". . . conclusions drawn from one average but not confirmed by the other, are sometimes misleading, and should always be treated with caution. . . ." (June 26, 1925)

"Once more it is worth while to emphasize that the movement of these two averages is deceptive unless they act together." (June 9, 1915)

"In the studies of the price movement, based upon Dow's theory . . . it has been repeatedly found that the two averages of twenty railroad stocks and twenty industrials must confirm each other to give an authoritative prediction." (July 8, 1922)

"Indeed it may be said that a new high or a new low by one of the averages unconfirmed by the other has been invariably deceptive. New high or low points for both have preceded every major movement since the averages were established." (May 10, 1921)

"The indication is always stronger when both the industrials and the railroads make such a new high level about the same time . . ." (July 16, 1919)

"They are frequently misleading where one group breaks through the line and the other does not. When, however, the movement is simultaneous there is a uniform body of experience to indicate the market trend." (April 16, 1914)

"One of the shortest ways of going wrong is to accept an indication by one average which has not been clearly confirmed by the other." (*The Stock Market Barometer*)

"It is by no means necessary, as experience shows, that the low or the high point of a primary movement should be made in both averages on the same day. All we assume is that the market has turned, with the two averages confirming, even although one of the averages subsequently makes a new low point or a new high point, but is not confirmed by the other. The previous lows or highs made by both averages may best be taken as representing the turn of the market." (*The Stock Market Barometer*)

"This illustration serves to emphasize the fact that while the two averages may vary in strength they will not materially vary in direction, especially in a major movement. Throughout all the years in which both averages have been kept this rule has proved entirely dependable. It is not only true of the major swings of the market but it is approximately true of the secondary reactions and rallies. It would not be true of the daily fluctuation, and it might be utterly misleading so far as individual stocks are concerned." (*The Stock Market Barometer*)

Students of the averages will find one interval when the action of rail and industrial averages ceased to confirm one another. During and immediately after our participation in the World

War, the railroads were operated by the federal government with a fixed return guaranteed to the roads. This situation eliminated speculative activity from that group during that period, causing the railroad stocks to fluctuate with bonds because their return was fixed. For this reason, students studying the averages will find it advisable to omit the period from consideration.

CHAPTER XIII

DETERMINING THE TREND

Successive rallies penetrating preceding high points, with ensuing declines terminating above preceding low points, offer a bullish indication. Conversely, failure of the rallies to penetrate previous high points, with ensuing declines carrying below former low points, is bearish. Inferences so drawn are useful in appraising secondary reactions and are of major importance in forecasting the resumption, continuation, or change of the primary trend. For the purpose of this discussion, a rally or a decline is defined as one or more daily movements resulting in a net reversal of direction exceeding three per cent of the price of either average. Such movements have but little authority unless confirmed in direction by both averages, but the confirmation need not occur on the same day.

The significance of rallies in a secondary reaction in a bull market is explained by Hamilton as follows: ". . . On the well-tested rule of reading the averages, a major bull swing continues so long as the rally from a secondary reaction establishes new high points in both averages, not necessarily on the same day, or even in the same week, provided only that they confirm each other." (Dec. 30, 1921)

It should always be remembered that a new high or low by one average, unconfirmed by the other, is deceptive. Such action frequently denotes a change of a secondary nature, although sometimes proving to be of primary importance.

The authority of new highs or lows which are properly confirmed remains in force until cancelled by some later definite confirmed action. If, for instance, new highs are made in a primary bull market, the prediction is valid that the bull market will continue for a considerable time. Moreover, if one average later retraces its advance to a point below its old high, or even below a previous low point, but the other average fails to confirm the action, it is proper to infer that the previous bullish indication is still in force. Hamilton explains this as follows: "The barometer does not give indications every day and all the time; according to Charles H. Dow's theory, an indication remains in force until it is cancelled by another, or re-enforced in some way, as, for instance, when the industrial average confirms the railroad average or vice versa." (Sept. 23, 1929)

If, after a severe secondary reaction in a primary bull market, the ensuing rallies fail to go to new highs within a reasonable time and a further drastic decline occurs extending below the low points of the previous reaction, it is generally safe to assume the primary trend has changed from bullish to bearish. Conversely, when, after a decline has carried both averages to new low ground in a bear market, an important secondary reaction has taken place and the next decline fails to carry either average to a new low, one may infer that the primary trend has changed from bear to bull if the next rally carries both averages above the high points of the last important rally. Few exceptions to this rule can be found in the charted averages when examined over a 35-year period.

Many traders try to apply this rule to minor reactions, forgetting that a normal secondary reaction generally lasts from three to 12 weeks and retraces from one-third to two-thirds of the primary movement since the last important secondary reaction. The best way for the students to gain a complete understanding of the significance of small rallies and declines is to study the charted daily movements over the entire record of the averages.

According to Hamilton, "Dow always ignored a movement of one average which was not confirmed by the other, and experience since his death has shown the wisdom of that method of checking the reading of the averages. His theory was that a downward movement of secondary, and perhaps ultimately primary, importance was established when the new lows for both averages were under the low points of the preceding reaction." (June 25, 1928)

Because a lucid explanation of the significance of rallies and declines has always proved so difficult, and because a proper understanding of the rise and fall of prices as compared to previous similar movements is of such vital importance when using the averages as a forecasting device, it is perhaps wise to offer a second quotation which is merely a repetition, although phrased differently: "Whenever a series of rallies and declines have occurred in the day to day movement, always confirmed by both rail and industrial averages, and the rallies carry above immediately preceding high points, with declines failing to penetrate recent lows, the implication is bullish for the immediate future, but not necessarily indicating a primary bull trend."

When a series of such rallies and declines of both averages have penetrated the highest points previously attained in a primary bull market, it is generally safe to infer that the primary bull trend will continue for a considerable period of time. Conversely, successive rallies and declines, with highs failing to penetrate the immediately preceding high points, and the ensuing declines carrying below previous low prices, afford a bearish implication for the immediate future, although not necessarily implying a primary bear trend. On the other hand, when a series of rallies and declines break through the lowest prices of a primary bear trend, the probability of much lower prices is generally a reasonable inference. When declines in a primary bull market result in violating the lowest points encountered during the last major secondary reaction of that market, it may generally be assumed that the primary trend has changed from bullish to bearish; the converse, of course, is usually a dependable means of determining when a bear primary movement has changed to the beginning of a bull market.

Occasional exceptions can be found, and it is proper that this should be true, for otherwise these rules would constitute a sure way of beating the stock market. Such a method would, of course, very quickly result in there being no market.

CHAPTER XIV

LINES

A "line" is a price movement extending two to three weeks or longer, during which period the price variation of both averages move within a range of approximately five per cent. Such a movement indicates either accumulation or distribution. Simultaneous advances above the limits of the "line" indicate accumulation and predict higher prices; conversely, simultaneous declines below the "line" imply distribution and lower prices are sure to follow. Conclusions drawn from the movement of one average, not confirmed by the other, generally prove to be incorrect.

The portion of the Dow theory which pertains to "lines" has proved to be so dependable as almost to deserve the designation of *axiom* instead of *theorem*. However, "lines" do not occur frequently enough to satisfy most traders, with the result that many endeavor to see "lines" that do not exist. Moreover, many traders insist on forming conclusions from a "line" in one average not confirmed by the other—a very dangerous practice. There are others who, seeing a line forming, try to guess the direction in which the averages will break through, putting out their stocks and hanging on to them regardless of the fact that their judgment may be proved wrong by subsequent movements of the averages. "As a matter of fact, when a 'line' is in process of formation it is the hardest thing in the world to tell either the nature of the selling or that of the buying. Both accumulation and distribution are at work, and no one can say which will ultimately exercise the greatest pressure." (May 22, 1922)

There are people who insist on trying to place an exact mathematical interpretation on the duration or height of a line, but this cannot be done successfully. The allowable price variation must be considered in connection with the prevailing activity of speculation and be compared with the violence or lack of violence of preceding fluctuations. This is one of the reasons why successful application of the Dow theory to speculation must be considered both an art and a science. Anyone attempting an exact mathematical interpretation of the Dow theory is placing himself on a parity with the surgeon who tried to remove an appendix by cutting two inches deep at a point 38 inches above the patient's instep, regardless of the age, sex, height, or contour of his patient.

Hamilton said that we could always depend upon the breaking of a line as indicating a change of the general market direction of at least secondary, and occasionally even of primary, character.

In discussing "lines," certain of the following excerpts define height rather exactly. It should be remembered that these comments were written years ago when the averages were generally below 100. Later in this chapter, Hamilton's comment will be quoted on the subject of appraising "lines" when average prices had gone far above the levels of earlier years.

A typical early comment on the subject of "lines" follows:

"Scrutiny of the average figures will show that there are periods where the fluctuations for a number of weeks are within a narrow range; as, for instance, where the industrials do not sell below seventy or above seventy-four, and the railroads above seventy-seven or below seventy-three. This is technically called 'making a line,' and experience shows that it indicates a period either of distribution or of accumulation. When the two averages rise above the high point of the line, the indication is strongly bullish. It may mean a secondary rally in a bear market; it meant, in 1921, the inauguration of a primary bull movement extending into 1922.

"If, however, the two averages break through the lower level, it is obvious that the market for stocks has reached what meteorologists would call 'saturation point.' Precipitation follows

—a secondary bear movement in a bull market, or the inception of a primary downward movement like that which developed in October 1919." (*The Stock Market Barometer*)

Some years ago a "line" was described in the following language: "Many years' experience in the stock market, tested by Charles H. Dow's theory of its movement, has taught students the significance of a 'line' in the averages. To be of real value the requirements are strict. The industrial and railroad averages should confirm each other. The period taken should be long enough to afford a real test relative to the volume of trading. The fluctuations from day to day should be so narrow that they can be confined within a range of less than four points. Given these conditions an important deduction may be drawn." (May 8, 1922)

Another explanation follows: "We can satisfy ourselves from examples that a period of trading within a narrow range—what we have called a 'line'—gaining significance as the number of trading days increases, can only mean accumulation or distribution, and that the subsequent price movement shows whether the market has become bare of stocks or saturated with an oversupply." (*The Stock Market Barometer*)

On March 17, 1909, Hamilton commented: "The net variation between March 3 and March 13, inclusive, was less than 3/8 of 1%. This curious seesaw movement occurs only very occasionally and quite often precedes a broad change in the general market swing." An advance which carried prices up 29 per cent occurred when the averages broke out on the top side of the "line" referred to at this time.

Useful inferences may sometimes be drawn from the very absence of price movement, as Hamilton has pointed out. "When the average price of stocks shows merely nominal fluctuations, it is still possible to draw useful inferences from the condition. In such a case 'they also serve who only stand and wait.'" (Sept. 20, 1910)

Hamilton's conclusions as to the duration of the validity of the forecast value of "lines" were once stated as follows: "Previous experience teaches us that after a line at the top of the movement has been broken through on the downward side, as in the case both of the industrials and the railroads, it would be necessary for the last high point to be reached again before we could assume anything like a bullish indication in the average." (March 6, 1911)

A perfect example of a "line" is the period between May 4 and July 31, 1911, when the "line" was broken on the bottom, a precipitous decline followed which proved to be the end of a bear market. While this "line" was being made, Hamilton wrote: "A long line, such as the averages have described in the past six weeks, may even, with a limited volume of business, be taken as indicating one or two things. Either stocks have been successfully distributed at the new high level, or an accumulation has been in progress sufficient in the aggregate to warrant the assumption that a strong section of opinion believes prices should work higher." (July 14, 1911)

On January 17, 1912, while a "line" was being formed which was followed by an almost uninterrupted advance of many months, this was written: "It is remarkable that in that period the average price of twenty active railroad stocks has not touched 115 on the one hand or 118 on the other; and the industrial price shows a maximum of 82.48 and a minimum of 79.19 in the same period. This is a striking continuance of what may be called a 'line' of accumulation or distribution, established more than a week before our previous price movement discussion was printed. Such a narrow fluctuation, to the experienced student of the averages, may be as significant as a sharp movement in either direction. If the long pause in the price movement has been made in order to accumulate stock without advancing prices, the result ought to show soon, when the price in both averages crosses the limit of the line in the upward direction. Let it be observed that the word 'line' is here used in the market sense, and does not mean strictly 'length without breadth.' It means length with very little breadth

—less than three points in the railroad stocks and a little more than that in the industrials."

Because "lines" are sometimes confusing, Hamilton's comment on Sept. 8, 1913, is helpful: "For nearly a month in the case of each of the averages, prices have fluctuated within little more than two points range. On August 28, the industrials advanced above this line, but the railroad stocks did not confirm. On September 3, the railroad stocks broke through on the down side, but the industrials held their own. To readers of the averages this constitutes a standoff, especially as both averages are now well within the old range. A simultaneous movement in either direction, but especially downwards, would, on previous experience, give an important lead on further movements." (Sept. 8, 1913)

Hamilton wrote a great deal during 1914 on the subject of "lines." He evidently felt that a bull market should be in progress, whereas his "lines" insisted on showing distribution. In later years, he always insisted that these "lines" represented the periods of distribution of Germany's American securities in preparation for the World War. An excerpt from an editorial written April 16, 1914, is typical: "For seventy trading days previous to April 14, the average price of the twelve industrials stocks did not go above 84, or below 81. For forty days before that date, the average price of twenty active railroads never went above 106 or below 103. Here is a range of three points for the two averages kept for comparison by *The Wall Street Journal*, and they simultaneously broke through the 'line,' on the lower side, on April 14.

"On all previous experience of the averages, the indication is so bearish as to point to a resumption of the primary bear market which set in early in October, 1912."

Students were warned that a line in one average alone has no forecasting value when Hamilton wrote that ". . . all past experience of the average has shown that unless such a line is made simultaneously by both the industrials and the railroads it is more apt to be deceptive than not." (March 20, 1916)

With the higher prices prevailing in 1926, Hamilton recognized the need for allowing more liberal limits for "lines" and declared, "It should also be said here that we may allow ourselves more latitude in the limits of such a 'line' in view of the high figure of the average, especially in the industrial group." (Oct. 18, 1926)

That he considered the action of the market in the spring of 1929 as being equivalent to a "line" is indicated in this excerpt from a discussion of the price movement written July 1, 1929: "It will be clearly seen that the sharp and extended fluctuations, especially in the industrial average, have amounted in effect to a distributive period not at all dissimilar to that which has occurred at lower levels when the averages have made a 'line.' Such a 'line' indicated either accumulation or distribution, and the movement out of it in either direction has historically carried market significance. At these high levels a much wider range of fluctuation in a distribution period is only to be expected. The advance of both averages above that area is a clear indication that a large quantity of stock has not only been distributed but effectively absorbed, presumably by investors or those who can finance their purchase by taking the stock off the market." (July 1, 1929)

An examination of the daily price movement for this period will prove of interest to students. In September, 1929, just after the peak of the late bull market had been attained, but at a time when few traders expected the approaching crash which shook the world, Hamilton detected a "line" while the railroad and industrial averages were within 10 per cent of peak prices. Writing about this in *Barron's* on Sept. 23, 1929, he said in part: "It follows that with an industrial average above 300 a wider flexibility is to be expected, although the principles upon which Dow reasoned are undisturbed. In his time an average would make what he called a 'line,' with a fluctuation up or down confined for weeks at a time within a three-point range. . . . But at the present high level of the industrials a wider range for this area of distribution or accumulation may be safely assumed."

In the opinion of this writer, there is an interesting and perhaps useful field of research to be explored in examining the relationship of the breadth of "lines" to volume of trading, or perhaps a better correlation could be worked out by using the number of stock tickers in service. The force of the market is largely represented by the total stock sales, and the more force applied the greater the resultant action or reaction. It has been noticed that the tendency of "lines" is to broaden near peaks of bull markets, as does the volume of trading. On the other hand, "lines" forming near the bottom, or in very dull periods, are correspondingly narrow.

CHAPTER XV

THE RELATION OF VOLUME TO PRICE MOVEMENTS

A market which has been overbought becomes dull on rallies and develops activity on declines; conversely, when a market is oversold, the tendency is to become dull on declines and active on rallies. Bull markets terminate in a period of excessive activity and begin with comparatively light transactions.

The subject of the relation of market activity to the price movement is one in which many contradictions appeared in Hamilton's writings. He repeatedly told his readers to ignore everything except the movement of the averages and that this movement discounted and appraised even the activity of the market. Nevertheless, he seems to have used the volume of transactions all through the years, and his conclusions based particularly on comparative activity seem to have been both well considered and effective.

At the risk of confusing the reader, it seems best to quote Hamilton wherein he denied the usefulness of volume, and then to show that he repeatedly used this datum in summing up his case before reaching some of his conclusions.

The following excerpts present the case against considering market activity in arriving at conclusions:

". . . it should be said that the price average by its very nature discounts everything. Dullness and inactivity are but symptoms, and for these the average allows, as it does likewise for activity, unexpected news, dividends and everything else contributing to make up the fluctuating market price. This is why the volume of trading is ignored in these studies. In the quarter of a century of the price movement recorded in the Dow-Jones and Company averages, the volume of business has borne little perceptible relation to the tendency of prices." (June 4, 1913)

"The averages have looked as if they wanted to go up, although some students might argue that the small volume of business detracted from the importance of such changes as there were. Nevertheless, the tendency has been distinctly bullish. So far as volume is concerned we prefer to neglect it in these studies, arguing that this, as well as all other considerations, may be eliminated in the comparison of extended price movements over any considerable period of time." (April 5, 1911)

On Jan. 5, 1911, Hamilton wrote: "We prefer to neglect volume and the character of the trading in these studies, believing that the average itself, being absolutely impartial, makes allowances for these factors as well as for the chapter of accidents, the conditions of trade, the tone of the money market, and the temper of the speculating public and even the character of the investment demand." On October 18 of the preceding year, he had stated: "One strong feature of the advance is that the volume of trading has increased with each successive daily gain in price. Such a movement is apt to culminate in one or two days of noticeably heavy trading, but the essence of the analysis of averages is that they are taken as reflecting these and all other factors." The latter statement is an interesting contradiction, for he was evidently influenced by volume, although at the same time claiming that the averages discount the significance of market activity.

The writer hazards the guess that one reason for Hamilton's attitude on this important point may have been that he did not have the datum which would enable him to study the relation of activity to price movement. Such an inference seems reasonable in view of the following extract from an editorial written in 1910: "We are aware that there are good arguments in favor of simultaneously considering the volume of business with the average price movement, but there are practical objections to that method. *To give such a comparison any value, it would be necessary to establish the volume of business day by day over a quarter of a century,* when we should probably find that the averages themselves had made allowance sooner or later for this influence, as well as for all others." [7] In this connection, it is interesting to note that his book, *The Stock Market Barometer,* contained a chart of the averages showing both the monthly price range and the *monthly daily average of sales.* If Hamilton really thought students should ignore volume, why was the volume included in this chart? [8]

When this book was planned, the writer determined not to digress from Hamilton's interpretation of the Dow theory, but the volume of trading has proved to be such a useful guide in attaining proficiency in the art of forecasting market trends that it is necessary to urge all students to study intently the relation of volume to price movement. Justification for offering this advice lies in Hamilton's casual but successful use of the relation of market activity to price movement when forming his conclusions.

At one time, when the end of a bull market was near, he noted the increase of volume and commented on the fact that such excessive activity was not advancing prices. He illustrated the mechanics of the situation with one of his pleasing and apt illustrations: "The economical steaming capacity, on 100 tons of coal a day, of a 2,000-ton steamer may be 12 knots. It takes 130 tons to get her up to 13 knots, and possibly 200 tons to make 15 under forced draught. . . . It may be taken as a natural rule that when the market's 'economical steaming capacity' has been reached,

---

[7] My italics.

[8] The experience of the writer in procuring daily volume figures is illuminating and perhaps suggests why Hamilton failed to utilize this factor in his recurring comments on the market action of the averages. The complete figures for 35 years were needed for private research and for inclusion in a portfolio of charts of the averages then being prepared for publication. An effort was made to obtain the datum from large statistical organizations, from newspapers, and even from the offices of the New York Stock Exchange. No one seemed to have the daily figures. It proved necessary to search the files of *The Wall Street Journal,* day by day, and this method was finally resorted to in order to obtain the complete record. It seemed that everything on volume was available except daily totals; the daily average of trading, monthly totals, etc., could be obtained—but not the daily totals. Since the publication of the charts referred to above, a week seldom goes by without a request for the tabulated volume figures from some statistician or organization whose address is usually in the Wall Street district.

there are at least some engineers who are expending a great deal more fuel for a very small gain in speed." (Jan. 21, 1909)

Examination of charts of the daily movements of the averages and volume of trading over a long period of years demonstrates that the tendency is for volume to increase whenever new highs or new lows have been made in primary bull or bear markets, with such an increase frequently progressing until something like a climax indicates a temporary reversal of the movement. Hamilton recognized this phenomenon, as shown by this portion of an editorial appearing on July 21, 1908: "This crossing of a preceding high point is usually significant of a bull swing in the stock market. It is also to be noted that the market is broader at the present level than it was at the May 18 level."

There can be no question that Hamilton recognized volume as a helpful factor in interpreting the movements of the averages. The following paragraphs, taken from editorials, prove this conclusively:

"One good sign also for the student of the market from such records as this, ignoring supposed outside factors such as tariff revision and industrial conditions, is that the volume of business has steadily improved during the advance. This is usually a good indication, as there is plainly not much stock in the market. A market which has been overbought shows it very plainly by becoming dull on small rallies and developing activity on declines." (March 30, 1909) This was written as part of a very accurate bullish forecast.

After an advance of three months in the spring of 1909, at a time when a secondary decline would have been in order, Hamilton noted on May 21 that "On the recession the market has become dull and narrower." The decline to which he referred amounted to less than 2% and the volume indicated that the advance would be resumed. This proved to be the case.

Near the end of an extended bull market, when every little recession was regarded as a possible beginning of a bear market, a considerable decline occurred, with the volume dropping about

50 per cent on the recession. Hamilton warned his readers not to sell the market short because the volume died out on the recession. He declared that "Various meanings are ascribed to reductions in the volume of trading. One of the platitudes most constantly quoted in Wall Street is to the effect that one should never sell a dull market short. That advice is probably right oftener than it is wrong, but it is always wrong in an extended bear swing. In such a swing the tendency is to become dull on rallies and active on declines." (May 21, 1909) [9]

At one time, when a new set of bull market highs was made, he considered that the movement had exceptional authority because "New high records for the movement were recorded on Monday and Tuesday, while the volume of trading has been broad enough to give importance to the movement." (April 22, 1909)

In September, 1910, he called the turn on the top of a secondary rally in a bear market when to many it would have appeared to have been the beginning of a bull market. At that time, the averages alone gave no indication of weakness, but the decreasing volume evidently caused Hamilton to write as follows: "In the present bear market the average prices rallied rapidly up to August 17, but having exhausted the secondary or upward swing, the strength evaporated, both in respect of market movement and the volume of trading, and we have been hopelessly in the doldrums ever since." (Sept. 20, 1910)

At another time, he explains how a professional would look with suspicion on a sharp rally in a bear market accompanied by a sudden increase of volume of trading: "It is probable that the professional trader would attach more importance to the present rally if the market had remained dull and inactive near the low level, with an appreciable time before recovering." (July 29, 1910)

Some good advice was passed out in the following editorial

[9] In studying the record of forecasts for 30 years, it is obvious that Hamilton could often have given his readers market "tips." One can imagine him perhaps wishing to display his skill and have his readers profit thereby, but restraining himself because of the dignity of his position. He repeatedly said that his newspaper could not descend to the level of competing with "tipsters."

comment: "There seems to have been a large distribution of stock on the advance, but such stock has been well absorbed, as the technical market movement shows. The market became dull on small reactions, showing increasing activity on any resumption of the advance. As any professional knows, this is a good indication that the strength is still on the buying side." (Feb. 6, 1911)

The respect with which floor traders regard volume indications was shown when he wrote that "For a few days at least the aggressive traders found activity on declines with dullness on rallies, and consequently took the short side of the market." (May 4, 1911)

In 1911, Hamilton unequivocally went on record as to the importance of considering market activity in relation to price movement when he wrote that "In studies of the price movement inertia has its value as well as activity, and not infrequently gives an important indication of future changes of a more radical character." (July 14, 1911)

Two days before a drastic decline, an editorial appeared which included the following: "Trading on the recovery showed a tendency to stagnate, and the market only became active on declines which, to the professional, is a fairly good indication of a continued bear movement." (Sept. 9, 1911)

The lows of the 1921 bear market were made in June and August, and Hamilton called the turn within four points of the bottom. On the following December 30, noticing that the market became dull on declines, he casually warned against further short selling: "One of Wall Street's old maxims was, 'Never sell a dull market.' Rallies in a bear market are sharp, but experienced traders wisely put out their shorts again when the market becomes dull after a recovery. Exactly the converse is true in a bull market, where traders buy stocks if the market becomes dull following a reaction."

A systematic study of the charted movement of the averages and daily trading discloses that trading is heavier in bull than in bear markets, and that in secondary reactions in bull markets one is generally safe in assuming that the market is at least temporarily oversold when volume decreases after a decline. Very often, a rally is likely to be imminent. On the other hand, when a secondary rally has occurred in a bear market, with activity dying out after the advance, it is reasonable to conclude that the market is overbought and that a further downward trend is near if a tendency towards increased activity is noticeable on declines.

Although Hamilton never referred to a climax of volume as such, any student of the charts can see that turning points of secondary importance are frequently signaled by a violent increase in the volume of trading.

In emphasizing the importance of volume, the writer does not, of course, intend to convey the idea that volume of trading is as important as the movements of the industrial and rail averages. The latter are always to be considered as of primary importance. Volume is of secondary significance, but it should never be overlooked when a study is being made of the price movement.

CHAPTER XVI

DOUBLE TOPS AND DOUBLE BOTTOMS

"Double tops" and "double bottoms" are of but little value in forecasting the price movement and have proved to be deceptive more often than not.

Hamilton stated on more than one occasion that he did not attach great importance to inferences drawn from "double tops" or "double bottoms." It would be interesting to know who was first responsible for convincing the public that such phenomena formed an integral part of the Dow theory. Such an impression does unquestionably exist.

Whenever a market movement approaches a previous high or low point, we are sure to read a great deal of useless speculative comment about conclusions to be drawn in the event of a "double top" or "double bottom" being made. Frequently, such comment will be prefaced by the statement that "according to the Dow theory, if a 'double top' is made by the industrials," etc. Every student of the Dow theory knows that no proper inference may be drawn from the action of one average alone, and it is a rare occurrence when both averages make simultaneous "double tops" or "double bottoms." Moreover, when this has happened, it has perhaps been merely a coincidence. If one counts the important secondary movements for 35 years, he will find that only a negligible number terminated in a "double top" or "double bottom."

Instead of looking for "double tops" or "double bottoms" as a clue to a possible change of trend at critical times when the averages approach old highs or lows, the students of the Dow theory would do better to remember that failure of both averages to penetrate previous highs indicates lower prices; that failure to penetrate previous lows suggests that higher prices are apt to follow; and that if one average goes through a previous high or low point without the other average confirming the movement, any inference drawn from the movement may prove to be erroneous. Incidentally, a comparison of the charted movements of *The Annalist* and *Standard Statistics Company, Inc.,* stock averages reveals that a "double top" or "double bottom" occasionally occurs in one set of compilations without being apparent in the other. It has been shown how Hamilton used the "double top" theory in 1926 in erroneously concluding that a bull market had terminated. In fact, he was so eager to justify his belief that he even used a "double top" of the industrial average alone.

It is also worth noting that although several "double bottoms" have occurred at the endings of bear markets, Hamilton apparently did not consider such an occurrence as important in calling the "turn."

A glance at the diagram on page 42, which pictures through the Dow-Jones averages the termination of nine bear markets, discloses that three might be said to have had a "double bottom" of *one average only;* three had "double bottoms" in both averages, while the other three gave no indication of "double bottoms."

In 1899 and 1909, "double tops" in both averages may be said to have occurred at the peaks of bull markets, but no such phenomenon occurred at the termination of the other seven major advances. However, it is true that many important secondary reactions have terminated in "double tops" or "double bottoms." For example, in the fall of 1898 a big reaction in a bull market terminated in "double bottoms" of both averages, followed by a strong advance; on the other hand, in the spring and summer of 1899 a perfect set of "double tops" gave a false lead, for the market soon ran through these highs to an extent which would have been disastrous to a trader making short sales on the basis of these "double tops." Early in 1900, during a bear market, the industrials showed a "double top," unconfirmed by the rails, which proved to be the ending of an important secondary rally. In 1902, during a bear market, both averages made a "double bottom" which its proponents would have construed as bullish, but these "bottoms" were soon violated and one of the most drastic declines on record occurred.

A perfect "double top" occurred in the rail average at the 1906 highs, with a severe decline following. In the spring and summer of 1907, there was a reaction in which both "double tops" and "double bottoms" appeared; the tops were not violated, but in a few weeks the bottoms were broken by a decline in which the industrial average lost over 30 per cent of its value. In the spring and summer of 1911, "double tops" were made in both averages, followed by a considerable decline in the industrials and a less violent one in the rails. During the bear market preceding the World War, both averages made "double tops" within 12 per cent of the bottom of that market. Short trades made on the showing might have resulted in losses, for the careful trader would, perhaps, have waited until a decline of a few points had taken place before accepting the "double top" as a clear signal to sell stocks.

There are any number of similar manifestations of the averages which could be described, but any student making a painstaking analysis of the subject is certain to conclude that inferences drawn from the theory of "double tops" or "double bottoms" are more apt to be misleading than helpful.

In July and August, 1930, during our greatest bear market, a perfect "double bottom" was made by both averages. This manifestation of resistance to the downward trend was eagerly seized by many financial writers as heralding the end of the bear market, but within a few weeks the primary downward trend was resumed, with the industrial average losing about 60 points in 90 days. More recently—in the winter of 1931–1932—"triple bottoms" appeared in both the industrial and rail averages, but the market soon resumed its downward trend in no uncertain fashion.

In summary, it may be said that "double tops" and "double bottoms" have not the significance which nine out of ten speculators give them.

CHAPTER XVII

INDIVIDUAL STOCKS

All active and well distributed stocks of great American corporations generally rally and decline with the averages, but any individual stock may reflect conditions not applicable to the average price of any diversified list of stocks.

The investor who studies values may be well informed as to the worth and earning power of certain corporations, but if he does not understand market trends he will be an unsuccessful speculator. The reason for this dogmatic assertion is that sound stocks generally advance in a bull market, and decline in a bear market, no matter what their intrinsic value or earning power may be, although the status of an individual company may cause any particular stock to advance or decline to a greater or lesser extent than is true of a group of representative equities.

Every broker knows how many of his customers insist on buying sound stocks during a bear market, basing their judgment on dividend records, price-earnings ratios, and strong cash positions. After the purchases are made, the steady pressure of liquidation may whittle away the quoted values until the disgusted buyer sells his stocks. By that time, he has forgotten his reasons for buying them and is very apt to blame the "bears" for his loss. However, the bears are not to blame. He should blame no one but himself, because if he really bought his stocks as an investment, basing his purchase on soundness of values, then price fluctuation makes no difference inasmuch as he owns an unvarying proportion of equity in these corporations, regardless of the quoted price of the stock. However, if such an investor desires to handle his funds in an efficient manner, he must understand market trends as well as balance sheets.

Then there is the unsuccessful speculator who does not understand balance sheets and does not want to. In addition, he knows nothing of market trends and is too ignorant or too lazy to learn. He buys stocks because he has suddenly discovered that prices are far below a point where some friend told him they would be "a good buy." Over a period of time, losses are inevitable to such a speculator.

This brings us back to the fundamental proposition that the occasions are rare indeed when an individual stock will advance, and hold that advance, when the Dow-Jones averages are declining; conversely, it is seldom that any stock declines when the averages are advancing. Any novice at speculation can verify the truth of this statement by comparing the action of the averages day by day with the price fluctuation of any dozen stocks.

CHAPTER XVIII

SPECULATION

The man who marries takes a chance, as does the man who goes to war, or who buys his son a college education. The father speculates on the boy's ability to develop useful habits and the power of concentration, just as the merchant who buys a shipment of overcoats for fall sale is speculating on the weather and the ability of his customers to purchase them. Do we criticize these ventures? No, because intelligent speculation is conceded in these cases. The intelligent speculator must not be compared with the board room pest who neglects his business because of his market dabbling. It is almost an axiom that the dabbler loses his money, while the intelligent speculator, if not successful, at least limits his losses to a sum which he can afford to lose.

Jesse Livermore was once quoted in *Barron's* as saying that "All market movements are based on sound reasoning. Unless a man can anticipate future events his ability to speculate successfully is limited. Speculation is a business. It is neither guesswork nor gamble. It is hard work and plenty of it."

Speculation is both an art and a science. Its morality is frequently questioned, but regardless of whether it is right or wrong, it is vitally necessary to the business progress of any civilized nation. Without speculation, our transcontinental railroads would never have been built, nor would we today have electricity, telephones, radios, or airplanes. Most people have unpleasant memories of losses incurred through the purchase of stocks in radio and airplane manufacturing concerns, but every subscription to the stock of a company which later fell by the wayside was, directly or indirectly, a contribution to progress in that industry.

Speculation, even of the rampant variety, has its uses, because when prices are being whirled upward at a startling rate, the promotion of capital for new business ventures is easy. From capital so acquired, many enduring businesses have been developed. The development of our great western states was largely the result of such speculation. Hamilton thought speculation and good business were blood brothers, as is indicated by the following extract: "The speculation in stocks itself creates exactly the confidence which stimulates an expansion of general business. This is really only another way of saying that the stock market is a barometer, acting not upon the news of the day, but upon what the combined intelligence of the business world can anticipate. The prediction of better general business in sight is positive and trustworthy." (May 22, 1922)

The distinction between speculation and gambling is difficult to define, because speculation necessarily entails the taking of chances which might be construed as gambling, just as it is equally certain that some forms of gambling contain an element of speculation. Webster's *Dictionary* suggests that to speculate is to buy or sell with the expectation of profiting by a rise or fall in prices; or to engage in hazardous business transactions for the chance of unusually large profit. This definition would certainly apply to a marginal transaction in stocks. The same authority defines gambling as a game for money or other stakes, or the hazarding of something on a chance. A strict construction of this definition would make it appear that a speculator buying 100 shares of Steel and placing an open sell order two points above the execution price, with a stop-loss at two points under that price, might be considered to be gambling. Certainly many traders consider such a transaction as a gamble and not speculation. Brokers in stock market circles explain the difference by saying that when a man bets on a horse to win a race, his bet does not have the slightest influence on the pony's speed, whereas when he buys or sells 100 shares of Steel on the New York Stock Exchange, regardless of whether he does or does not regard it as a gambling transaction, the purchase or sale of that 100 shares does influence the price of the stock. A carefully planned raid on Steel might depress it, and such a coup would be a successful speculation rather than a gamble. The laws of our country generally sustain speculation but condemn gambling.

There is no mathematical formula which will indicate a method of successful stock speculation, nor are there any set rules which, if followed by a trader, will always enable him to make money on stock trading. On the other hand, certain rules and theorems —the Dow theory being perhaps the best—can certainly be of invaluable assistance to the speculator. This book has failed of its purpose if it has not outlined a method of appraising market trends by means of the Dow theory, but the reader must understand that application of the theory depends upon the time and the man. Unless the speculator will practice endless patience and self-discipline, the Dow theory will not prevent his losing money. Any trader using the theory must think for himself and must at all times follow his own conclusions, being careful, of course, that his desire is not influencing his judgment. It is certainly much better for him to make a mistake based upon his own conclusions, and then to learn why the mistake was made, rather than to guess at the market. Self-reliance and hard work are necessarily the foundation of successful speculative efforts, in which probably 20 men fail where one succeeds.

Nearly every book on speculation lays down certain axioms which are vital to success, all of which are generally well considered, but only the exceptional man can profit by another man's advice. Therefore, it is perhaps useless to attempt an explanation of the dangers of pyramiding stocks. The temptation to realize an enormous profit generally induces a trader to try it, and only the hard school of experience can convince him of the actual risk inherent in such a market operation.

Hamilton believed that it was much better to increase a line on rising prices than to average on falling prices, and the advice is worth remembering. No trader should buy a stock unless he believes it due for an advance. There are, of course, some men who buy stocks on a declining market to put away as permanent investments. No criticism is intended of that market operation.

The first thing a trader must learn is that his commitments should at all times be limited to an amount which he can, if fate decrees, afford to lose. A young speculator once told a veteran trader that his speculations were bothering him and that he could not sleep at night. The veteran's advice was, "Reduce your line down to the sleeping point."

Hamilton often said that the majority of opinion in the Street was seldom right. Assuming him to have been correct, then the trader who understands the Dow theory should not hesitate to put out a short line of stocks if the market action indicates to him that this would be a wise move, even though sentiment on Wall Street is overwhelmingly bullish. Many times when Wall Street was bullish Hamilton would remark that there was entirely too much company on the constructive side; at other times, when public opinion was extremely bearish, he would warn his readers that there was too much company on that side and that the Dow-Jones averages were saying that the market was perhaps oversold. Hamilton seemed to be able to take the measure of the stock market by means of his understanding of the Dow theory and to forecast its subsequent action in much the same manner that a good doctor forecasts the recovery of a patient after examining the charted record of his temperature, pulse, and respiration.

However, even the most capable speculator will occasionally run into a chapter of accidents completely nullifying or destroying the results of careful planning. It is obvious that no system or theory could have allowed for the San Francisco earthquake, nor could any theory have allowed for the Chicago fire of many years ago.

Statistics are, of course, valuable, but they must always be subordinated to a view of the market as reflected by the averages, as those who confine themselves to statistics as market guides have never proved to be true prophets. Mark Twain is once supposed to have said, "There are three kinds of prevarication: lies, damn lies, and statistics."

Any person who tries to be in the market at all times is almost certain to lose money, for there are many periods when even the most skillful trader is in doubt as to what will happen. A good market axiom is, "When in doubt, do nothing." Moreover, if a trader has made a serious mistake in judging market trends and, in so doing, has realized a substantial loss, he should get out of the market entirely and stand on the side lines until he has recovered his poise.

No one but a floor trader can speculate successfully on the minor rallies and declines which are constantly taking place in every market. In secondary movements, such a trader has every advantage over the outsider. It is his business to take advantage of these turns, and he is in a position to appraise the technical situation and to sense the minor changes in market sentiment long before a change can be apparent to the man on the Street. Hamilton often remarked that "In the long run, in speculation as in everything else, the professional will win oftener than the amateur."

The speculator reading the tape, whether in New York or in the Far West, can sometimes realize when a testing of market sentiment is taking place on the floor of the exchange. At such times, it will be noticed that a few leading stocks may be pushed upward. It is a not infrequent occurrence to see pressure being put upon the same stocks a little later. The result of this test cannot be understood by the outsider, but it frequently indicates to those making the test that the public will not come in on the long side or sell stocks on the decline. It is by means of such testing that the professional decides whether there is more room on the top or on the bottom at that particular time.

Brokerage charges, taxes, odd lot penalties, and the bid and asked differential build up an overhead resulting in deadly odds against making money while indulging in "in and out" trading, but many men who have the necessary capital, courage, and caution, together with the ability to acquire first hand information by endless study of market trends and corporation balance sheets, can and do overcome these odds.[10] Few speculators take the trouble to calculate the terrific odds running against speculative profits. The only possible way in which such odds can be overcome is by an understanding of trends and values and by following Hamilton's advice that speculators should learn to take losses quickly and let their profits run. He believed that pride of opinion was more responsible for losses than any other single factor.

Back in 1901, while writing an editorial on speculation, Dow said: "If people with either large or small capital would look upon trading in stocks as an attempt to get 12 per cent per annum on their money instead of 50 per cent weekly, they would come out a good deal better in the long run. Everybody knows this in its application to his private business, but the man who is prudent and careful in carrying on a store, a factory or a real estate business, seems to think that totally different methods should be employed in dealing in stocks. Nothing is further from the truth."

No one has ever given a satisfactory explanation of the obvious fact that many successful merchants, manufacturers, or hotel keepers will risk their earnings of years in stock speculation, a business about which they know nothing. These men almost invariably assume stock trading requires no knowledge or study, although they would not think of risking any considerable portion of capital in the expansion of their own business without most carefully canvassing the possibilities of the return to be earned on the funds so expended. Even if they subscribe to some advisory service, they too often trade on the tips and gossip of the board room. However, assuming that they do trade on the advice of an advisory service, it is the exception when the subscriber makes a thorough investigation of the ability of the men operating the service or of the accuracy of their forecasts over a number of

10 Increased federal and New York State taxes on stock sales and transfers, voted in 1932, have substantially added to the tax handicap faced by the trader.

years. It is an obvious fact that if the advice given by these services were as good as they are often said to be, the men operating them might better employ their substantial investment directly in market activities.

Speculators who "go broke" are usually those who fail to devote as much time to studying the subject of speculation as they devote to the risking of an equal sum or money in their own business. These individuals will seldom admit that their ignorance is responsible for their losses. They prefer to accuse "Wall Street" and "bears" of having cheated them out of their money in some mysterious fashion. They fail to realize that no profession requires more hard work, intelligence, patience, and mental discipline than successful speculation.

Perhaps less money would be lost by amateur speculators if they had a clear understanding of the results actually accomplished by professionals. It is not unreasonable to assume that a floor trader with $1,000,000 in his speculative fund would, over a period of years, be satisfied with an annual appreciation of 20 per cent. Indeed it is very doubtful if there are many who have done as well as that. But the man operating with a $2500 fund is not content with any such rate of increase. He ventures into a game about which he knows nothing and confidently expects to do far better than that. Several veteran speculators—men who have accumulated huge fortunes in the Street—have placed the average appreciation which may reasonably be expected over a period of years at about 12 per cent. Money compounded at that rate will about double itself in six years. However, the market dabbler can hardly expect to get any such results over an extended period of time.

CHAPTER XIX

STOCK MARKET PHILOSOPHY

Hamilton had the knack of seasoning technical subjects with pithy comments and useful bits of market wisdom accumulated during his many years of observing the habits of Wall Street. These comments have little or nothing to do with the Dow theory, but anyone reviewing his work cannot but be impressed with certain of his observations. Perhaps he was trying to hammer home something he knew would be useful to his readers; on other occasions, he was expressing veiled contempt for the ignorance of certain editors who wrote in ill-considered fashion on financial subjects. Occasionally, some foolish letter from a subscriber may have inspired him to use a familiar simile. At any rate, the following typical excerpts, chosen at random from his editorials, are worth reading.

During a bear market, certain editors proclaimed a typical secondary rally as being the first stages of a bull market. In disagreeing with them, he wrote: "One swallow does not make a summer, and one rally . . . does not make a bull market." (July 8, 1908)

At another time, when tipster services were predicting great things during the final stages of a bull market, readers of *The Wall Street Journal* were warned that "The tree does not grow to the sky." (Dec. 23, 1908)

"It is interesting, and not unilluminating, to hear that certain well-known houses are large lenders of stocks in the loan crowd. This would indicate a corresponding short interest. But it by no means follows that the people borrowing could not deliver the stock if they chose. Indeed, if they had more to sell from the same sources it would be to their manifest advantage to create the im-

105

pression of a vulnerable bear account. Experienced Wall Street is skeptical of such indications." (Aug. 25, 1921) This was written at a time when some writers were confidently predicting an advance in the market based on a splendidly advertised short account. The quotation contains sound market logic.

When stocks were within three points of the 1921 low, the following appeared: "There are plenty of wise saws and modern instances to show that the investor seldom buys at the bottom and rarely or never sells at the top. Cheap stocks are never attractive. This is no paradox but a matter of market record. If cheap stocks were attractive there would be an active market today, with an interested and even excited public. . . . There are not enough . . . customers to go around." (March 30, 1921)

Discussing the mental attitude of the investor who thinks he has bought on value and earnings, Hamilton wrote: "He may be able to pay for his stock, but he can not forget about it, he thinks he must read the price list every morning." When he sees his stock down a few points, "He says he will take his loss and remember the lesson. He is entirely mistaken about the lesson, and what he is forgetting is not his loss but the reason why he bought the stock." (March 30, 1921)

The following comment is well worth remembering as an explanation of why the best stocks frequently seem to decline, when, based on earnings and sound value, such a drop appears anomalous: "In a market unsettled by long liquidation . . . it is easy to forget that good stocks are often more vulnerable than bad ones. The market for good stocks is real, and that for the bad ones is nominal . people who have to meet loans liquidate what can be sold at some price because they hold other things which cannot be sold at any price." (March 30, 1921) Of course, reference was made to the large operator who liquidates a big line of sound stocks in order to protect his loans. He would no doubt prefer to peddle out his "cats and dogs," but is unable to do so because of a thin market.

In criticizing his own work and defending the Dow theory, he wrote: "Studies of the price movement . . . were wrong for the most part when they departed from Dow's sound and scientific rule." (Aug. 8, 1919)

His editorials often encouraged his readers to buy stocks when a severe secondary movement had occurred. At one time, he wrote: ". . . at the worst . . . the recession has not amounted to more than what the French call 'reculer pour mieux sauter'—stepping back to jump better." (July 14, 1911) Hamilton had rare ability in appraising secondary reactions, and to those who believed in this ability a repetition of this pet phrase always appeared as bullish advice.

At various times between 1924–29, Hamilton commented on the expansion of speculation and investment. He noticed that distribution was getting wider each year, not only in the number of stockholders in leading companies, but also because the whole country was participating in activities formerly confined largely to a few important financial centers. He was perhaps one of the few, if indeed not the only one, who foresaw the danger this new element might inject into a period of drastic liquidation. The warning in the following excerpt was written in 1925, with the same thought expressed several times between that year and the 1929 crash: "The technical condition of the market should always be kept in mind. . . . Should something arise of an unexpected character to disturb public confidence there would be a large volume of selling from all over the country, such as Wall Street could not calculate with anything like the degree of certainty possible in the past, when it knew that the bulk of the bull account was being carried in New York." (March 9, 1925) Those who were unfortunate enough to have been caught in the drastic liquidation following the 1929 peak realize the wisdom of this forecast.

To readers of *The Wall Street Journal* who were fond of writing its editor long letters pointing out what they considered as unquestionable inferences to be drawn from their own systems of speculative analysis, Hamilton replied editorially: "It cannot be too often said that the road to ruin lies in dogmatizing on charts, systems and generalizations." (March 17, 1909) Charts are as necessary for those who use the Dow theory as ledgers are to a bank, but the student must refrain from a dogmatic or too precise interpretation. We all know how seldom the market performs exactly as expected, which led Hamilton to declare that "There is something almost uncanny about a market which acts exactly as it has been expected to." (May 19, 1906)

Once, when the prosperity ballyhoo was being handed out in the excitement of a bull market, Hamilton warned his readers as follows: "By all accounts we are to have a great bull market in the next six months when the public is to take stocks at the top. So far the judicious distribution of ground bait has not attracted fish in any great numbers." (Dec. 20, 1909) It is a matter of interest that this was written only a few days before the peak of a bull market. He saw very clearly that the fish (suckers) had swallowed a little more of the bait than they could digest.

At another time, Hamilton wrote: ". . . long experience of the stock market would indicate that one of the indications of the best buying is the excellence of its disguise. Other things being equal, notorious 'inside selling' is rather a bull argument. People with a lot of stock to distribute do not usually go abut it with a brass band." (Jan. 16, 1923) This was one way of warning us that market news is frequently deceptive. Had Hamilton lived through the troublesome years of 1930–31, he might have warned some of us not to swallow the "ground bait" so freely offered during that time. It is inevitable that powerful interests should use every effort to hold stocks up while distributing their holdings.

On April 27, 1923, Hamilton did not think that ". . . the school-room economics to which we have been asked to listen . . ." could upset the implications of the Dow theory.

". . . The Dow-Jones averages . . . have a discretion not shared by all prophets. They are not talking all the time." (Dec.

17, 1925) This is valuable advice for some of the high-priced advisory services.

"Every experienced Wall Street trader knows that the operator who has been on the right side of the market, getting in and out but increasing his commitments from his profits over an advance of 100 points, does not need a decline of anything like that extent to leave him worse off than when he started. He is usually found pyramiding at the top and a relatively small decline wipes him out." (Dec. 12, 1928)

"It is a commonplace of Wall Street that there is no news in a bull market; and it is true that the publication of the reason for a rise in a stock quite frequently marks the termination of the movement." (April 1, 1912)

During a bear market, when Wall Street was being criticized by politicians, the irritated Hamilton wrote: "For goodness' sake, cannot we inaugurate a condition of real Americanism, where we are allowed to blow our own noses? There has scarcely been an occasion in its history when the New York stock market has not perceived dangers ahead long before anybody else and safely liquidated itself accordingly." (Nov. 12, 1924)

Hamilton wrote in *The Stock Market Barometer:* "It would be possible to offer endless instances of people who lost money in Wall Street because they were right too soon."

"A normal market is the kind that never really happens." (May 4, 1911)

"Everybody speculates nowadays and it is a matter of many years' experience that everybody's judgment is not so good as somebody's." (Dec. 8, 1928)

Shortly before the end of the bull market of 1929, this pertinent paragraph appeared: "The people who have been active in the stock market, pyramiding their speculative position in the usual way, are for the most part those with affairs of their own which should not be neglected or minimized." (Dec. 8, 1928)

The Wall Street Journal has wisely refrained from the annual forecast habit so freely indulged in by many papers. In commenting on this practice, Hamilton wrote: "As a rule the reviews are better than the forecasts and before the new year is a week old the forecasts are forgotten." (Jan. 1, 1929)

During May, 1922, bear propaganda was being handed out; the public was told that pools were unloading, that stocks had advanced too rapidly, etc. *The Wall Street Journal* was never a party to such proceedings, and hoping to protect his readers, Hamilton issued this editorial warning: ". . . it is submitted that stock market 'pools' . . . do not usually do their selling with a brass band." (May 22, 1922) It is a matter of interest that the market subsequently made a rapid advance for about five months, without a reaction of consequence.

"The man who picks the wrong stock for a speculative purchase, or, more rarely, the right stock at the wrong time, must always find someone else to blame for his defective judgment. He has no use for the stock market as a barometer of the country's business. He believes he can make money by reading the barometer first and reading the business afterwards, or not studying it at all. Is it still a hopeless task to tell him that he should exactly reverse the process? It has recently been demonstrated at Wellesley Hills, that the attempt to do both things leads to inextricable confusion." (July 30, 1923)

"The speculator . . . cannot expect any stock, except under the most unusual circumstances, to advance profitably against the general current of the market."

This comment on the morality of speculation gives us Hamilton's view on the subject: ". . . I do not believe the moral question enters into speculation at all, provided it does not degenerate into gambling with what is, in effect, other people's money."

Apparently wearied by letters from his readers asking for more frequent market advice, Hamilton for a long time abandoned his efforts, giving his reasons as follows: "There was no desire here to appear in competition with Mr. Babson and the less sanctified minor prophets. It was because discussions on the price movement in *The Wall Street Journal* were construed as stock tips that they were abandoned."

It would be interesting to know how many of Hamilton's readers acted on his last forecast published only a few weeks before his death. On Oct. 26, 1929, he wrote: "So far as the barometer of the Dow-Jones average is concerned it has been clear since last Wednesday (October 23) that the major movement of the market has turned downward." This is a fitting epitaph to an extremely useful career, for it must be remembered that the large majority of stock market prophets were still imbued with the "New Era" doctrine.

APPENDIX

THE EDITORIALS OF
WILLIAM PETER HAMILTON

The Wall Street Journal: Dec 5, 1903

Considering the extraordinary advance in wealth of the United States during that period, considering that railroad mileage has not increased in anything like the ratio of increase in surplus earnings, and finally considering that the ratio of increase in surplus earnings available for dividends has been at all times in excess of the rise in market prices and at the present time shows a larger percentage on market price than at any time since the boom started, the question may well be asked whether the decline in stocks has not culminated? There is at least some evidence in favor of an affirmative answer to that question.

The Wall Street Journal: December 7, 1903

DEVELOPMENTS OF THE WEEK

The market was strong, practically without recession throughout the week ending December 5 and prices advanced quite materially, with a great increase in transactions. The average price of twenty active railroad stocks which closed at 93.15, November 28, rose practically without intermission to 95.79 on Friday, December 4, and finished the week at 95.16. This is the highest point reached by the averages in pretty nearly three months. The most active stocks in the railroad list were Pennsylvania, about 500,000 shares (half stock), and an advance of 4½ points in the price; Union Pacific, 230,000 shares, and an advance of 3½ points; Rock Island, with nearly 200,000 shares, advancing 3 points; Atchison, 150,000 shares, advancing 2½ points; Brooklyn Rapid Transit, 250,000 shares, and an advance of 10 points; St. Paul, 125,000 shares, advancing 4½ points; Erie, 135,000 shares, advancing somewhat better than a point; Missouri Pacific, 110,000 shares, advancing 4 points; Reading, 170,000 shares, advancing 5 points, and Southern Pacific, 100,000 shares advancing 1½ points. In industrials, 450,000 shares of Steel preferred stock were done at an advance of 6½ points; 240,000 shares of Amalgamated Copper, at an advance of 4½ points, and 100,000 shares of Sugar, at an advance of 5 points. Sharp advances, moreover, occurred in a number of less active specialties in both the railroad and industrial list, the feature in the latter being the recovery in preferred stocks that has been attacked in the preceding week.

Undoubtedly the principal motive power in the advance came from the covering of a very large short interest, which proved to be more widely extended than the street generally had appreciated. It has been fashionable to sell stock short for some months and evidently more people have been in the fashion than has been generally supposed. It is worth noting that the rally in progress during the week practically dates from the latter part of September, since which time pressure upon the market has failed to bring large offerings of stock. The importance of this is in the fact that this is the first long rally, in point of time, that the market has had since fourteen months ago, when the great decline started. A good deal of evidence has accumulated tending to show that the decline in prices culminated in the early fall. Bearing in mind the fact that values, as expressed in railroad earnings, are still increasing, it must be said that there is great presumption in favor of the market having reached a level where investors may reasonably consider it safe.

The Wall Street Journal: September 17, 1904

ARE PRICES RISING OR FALLING?

We have often pointed out that there are three movements in the market which are in progress at one and the same time. These are—first, the day-to-day movement resulting mainly from the operations of the traders, which may be called the tertiary movement; second, the movement usually extending from twenty to sixty days, reflecting the ebb and flow of speculative sentiment which is called the secondary movement; and, third, the main movement, usually extending for a period of years, caused by the adjustment of prices to underlying values, usually called the primary movement. It is a very important thing to determine in which direction the primary movement is taking place, as this is the movement that concerns investors. No more interesting question, therefore, can be asked at the present time than whether prices are rising or falling on the primary movement.

On Dec. 5, 1903, we printed an article dealing with the movement of prices, the concluding paragraph of which was as follows:

"Considering the extraordinary advance in wealth of the United States during that period, considering that railroad mileage has not increased in anything like the ratio of increase in surplus earnings, and finally considering that the ratio of increase in surplus earnings available for dividends has been at all times in excess of the rise in market prices and at the present time shows a larger percentage on market price than at any time since the boom started, the question may well be asked whether the decline in stocks has not culminated? There is at least some evidence in favor of an affirmative answer to that question."

The events of the last nine months make it reasonably clear that the suggestion contained in the foregoing was correct. There has been a large advance since that time as measured by the average of twenty active stocks. It is worth while once more to recite the leading facts of the case. The average of the highest prices reached by the twenty active stocks used in our average compilations during the great boom which culminated in September, 1902, was 134.53. The highest average closing bid of those stocks in the boom was .... 129.36 The lowest prices touched by these stocks in 1903 on the

decline averaged 86.68
The lowest average closing bid in 1903 was 88.80
The decline from the averaged high points to the averaged low points was 47.85
The decline from the highest averaged closing bid of 1902 to the lowest averaged closing bid of 1903 was 40.56

In September last year the rally began (from what now appears to be the bottom of the decline) from the closing bid of 88.80 on September 28, 1903. The market rose with substantially little check until Jan. 23, 1904, on which date the averaged closing bid was 99.78. This was an advance of 10.98, accomplished in a period of 117 days. It was followed by a decline to 91.31 average closing bid on March 14. This decline amounted to 8.47, and was accomplished in 51 days. A rally followed to 97.58 on April 11, being 6.27 in 28 days, and a decline then ensued to 93.55 on May 16, being 4.03 in 35 days.

Since May 16 the market has advanced without a setback of as much as 3 points on the active stocks, and on September 10 the average closing bid was 108.12. The average of the high prices on the movement, moreover, reached 110.45, being 16.90 above the closing bid on May 16 and 21.65 from the lowest closing bid in 1903. On this advance, therefore, the market recovered one-half of the entire decline from the highest prices of 1902 to the lowest prices of 1903, and more than one-half of the decline from the highest closing bid of 1902 to the lowest closing bid of 1903. On Sept. 10 the market had been advancing for 117 days.

It is characteristic of the main or primary movement that the secondary swings in the same direction as the main movement are accomplished more slowly than what might be called the eddies. In the great decline of 1903 the downward secondary swings averaged 32 days while the rallies averaged but 12 days. Since Sept. 28 last the declines have averaged only 42 days, while the advances have averaged 87 days. This would, therefore, indicate that there has been a change in the primary movement, which was evidently downward until a year ago. The evidence, in fact, goes to show that the primary movement is upwards at the present time.

It must further be said that the extraordinary stability in railroad earnings, the comparative stability of bank clearings, pointing as they do to a large volume of business in progress and the soundness of foreign trade figures, despite some falling off in export balances, are also evidence that the decline in security prices has not been followed by general business depression for which no particular causes would seem to exist at the present time. Failing a large diminution in the maturing crops of corn and cotton, there is apparently nothing in sight to lead one to believe that railroad values are not on the whole maintaining their high position, and that as time goes on this will bring a further appreciation of prices. Much will depend on the coming winter, which will at all events bring a clear indication of the general trend of values. In the long run values make prices. It is safe to say that if present values are maintained, present prices are not on an average high enough.

It must further be remembered that the continued increase in the production of gold is a most powerful factor, which cannot fail to be felt in the future as making for higher prices of securities other than those of fixed yield.

The Wall Street Journal: October 20, 1904

THE MARKET'S POSITION

On Tuesday evening the average closing bid price of the twenty active stocks was almost exactly twenty points above the average closing bid on May 15. In other words, the market has had at least a "twenty point advance" all round so far as the general average goes. Taken by itself, this is an important fact more especially when to it is added the fact that at no time during that advance was there an important interruption or setback. As a result of the rise the market as a whole now stands at about the level at which it stood in the fall of 1901 after the excitement in connection with the late President McKinley's assassination had passed away. The highest average closing bid in 1902 was somewhat over 129, while the lowest average closing bid in 1903 was below 89, a decline of something like forty points. Of these forty points there have now been recovered in round figures about twenty-five points—this being over 60% of the whole decline.

This is, of course, an important recovery when looked at in this way. It is, however, but fair to note that the great decline in prices during 1903 occurred actually in the face of increasing railroad earnings, for the net earnings of all the railroads taken together in the year ended June 30, 1904, were the largest in the country's history. Thus, during the long decline of 1903, values were in many cases actually rising while prices were falling, and allowing for increased capitalization charges, etc., values as a whole certainly did not decline appreciably. Notwithstanding the fact that there was no decrease in railroad earnings in 1903, earnings at present are materially in excess of those of last year and there are clear indications that the net earnings of railroads in the current fiscal year will be well ahead of those of last year, and will be much the largest in the history of the country.

If we suppose, therefore, that the prices of 1901 were not unreasonable as referred to the values of that year or even of the year following, it is clear that present prices are not high by comparison with present values. The line of values even allowing for increased capitalization is probably, at this moment, higher than at any time since the recovery began. In the spring of this year the discrepancy between the line of prices and the line of value was, undoubtedly, very large and the probability is that at the present time it is still considerable. To some extent at least the movement of the past five months must evidently be regarded as a process of adjustment of prices to values, and so far as surface indications go it would seem that values are likely to tend upwards for at least another year. Whether prices will follow is something that time alone can tell. In the long run, however, eliminating eddies and cross currents of speculation, values make prices.

The Wall Street Journal: April 16, 1906

THE PRICE MOVEMENT

During the past week there has been quite an interesting development in the price movement of the active stocks. The last low point of twenty active railway stocks was touched on March 5,

1906, when the average price was 128.54. There was an irregular rally from that point to 133.13, reached on April 2, 5 points below the record of the averages and the top of the year of 138.36, recorded on January 22nd. There was a reaction during the week to 130.07 or within 1½ points of the low of March 5th. Had the price of the twenty stocks broken below that figure previous experience of the averages shows that the movement indicated would have been something more than a moderate reaction and rather in the nature of a new downward swing.

As it is, prices have now recovered to within exactly a point of the high price recorded April 2. If the present movement carries them beyond that figure there will be fair evidence of a new independent upward swing. Tested over a number of years the averages show that the decline after a long advance is usually about half recovered, and that the market then backs and fills between the old low and that point until a new impulse develops. What is really implied is that the technical position of the market, after a rally based mainly on its oversold condition, is adjusting itself with about a level chance, other things being equal, of new buying or new selling starting an independent movement.

The position is interesting especially in view of the changes in outside influences. There is fair evidence that the stringent money conditions have been largely ameliorated by the engagement of gold abroad, the check to the outflow of currency to other points, the return of the pension checks, the money attracted by high interest rates and the generally easing money conditions all over the world. The political horizon also is clear. The only uncertainty is the pending Russian loan and it may be taken, from the recent action of the Bank of England and the fact that Paris did not outbid us for gold in London, that it has been prepared for.

The Wall Street Journal: May 2, 1906

THE MARKET MOVEMENT

In a space of eleven trading days, from Wednesday, April 18, the day of the San Francisco earthquake and fire, to Saturday, April 28, there was a decline of 10.77 points, from 132.66 to 121.89, in the average price of twenty active railroads. There was a rally of 2.17 on Monday, followed by a new break of 3.36 on Tuesday, making a total loss of 11.96 since the earthquake. Such a decline in so short a time is abnormal. Even in panics the fall has not been so severe on the average, although, of course, much more considerable in individual stocks. Declines to some extent corresponding have, however, been recorded over a longer interval of time, and it will perhaps be instructive to compare what the market did afterwards.

There was a curiously parallel movement about the same time last year. On April 17, 1905, the price of twenty active railroad stocks was 126.39, from which there was a decline extending over the Easter holidays, in ten trading days, of 8.58 points. This is the closest parallel we have in the averages. The low point was recorded on April 29. The market rallied 3 points by May 2 to 120.63, selling off again below the old low point, and failing to recover until after May 22, when 114.52 was touched. From that figure we had the most important advance of 1905, and by the 29th of the following August prices had advanced to 132.19, a gain of 17.67 points.

So far as the averages are concerned panic declines are not as serious as they look at the time. Between May 1, 1901, and May 9 the average of twenty railroad stocks declined 14.49 points, but it should be observed that only a relatively small part of this decline was made on the actual day of the panic. In practice it is found that very sharp breaks have quick recoveries, and on that occasion the recovery was so quick that many of the losses were wiped out in the afternoon.

In each of the instances noted it will be observed that after a very considerable break in a short period of time, about 40% of the decline was recovered, largely on the covering of shorts, and, of course, partly on investment buying; While afterward there was a gradual and much slower downward movement, carrying the average price to the old low point or below it. In April of last year, for instance, the low point was touched on April 29, and after a rally of under 4 points the averages fell back to 114.52 before they recovered.

This was the case in the panic of

December, 1899, except that after a decline of over 13 points between September 5 and December 22, the averages recovered a little over 6 points and then did not touch the old low figure again, although the high price of September, 1899, was not reached again until late in the following year.

The Wall Street Journal: May 19, 1906

THE PRICE MOVEMENT

There is something almost uncanny about a market which acts exactly as it has been expected to. The movement of the average price of twenty active railroad stocks has shown such extraordinary conformity to type that people who take this method of gauging the extent and strength of the market movement are very much impressed. The market has, in fact, done exactly, so far as the average price movement is concerned, what might have been expected from similar movements analyzed over a period of many years.

The market saw its top for at least a considerable period on January 22nd, when the average price of twenty active railways was 138.36. Serious and sudden as the decline on the San Francisco disaster was, it is now plain that money market conditions, the poor demand for bonds, the locking up of free capital in real estate and other industrial enterprise and other factors were working for lower prices in any case. The decline was evidently due and only came quicker than was expected. In such a decline a rally of from 40% to 50%, usually of a rapid character, has been a comparatively uniform experience. From the high price of 138.36, the averages receded to 120.30 by May 3rd, or 18.06 points. At the close of the market on May 11th the average price was 128.16, a rally of 8.10, or a shade under 45% of the decline.

It will be seen that the recovery was strictly according to schedule. It was extraordinarily rapid and after the advance the market has begun to sag slowly in much the same way as from previous rallies following a severe decline. The recovery was made in seven days, at the rate of 1.12 points a day, while the decline has been irregular, accompanied by individual recoveries. It has not carried the market down far

from the top of the rally, after six days of trading, as the closing figure 126.90 shows.

The severe decline, the rally from May 3rd and the heavy irrregular tone and sagging tendency of the past six days are all typical of the action of the market after a severe shock. Following the panic of 1896, the Flower panic, the December panic of 1899, the Northern Pacific corner, and the sharp decline from September, 1902, the market rallied in very much the same way and then gradually sold off, in spite of individual strength, until a point somewhere near the old low was reached, when a narrow, traders' market developed until a real new impulse gave a new direction. The unexpected happens in Wall street oftener than anywhere else, but the experience of these typical occasions is worth recalling.

The Wall Street Journal: June 29, 1906

THE WALL STREET BAROMETER

Speculation is essential not merely in the market for stocks but in any market. Somebody must take chances. The pound of coffee sold across the counter contains greater or less profit to the retailer as he judges the wholesale market correctly. Every market must therefore adjust itself not merely to present conditions but to future conditions. In this respect stocks are like any other commodity, but they cover so wide a range of interests that a general movement in them may, and frequently does, reflect a change in general conditions outside.

In this respect the Wall street market is something of a rational barometer. It is the constant phrase of the street that a movement is over "when the news is out." Stockholders and intelligent speculators operate not on what everybody knows, but on what they alone know or intelligently anticipate. We have often had the spectacle of a general decline in the market, only followed six months afterwards by a contraction in business, or a general advance in the market anticipating by an equal time improving industrial conditions not then obvious.

It is the business of Wall street to sell securities to the public. Wall street anticipates that when the business improvement it expects matures, the public will take stocks off its hands. This is really what establishes a bull market. Favorable conditions inside and out of Wall street act and interact until the necessary impetus for a stock boom is developed. In the summer of 1904 when the unskilled observer was convinced that the McKinley boom was over and industry on the down grade, professional Wall street was buying stocks. It correctly estimated the vast recuperative power of business. The average price of twenty active railroad stocks advanced nearly thirty points in that year with a continuous gain between the latter part of May and the beginning of December.

It must always be remembered, however, that there is a main current in the stock market, with innumerable cross currents, eddies, and backwaters, any one of which may be mistaken for a day, a week, or even a longer period for the main stream. The market is a barometer. There is no movement in it which has not a meaning. That meaning is sometimes not disclosed until long after the movement takes place, and is still oftener never known at all; but it may truly be said that every movement is reasonable if only the knowledge of its source is complete.

What the barometer needs of course is expert reading. At the present time the stock market, which, touching the highest point ever recorded on January 22 of this year, has made an irregular reaction. The decline at one time extended in the case of twenty active railroads to over eighteen points, and in the case of twelve active industrials, to almost as much. Even now after very substantial rallies the market has worked off from the recovery point of last April and is even six points below the best quotation of the current month. On the surface, crop prospects, industrial conditions and the money market are all as favorable as ever. Here is an opportunity for the amateur reader of the barometer. Is the market, or is it not, reflecting some change in fundamental conditions which shall justify the present quotations six months hence?

The Wall Street Journal: July 6, 1906

THE PRICE MOVEMENT

If the low average price touched by both industrial and railroad stocks on July 2 represents the culmination of a downward swing, the stock market is now in a very interesting position. It would be quite in accordance with the experience of past movements, if such were the case, and some reasonable inferences may be drawn. From the high level of 138.36, touched on January 22, 1906, by twenty active railroad stocks, and of 103.00 reached on January 19 by twelve industrials, there were declines in the former to 120.30 and in the latter to 86.45, both reached May 3 which represented the low point of the San Francisco earthquake decline. Since then the price of industrials has crossed the old low, while the active railroad stocks have sold within 1½ points of it. It is a uniform experience, over the years when such averages have been kept, that a panic decline is followed by a sharp rally of from 40% to 60% of the movement, and then by an irregular sag ultimately carrying the price to about the old low point. It seems to need this to bale out the weak holders who were helped over the panic. It could hardly be said that the break on the San Francisco disaster was exactly of the panic class, and the market in rallying recovered to 131.05% in the case of the railroad stocks, which is only 1.61 below the price at which the earthquake decline started. The rally, however, does represent about 60% of the decline since January 22, and the course of the market since has been curiously parallel to the movement observed after a panic rally.

It seems fair to infer that liquidation of very much the same kind as that following a panic has been necessary. It will be noticed that some closely held industrials, selling on a pool-created basis, have declined relatively little, while many stocks of undoubted value have lost heavily. This is simply another way of saying that people obliged to sell sold what there was a market for, probably in some cases to protect what could not be sold at all. The first decline in a panic is scare, and the second and slower decline is the demonstration of the general shock to confidence. May it not be reasonably inferred that some such similar shock was reflected in the decline in the market since June 11, carrying it down to the old low point or near it?

Another inference may be drawn on such an analogy. It is that the market is likely to wait for a new impulse at or somewhat above the low level. What that impulse may be, whether it will come from good crops, easy money or unquestionable evidence of a continuance of past prosperity, or whether from something of a depressing nature, it is impossible at present to say. Logically, if the impulse were known the movement would have already started and there would be no problem to solve. It can at least be said that the line of prices is well below the line of values, and that all signs at present point to fair weather.

The Wall Street Journal: August 4, 1906

PRICE MOVEMENT

There has not been a more typical development in the price movement of stocks in years than that of the recent past. Taking the twenty active railroad stocks whose average price has been used for many years in this paper for purposes of comparison, the advance has conformed to type very closely. The average price after approaching the old low point of May 3 resulting from the San Francisco disaster, developed a new impulse and has already rallied nearly nine points from the figure recorded on July 2.

This is quite in line with the usual action of a market which has received a shock, rallied and then sold off again. This is the normal movement and, while each part of it varies in extent, it has been the almost unvarying rule that on the second recession after the feverish rally the market balances within narrow limits waiting for a new impulse. Analysis of the price movement scarcely shows what that impulse was, but in the past month and particularly in the past fortnight there has been a vigorous upward movement which has all the character of an independent swing governed by influences of its own.

The highest point ever touched in the average was 138.36, on January 22 of this year. The lowest point of the year was 120.30 on May 3. From that low point the market on June 11th had rallied to a figure above that of present ruling. The upward swing now in progress therefore would gain considerable strength and authority if the price passed that recorded on June 11th.

So far as the averages are concerned, and leaving outside considerations apart, an advance of over eight points to a figure above that of January 22 would still be necessary before it could be said with a strong show of reason that the bull market which terminated in the beginning of the year had been surely re vived.

The Wall Street Journal: August 21, 1906

IS IT A BULL SWING?

Since the average price movement was last discussed in these columns, a surprising change has come over the complexion of the market. In nine working days the twenty active railroad stocks have advanced very nearly seven points. It is necessary to go back to last May to find a market movement so general and considerable, and it is more noteworthy as the greater part of it was made in three days.

After the market turned and hardened from July 2nd, it was pointed out in these columns that an independent movement was due, and that it was possible that the new impulse the market had been waiting for had been found. The reasoning was based upon the action of stocks from Jan. 22nd, when the twenty active railroad stocks touched 138.36, their record, up to and after the fluctuations arising out of the San Francisco disaster. The market from January was probably on the down grade, but the decline was of course enormously accelerated by the earthquake.

As in every other severe decline caused by some acute development of the same kind, the market after rallying rapidly to a point rather more than 50% of its loss, made an irregular slow decline, until on July 2nd 121.76 was touched, or only 1.46 above the earthquake low of 120.30 made on May 3rd. It was pointed out then that the market had completed the usual pendulum swing. The point of equilibrium had been reached, and it was necessary before a new movement developed that a fresh influence should be felt.

At the time it almost looked as if the new influence might be a bearish one. The market hovered near the old low point, and would certainly have looked very depressing if the average price had broken through it. There was nothing to indicate that the greater financial interests were taking special pains to protect prices, and so far as the public was concerned, faith was small and hope delayed. It was obvious that an advance of 16 points was necessary to carry the average price past the old January high, while less than two points would have broken stocks through the earthquake low.

From the beginning of July, however, a distinct independent movement set in, checking occasionally, and not indeed stimulating any specially large volume of business, but gathering strength, and giving plain indications that underlying the movement must be some definite cause. Up to the time when the Union Pacific and Southern Pacific dividends were first talked of, the movement might have meant anything.

Even a week ago, before any but a privileged few could have had any conception of the size of the Harriman dividend declarations, quotations had already passed the highest point of their rally at the San Francisco earthquake. It is fairly certain now that the underlying influence was a new departure in railroad dividend policy, intelligently anticipated. The market shows it, and particularly so in the advance in the average price of over four points since the dividends were made public. At the present figure of 136.98, the average price is already within two points of the old January high record. If the outlook was bearish with a possibility of the earthquake low being passed, it is reasonable to admit that it is bullish with a new top almost in sight.

The volume of business after the declaration of the dividends in question must show more than manipulation. It is absurd to suppose that within the two hours of a Saturday's trading any single interest could possibly manipulate 1,-600,000 shares. The only inference possible is that the public has at last to some extent taken hold. On the enormous profit taking sales of Monday, it was evident new buyers were forthcoming. If, therefore, buying in this volume carries the average price above 138.43, we can only suppose that the long decline between Jan. 22nd and July 2nd represented a somewhat extended bear swing in a bull market which will have resumed its sway.

The Wall Street Journal: September 6, 1906

AN IRREGULAR PRICE MOVEMENT

On Saturday, August 25th, the average price of twenty active railroad stocks touched 137.06, the highest figure since January 22nd of this year. Since that date there have been some remarkable fluctuations in individual stocks and a curiously unsettled price movement which will bear analysis.

After the violent fluctuations involved in the adjustment of prices to the San Francisco earthquake the market may be said to have turned on July 2nd, when the average price of twenty active railroad stocks was 121.76, or only a little more than a point above the low level reached on the earthquake decline. From the beginning of July up to August 25th there was a consistent advance very occasionally interrupted to a figure only 1.30 below the highest figure ever touched by the average.

In the eight trading days since the high figure of Aug. 25th was reached the extreme fluctuation has been surprisingly small in the averages, when compared with the movement of individual stocks. Union Pacific, for instance, has advanced seven points and declined five in that time, and there have been fluctuations almost as considerable in a number of other stocks. The extreme fluctuation of the average, however, in that time has been 2.02 points, and even now the market is less than a point below the last high figure. In the violent fluctuations of Tuesday, when Union Pacific advanced five points and declined four, while St. Paul was equally irregular, the total change was .01%.

It will be noticed also that since the big trading days immediately following the Harriman dividend declarations the volume of transactions has fallen off. Even when stocks are selling off the market tends to get dull. This is a usual condition after a general movement arising out of special news, like the Harriman dividends, has been checked by a development which cannot be ignored, like 40% money. Stocks, in fact, are swinging backward and forward with a tendency to reach equilibrium and a coincident small volume of sales. Conditions are being adjusted to the necessities and possibilities of the money market. It cannot be said that the price movement really indicates anything more than the adjustment of an unusual but easily comprehended technical position.

The Wall Street Journal: December 15, 1906

THE PRICE MOVEMENT

As giving within certain limits trustworthy indications of the possible course of the market, the average price of twenty active railroad stocks as published in these columns is well worth study at present. There has been a well-defined movement in the recent past which may throw a little light on the ultimate meaning of the trading. Since this time last month there has been an extreme fluctuation of a trifle over 3 points, with a low of 134.35 recorded on November 15, and a high of 137.56 on December 11. Within these narrow limits the volume of business has been very considerable, although outside of the Hill stocks and St. Paul the individual fluctuations have not been extreme.

The average price has never crossed the old high of 138.36 recorded on January 22, although it has come very close to it more than once. The low was recorded on the earthquake break, and has not been so closely approached, although on the reaction after the rally which always follows a semi-panic break in the market, stocks for a day or so looked like going through that price. Such a development would, of course, have been a very bearish indication. Conversely, if the average price crossed the high of January 22, the bull point would be unmistakable.

It is a very good working rule that when a large number of transactions take place in a stock within a very narrow range of prices, that stock is either being accumulated or distributed, and the prices manipulated to facilitate one of those objects. By analogy, the average of twenty active railroad stocks should give such an indication, and very frequently does so. The three point fluctuation of the past month is apparently a case in point. At the close on Thursday the price looked like breaking through the last low point of November 15, and on November 26 very nearly the same price was reached. If afterwards stocks sold above the high of December

11, the indication would be decidedly bullish, and an advance beyond the high record of January 22 would make that assurance doubly sure.

If, however, the average eased off to a figure below the low limit of the present fluctuation, the indication would be bearish. It would not necessarily mean that the great bull market which has been in progress for the past six years would have terminated. It would rather indicate that we were in one of those periodic bear swings in a bull market which sometimes last for two months or more. In fact, a movement out of the rut either way would probably demonstrate with considerable accuracy whether stocks are being accumulated or distributed.

The Wall Street Journal: February 2, 1907

THE PRICE MOVEMENT

At various times after the severe decline in the stock market consequent upon the San Francisco disaster, the lessons of the average movement of stocks were very fully set forth in these columns. It was pointed out that the market had shown what practically amounted to a panic break. It was also remarked that the rally consequent upon that break had amounted to about one-half of its full extent. The situation was a little complicated by the fact that the market was moving downwards anyway, and that the San Francisco earthquake only accelerated the decline. On Jan. 22, 1906, the average price of twenty active railroad stocks touched 138.36, its record. On May 3 the price had reached 120.30, which marked the extreme of the downward swing.

As constantly happens after such violent movements there was a rally of rather more than one-half and the usual gradual sag to a figure very near the old low point. This ended on July 2 when the average was at 121.76. This is where the pendulum had exhausted its swing and was waiting for something to start it from a state of equilibrium. A movement set in, stimulated by the big crops and the enormous industrial prosperity of the country, which carried the average price up to 137.84 on Sept. 17. It will be seen that the second downward swing did not quite touch the old low, while the advance did not pass the record high of Jan. 22. If it had done the latter the inference that we were still in a big bull market would have been inevitable.

It was remarkable at that time, and again after the market halted, backing and filling up to Dec. 11, when the old high point was again approached, that the averages would give the best indication of the future course of the market. In two advances the old top had not been reached. After hovering within a point and a half of the May 3 record the market rallied a little on Thursday, but on Friday at last crossed the old low. It is true that the Northwest rights come off, but rights and dividends have been coming off ever since the averages were first instituted and such deductions average themselves like the prices. A short, but severe decline from Dec. 11 has carried us to a new low point.

If it would have been a bullish indication had stocks sold above the January high in the September or the early December movement, it seems fair to infer that a drop below the earthquake low suggests that something like a bear market has been established.

According to the late Charles H. Dow's theory, which is about the only intelligible system of regarding price movements, there are three movements always going on. One is the daily fluctuation, another is the short swing, lasting from three weeks to three months, which may be defined as a reaction in a bull market or a rally in a bear market, and behind all the great underlying movement extending over a period of years and practically corresponding to the recurring booms or depressions of every ten years or so which the world has seen even since it kept a record of its business.

There is no question that up to Jan. 22 last year we were in a bull market. What we have to inquire is did the bull market terminate then? The decline which culminated in the San Francisco earthquake might have been merely a secondary reaction. Both in September, and on Dec. 11 when the old high was approached again, this looked extremely probable. But for over a year, with occasional rallies the market has really had a downward tendency. The question is whether we are in the beginning of one of those great and gradual bear movements, varied by occasional brilliant

rallies, which mark a contraction in business after a great boom. A good deal will turn upon what happens after the present decline has exhausted itself. The real rallies in such a market are violent and stocks often recover in a few days a great part of the decline of weeks. Nevertheless the average certainly looks as if stocks were in more or less "orderly retreat."

The Wall Street Journal: July 12, 1907

A STUDY IN PRICE MOVEMENTS

Probably no institution has become better known in Wall Street than the average movement of stocks shown in Dow, Jones & Co.'s table of averages, corrected from day to day and extending over a period of some seventeen years in its present form. It has been possible in these columns to draw some valuable lessons from past market movements. The Wall Street Journal was able to point out by an analysis of the action of the market in past years, as shown in the average price of twenty active railroad stocks, that in 1905 the bull market had not reached its zenith. As a matter of fact it did not do so until Jan. 22, 1906, when the highest recorded price average of 138.36 was touched.

It was possible to point out during 1906, and particularly after the San Francisco earthquake, when the market price of the same stocks declined to 120.30, that the old bull market could not be considered as re-established unless the old high point was passed again. In the early autumn and before the market broke in the early part of December, 1906, for one of the severest declines of recent years, it was possible to deduce from the averages that indications favored a decline. The old high point of January, 1906, was closely approached on September 17 of that year at 137.84, and again on Dec. 11 at 137.56.

Special attention is drawn to these two high points in an effort to re-establish a bull movement which had culminated. It will be remembered that the weakest feature of the advance of the autumn of last year was that there was no public response whatever to attempts to manipulate prices. Somebody was filling up the market with long stock all the time. It is even fair to infer, now, that important banking interests were getting out of stocks as fast as they could, leaving other interests equally important, but less sagacious, to sustain an impossible level of prices.

In the recent past there has been a repetition of the price movement from the other end. The low point of the severe decline beginning in the second week of December, 1906, was reached when the average price of twenty active railroad stocks touched 98.27 on March 25, 1907. This was 1.44 points below the panic figure of 99.71 touched in the Harriman panic of March 14. Since June 3, when the old low point was approached and the average price declined to 99.50 the market has seen a rally to 107.23 last Saturday and a reaction of over three points.

It was possible to draw an important conclusion from the failure of the market on two occasions to pass its old high point of Jan. 22, 1906. In September and December of last year we came within less than a point of that figure. In the present decline we have once on June 3, come within 1.23 of the March 25th low figure of the big bear movement. If the market sells off again to a point very near that low, but not beneath it, and then rallies, it is fair to infer that a good recovery in prices will be in order. The second recession so far has not been sufficiently extended to base any conclusions upon. The next few weeks' trading should establish whether the bear market is to run further or whether a real recovery is to be established.

It is much too early to formulate axioms on price movements, but it may broadly be said that after tangible fluctuations two failures to pass the old high establish the presumption of a bear market. Conversely it may be reasoned that if the present market breaks through the low average price of 98.27, as of March 25, we are in line for a further decline, values, crops, earnings capacity and political conditions notwithstanding.

The Wall Street Journal: August 8, 1907

THE PRICE MOVEMENT

On July 12th it was pointed out in these columns that the average price of twenty active railroad stocks, which then showed a substantial rally from the low of 98.27, recorded on March 25th, 1907, would become very interesting if prices again approached the low figure. Since that date, there was a recovery of 9.41 points to the high figure at 107.68 on July 24th. Prices hung around that level until the Monday of the following week, when the first serious decline set in. In nine trading days the market has declined from 107.51 on July 27 to 100.90 last night, a loss of 6.61 points. The decline yesterday was one of the most severe that has taken place in the month of August.

The average price, therefore, is now only a trifle under three points above the last recorded low figure of the March break. It was said on July 12th that if that low figure were crossed again, all previous experience of market movements indicated a further extended decline, values, crops, earning capacity, and political conditions notwithstanding.

Probably no one will deny that we have been in a bear market since January, 1906, when the record high average price was touched. There have been strong rallies, noticeably in September and the early part of December of last year, but the long movement and the real current of the market has been downwards. Great swings like this may, and generally do, extend over a period of years. They are varied by sharp advances, frequently lasting from six weeks to three or four months. It is characteristic of a bear market that the rallies are always sharp, while relatively severe declines like that of the past nine days are the exception rather than the rule.

Technically, the average looks bearish. It has lost 72% of its recovery recorded between March 25th and July 24th. The decline as compared with the rally has been so sharp that it may be accidental developments only are indicated. On the figures and previous experience, the chance of going below the old low figure is at least as good as a resumption of the rally which culminated in July. The chapter of accidents is always against the market in such a position, because bear influences which would be neglected in boom times operate with increased power.

On the other hand, the normal tendency in August is upward. It is less so, however, when there has been a marked rise in July, which was the case this year.

The Wall Street Journal: October 14, 1907

DEVELOPMENTS OF THE WEEK

As a matter of fact, it might almost be said that we were just at the point where there was a promise of a turning of the tide. As the area of business contraction extends, it must inevitably produce a considerable slackening in the demand for money, and this will open to the easing up of financial conditions, so that at the beginning of the new year there ought to be a much better situation, so far as Wall Street is concerned, however wide may be the slackening in trade and industry. Wall Street seems to be about completing its period of readjustment, just at the time the readjustment outside Wall Street is beginning. The latter will afford capacity for financial recovery and equilibrium. Therefore, in spite of the immediate gloom that envelops the financial center, there seems a clearing ahead.

When the average price of twenty active railroad stocks was still above par on August 7, it was pointed out in The Wall Street Journal, the following day, that the market was only three points away from the low figure of March, and that if prices declined below that figure the indications would be decidedly bearish. The market has broken through the old low, and has established a new bear record. While this would indicate that we are still in a bear swing, it must be confessed that there is a tempting opportunity for drawing a false analogy. When a market has had a drastic break, it is apt to rally quickly on the covering of shorts and purchases made to restore confidence. What happens after that is the true test. If the price does not go below the low figure of the break, the indications over a period of years have been practically uniform that the worst has been seen. In the present case, however, the break has not been quite of that character, nor has it followed any sudden or startling rally. The market has been more or less on the down grade for the past three weeks, but the recovery in September has not been very

vigorous. To say that a new low point is always bearish involves a manifest fallacy, because there must come a time when the price cannot go any lower. A new low point after a panic and its typical recovery is one thing, but a new low in a liquidating market after irregular price movements is another. Some consolation can be drawn from the inference that a further sharp decline is not indicated in anything like so definite a way as it was in August.

The Wall Street Journal: December 25, 1907

THE PRICE MOVEMENT

When the low price of twenty active railroad stocks had declined, in a little more than a month, or from Sept. 21 to Oct. 29, from 101.03 to 83.49, it was pointed out that a rally was due, but that indications would be bearish if the so-called panic low price was crossed again. The rally from that price was decidedly feeble, and had only extended 2.42 points on Nov. 11, when the average price was 85.91.

It must be pointed out that in the strict sense of the word there has not been any real Stock Exchange panic in the present decline. A decline, however severe it may be, does not constitute a stock market panic unless stocks actually get out of hand. There was a moment in the afternoon of Oct. 24 when the market went as close to an actual panic as it ever did in its whole history. Union Pacific sold down to par with a rush after 2 p. m., and but for the Morgan pool, with its $25,000,000 of call money at 10%, the only thing which could have stopped the decline on that day would have been the gong to close the market.

The distinction is vital. After a real stock market panic, as distinguished from a severe decline, the average price has always shown a regular movement in which approximately 40 to 60% of the decline is recovered, and subsequently lost as the stock bought to protect on the panic comes out. It may be said, therefore, that such a movement after the "almost" panic of Oct. 29, could by no means have been expected. No one can say exactly where the decline started which ended temporarily then, and consequently no 50% rally was indicated, nor did any such rally occur.

There is, however, in the record of the average since Sept. 21, when the price was 101.03, a most interesting and symmetrical movement. The low price of Oct. 29, 83.49, was crossed on Nov. 15, and the downward movement did not stop until 81.41 was reached on Nov. 21. The total decline to the true low point of the year on this movement was 19.62 points. Prices rallied rapidly, and on Dec. 6 had recovered practically half of this decline, the average price being 90.56, which is 9.15 above the low, and 46% of the decline since Sept. 21. By Dec. 17 the price had reacted to 86.61, losing 43% of the rally. Up to Dec. 21 there was a still shorter swing, which carried the price up again to 89.35, while the reaction on Monday to 88.11 is just 45% of the small rally of the previous four days.

What has happened then is, successively, a decline of 19.62 points to the actual low of the year, a rally of 9.15, a decline of 3.95, a rally of 2.74, and a decline of 1.24. The resemblance to the oscillations of a pendulum, with a gradually diminishing arc as it approaches equilibrium, is positively startling. It is rarely indeed that the averages have given a more pictorial object lesson. The extent of the swing has diminished in absolutely regular proportion. The time of the swing also has shortened, as the first movement occupied 61 days, the second 15 days, the third 11 days, the fourth 4 days, and the last 2 days.

The market is coming to rest exactly as a pendulum would, and all that is indicated now is a period of unimportant fluctuations until an absolutely new impulse is given. We have seen the low price for the year in all probability. It no longer carries special significance so far as our method of reading the averages is concerned. It would require a severe decline to carry us below the 81.41 recorded on Nov. 21. This decline itself would really mean exactly that new impulse which the market is waiting for. An impulse might come from any one of a dozen directions. Cheap money in January might start a public buying movement. The absence of such a movement might cause liquidation of stocks supported and protected in the darkest days of the past year. No one

can tell, and one man's guess is as good as another's. What the average says, really, is that the market must be watched closely, in order that advantage may be taken of the first real lull after a decline which has extended over something more than twelve months.

The Wall Street Journal: January 10, 1908

THE RALLY SINCE THE PANIC

The average price of twenty railroad stocks last night was 92.86 which compares with 92.23 on October 21. The average price of twelve industrial stocks last night was 63.50, as compared with 60.81 last October. Thus the stock market has fully recovered all of the losses made during the panic.

The average railroad is now only two points lower than it was on August 24, and the industrial average is six points lower. The rally in the stock market has therefore, been pronounced, and gives the impression that it is one of those sharp fluctuations which follow an extreme low point and precede, at greater or less distance, a permanent turn in the tide.

The Wall Street Journal: January 13, 1908

DEVELOPMENTS OF THE WEEK

In the past week the stock market has made a substantial improvement, the average price of the active railways and industrial stocks being at one time 3½ points above the figure of the end of the previous week. It is pointed out in this place at the end of Christmas Week that the market had approached equilibrium after a long period of vigorous fluctuation, with a declining tendency, and that an independent new impulse was in order. Since that time there has been a movement of over seven points upward, and prices are now about the level of October, before the semi-panic at the end of that month.

The development is satisfactory, although it is hardly likely that we are to plunge immediately into a long sustained big bull movement. If we do, it will be for the first time in the history of any stock market.

The Wall Street Journal: July 8, 1908

THE PRICE MOVEMENT

One swallow does not make a summer, and one rally in the price list does not make a bull market. The market has had a recovery since the beginning of the week, and a little study of the average price of the active railroad stocks will not be uninstructive at present. The price of twenty active railroad stocks has once more crossed par, after fluctuating around that figure, with a somewhat unsettled tendency since the top of the main rally reached on May 18, at 104.45.

In seven weeks the market has failed to rally to that high level, and it cannot be said that the present recovery so far has any essential characteristics which differentiate it from similar movements in the middle of June, and even that in the short-lived advance of Monday, June 29. It may fairly be taken that the market turned in a generally upward direction after the panic of last October, and in spite of recessions of a more or less serious character, notably that following the January advance, we may say that there has been more or less of a bull market for the past nine months. The interesting point is whether the advance culminated in the second extended upward swing, that which terminated on May 18.

On previous experience of the average movement, a general upward tendency extending far upward of eight months, could perhaps constitute a bull market, however irregular, and however sharp the periodical setbacks might be. The bear market which it succeeded has lasted from January, 1906, to October, 1907, and this forms a long period for any broad price movement. Some recovery was naturally in order from the fact that the market had over-discounted bearish conditions, and it remains to be seen to what extent the rally of twenty points from the October low had discounted the modest recovery in general business.

It is always possible to manipulate the stock market in one direction or another for a short time, but it is not possible to devise a financial combination strong enough to manipulate the entire average movements of stocks over such periods as we are now dealing with. It may, in fact, be promised with fair safety that only the secondary swing of the market is liable to be increased or retarded by artificial means, and that the effect of manipulation upon the great price is almost negligible over a period of years.

There is nothing to show in the average price at present that the bull movement inaugurated after the panic is over, but the repeated rallies to near the high price of May 18 and the equally consistent failure to pass that point, call for careful scrutiny, as such a development often marks the end of a broad movement. It is only fair to say, however, that should the price of twenty active railroad stocks cross 104.45 on the present market movement, there will be a broad indication of a substantial further advance.

The Wall Street Journal: July 20, 1908

DEVELOPMENTS OF THE WEEK

During the past week the stock market has shown a fairly uniform tendency. The high point of the week before was passed on Tuesday.

Prices are now more than five points above the low figure which succeeded the high point of the year made on May 18. Industrial stocks, in fact, are nearly two points above that figure and the average price of twenty active railroads is less than half a point below it. This is an important movement and will look still more significant if the high point of the railroads is exceeded on the present advance. On all previous experience of the broad tendencies of the market, which are not seriously subject to manipulation, a further independent advance of some magnitude would be indicated, based on the temper of the Street and the public as distinguished from the incidents of the day.

The Wall Street Journal: July 21, 1908

THE HIGH POINT CROSSED

All students of the average price movement will note with interest the fact that the railroad average yesterday reached 105.20, which is 0.75 above the last high point established on May 18, when 104.45 was touched. This crossing of a preceding high point is usually significant of a bull swing in the stock market. It is also to be noted that the market is broader at the present level than it was at the May 18 (1908) level.

Apparently the usual August rise has started in a little ahead of time.

The Wall Street Journal: August 1, 1908

AGAIN CROSSING HIGH POINT

Again does the average price of railroad stocks break through the preceding high point.

On July 20 the average touched 105.25, crossing the previous high point of 104.45, made on May 18. Three days later the market had advanced to 106.24. That was the highest average until yesterday, when 106.76 was reached. To students of price averages this has the appearance of a bull swing. The market this year has started its regular August rise in July.

The Wall Street Journal: November 2, 1908

During the past week the average price of twenty active railroad stocks has twice, on Tuesday and Friday, approached within a quarter per cent of the high price of the year recorded September 9. As the market was active in the past year and in other years of recovery after severe depression, an advance to beyond the previous high point has always indicated a continuance of the broad bull movement. Experience shows also that the converse is true. If the old high point is approached more than once, but not passed, the subsequent break in prices indicates pretty clearly the termination of the main bull swing. The present movement is part of a tendency which has constituted a bull market since more than twelve months ago. The net gain on the week has not been large, but recoveries have carried further than declines. The movement of industrials is by no means so clear, and does not give anything like so plain an indication of the possible market change. On Saturday the market was heavy, and the railroad average, 109.57, was only slightly above that of a week ago.

The Wall Street Journal: November 28, 1908

THE PRICE MOVEMENT

Three days before the Presidential election it was pointed out in these columns that the average price of twenty active stocks (railroad) was rapidly approaching the previous high price of the year and of the bull movement reached September 9. It was shown then that a new high level had hitherto meant a further vigorous advance, and that anything of the kind about election time would have great importance in forecasting the future movements of the market.

On Nov. 2, the eve of the election, the average price of twenty active railroad stocks crossed the previous high point. In conformity with previous movements in the market a most vigorous advance set in, carrying average quotations up over seven points before the rise checked on Nov. 18th. It is rarely that a forecast based, as this necessarily was, upon strictly technical conditions so instantly and thoroughly justifies itself. Nothing can be more deceptive than to regard a whole market through the medium of two or three very active stocks. A limited number of stocks can be manipulated at one time, and may give an entirely false view of the situation. It is impossible, however, to manipulate the whole list so that the average price of twenty active stocks will show changes sufficiently important to draw market deductions from them.

The subject of stock market manipulation has about it a certain air of mystery, and consequently some sort of awful fascination to the small outsider, who believes that the limited number of so-called "insiders" are always in a position to arrange months in advance what the market shall do. The reputation of being able to do this thing is no doubt very valuable to some large operators, but the extent of their power has been most ridiculously exaggerated. All the manipulation in the world did not save such operators from tremendous losses in 1907. Since the panic the public has bought stocks on their merits, anticipating some improvements in business, and it is safe to say that the market might have advanced as much as it has done without any manipulation at all. Its top will be reached quite normally at the figure where the possible improvement in trade has been over-discounted.

The averages are now in a very interesting condition and may give another valuable lead before long. The average price of twenty active railroad stocks reached 117.51 on Nov. 17th, the top of the year. From that figure there was a reaction of not far from three points, but the price has now recovered and on Tuesday was within a point of that high. If that high figure is crossed there will be the strongest evidence, unless all previous experience goes for nothing, that the bull movement is far from culminating. If, on the other hand, the last high price were approached again, but not crossed, and a three or four point break followed, it would look as if the main swing, which has been operating since the panic, had for the present culminated.

The Wall Street Journal: November 30, 1908

In the past week the stock market has shown some irregularity, but on the whole a generally upward tendency. The average price of twenty active railroad stocks on November 21 had receded to 114.77, or nearly three points below the top of the year recorded on Nov. 17. The old high point has now been closely approached, and the movement is one calculated to stimulate public interest in the market. The public is not buying stocks in that indiscriminate way which was the feature of the trading immediately after the election. Business, in fact, has been marked by a resumption of the kind of stimulus which was found necessary during the long summer advance.

The course of price, judged by the average, is broadly upward, and there is nothing in the development of the week to contradict this theory.

The Wall Street Journal: December 14, 1908

The tendency of the stock market during the week has been irregularly upwards. After hesitating a little on Monday, there was a sharp advance on the following day, with irregular gains up to Friday, when some hesitation was shown and a recession in the average

price of the railroad stocks and the industrials. The trading has been marked by the heavy speculation in what Wall Street elegantly called "cats and dogs." There has been a decided increase in the amount of stock carried by commission houses for customers, and in view of this phase of the speculation, a deterioration in the character of the collateral in loans.

Taken altogether, the stock market situation is scarcely so strong as it was, although the establishment of a new high point in the average price of stocks has been an astonishingly consistent bull argument throughout the long advance of 1908.

The Wall Street Journal: December 21, 1908

A week ago the average price of twenty active railroad stocks was 118.18, the high point of the year. To a certain extent the market had acted consistently, as the previous high point had been crossed three or four days before, and that, in the present year, has always been an indication of a further bull movement. On Monday, however, the market developed serious hesitation. The only strong rally was on Wednesday, and a substantial net decline developed which carried prices back considerably below the previous high point of November 17.

From the appearance of the average price movement it looks as if there had been a systematic distribution of stocks. The average has not been below 116 or above 118.18 since Nov. 23. This means twenty-two trading days with an average showing of sales of not far short of a million shares. A rally above the last high figure would change the whole technical appearance of the market, but it must be confessed that for the first time in a long period the averages look bearish.

The Wall Street Journal: December 23, 1908

THE PRICE MOVEMENT

On the closing prices of last Saturday it was pointed out in these columns that for the first time in a long period the showing of this paper's averages looked bearish. On Wednesday December 9, the average price of 20 active railroad stocks crossed the previous high of Nov. 17, 117.51, and for four days afterwards the market showed strength above that level. During the present year the market has advanced materially every time a previous high point was crossed after a period of irregular fluctuation, rest or reaction. On the crossing of the old high this time, however, the market did not make so good a showing as usual.

Prices reacted below the November high point on December 15 and although it was crossed again on the following day, stocks have already had a sharp set-back. The 20 active railroad stocks are now one point below the high level of the year and lower than they have been since November 23. The 12 industrial stocks taken for the purpose of average comparison are now lower than they were on the day after the Presidential election. The tree does not grow to the sky, and it can be seen here that a bull point drawn from the average movement which has consistently made good since the panic of 1907 is at last withdrawn by the averages themselves.

For 22 trading days, from November 24 to December 20 inclusive, the average price of 20 active railroad stocks did not advance beyond 118.18 or decline below 116.01. In 19 days from November 24 to December 16 inclusive, 12 industrial stocks did not sell above 87.63 or below 85.15. It will be seen that in each case, during a period when these sales of stocks recorded on the tape averaged a million shares a day, the industrials and railroad stocks together did not fluctuate to the extent of 2½ points. This is a very striking exhibition and to most observers would indicate a period in which the market had been strongly held in order to facilitate distribution, especially as both the industrial and railroad stocks have broken through the line on the lower side.

It is a very large order to say that the big bull movement is over. If the averages in fact established a new high point for the year the indicator would have to make an average advance of one point and the 12 industrials one of four points. There is plenty of bull talk, and new bull arguments seem to be forthcoming every day. The average rise necessary, although not an unusually large one, or even approaching some of the upward swings of the present year, represents a very substantial movement when it is remembered that the whole list must move together, and that a 20 point advance in Union Pacific, for instance, would only amount to one point in the averages.

As the figures stand at present, the averages decidedly indicate the possible end of an important swing upwards, and they may also indicate the end of the fourteen months' bull market. This is a matter of pure conjecture, and it may be pointed out that this analysis, based solely upon the average movement of prices, is theoretical and does not profess to take account of general conditions.

The Wall Street Journal: December 30, 1908

THE PRICE MOVEMENT

When the average price of twenty active railroad stocks had declined to 115.20, or three points below the previous high figure of 118.18, it was pointed out in these columns that for the first time since the recovery from the panic of October, 1907, the indication was distinctly bearish. It is true that the market had once more given the bull point so uniformly correct throughout the long advance, in passing the old high figure of November 17. Such an advance has hitherto meant an active resumption of the bull movement, but the trading which developed showed a marked variation.

It is true that the November high point was crossed, but stocks acted sluggishly and even on the Thursday before Christmas, when the figure of December 12 was almost reached, the period of 26 trading days had been shown with a fluctuation of less than three points. This still looked rather like distribution, especially as the price had broken through the line on the down side on December 21, 1908. It is the more remarkable therefore, that the advance of the first days' trading after Christmas has cancelled the bearish indications, and renews the old bull point given so strongly as each previous high price of the year was crossed during 1908. Unfortunately the industrial stocks do not give anything like so definite a lead, but the price there, within the space of one week, has recovered three and a half points, and is now less than one and a half points from the high price of the year.

The highest price ever touched by the twenty active railroad stocks taken for comparison by the Wall Street Journal was made on January 22, 1906, when 138.36 was recorded. The low figure after the October panic of 1907 was 81.49, on November 22, representing a decline of 56.87 points from the high of the previous year. As the average price is now 119.80, it will be seen that we have recovered more than 38 points of that decline in 1908. The fall really extended over nearly twenty-four months and the recovery has so far occupied fourteen. A recovery of normal restoration of business after a panic depression, is very striking.

Conservative people in fact would say that the possible revival in business had been discounted a long way ahead.

It is worth remembering, however, that 1907 was in a large degree a rich man's panic, with the result that the decline was perhaps more severe than it usually is in such circumstances. There was a long period also when railroads could not borrow on any terms whatever; and during that time they were improving their properties out of earnings, without the opportunity to capitalize those improvements. Their strength consequently after the panic was such that a substantial advance was in order, even though railroad earnings at the time were showing severe declines. The roads had been well fed up and, just as the buffalo in times of famine lives off his hump, so the economies and wise expenditure when business was booming took care of the railroads in the lean year.

It looks from the railroad average prices at present as if the bearish indications of a week ago have been taken back and that a position largely favorable to some January advance is established. This possibility for the general market would be especially accentuated by an advance of one and a half points in the industrial average price, bringing it above the last high figure.

The Wall Street Journal: January 7, 1909

The present price movement is a striking example of one of those large swings of the market, extending in this instance over a period of considerably more than a year, which must find itself checked sooner or later. There has been a return of stocks to the market, and there is probably more stock in the Street now than there was when the public was rapidly absorbing promising securities at low levels. The difference between the high figure of the average of twenty active railroad stocks in 1906 and the low figure following the panic touched in November, 1907, was 57 points, a loss of over 41 per cent. The rally from that low figure up to last Saturday was 39 points or 68 per cent of the decline. There has been a considerable recovery in business as might have been expected after the exaggerated low point reached in the panic of 1907. Business, however, has not recovered 87 per cent of what it was in 1906, but that is the figure of the average price of twenty active railroad stocks as compared with the high of that year.

The Wall Street Journal: January 21, 1909

THE PRICE MOVEMENT

There is an interesting and somewhat tantalizing problem presented in the present fluctuations of the average price of stocks, especially since the beginning of the year. It may be said at once that neither the twenty active railroads nor the twelve industrial stocks, give any indication of the not infrequent January boom. So far from this being the case, the high point for the year was made in the railroads on January 2 and in the industrials on January 7.

The range of fluctuation in the railroad group since it took a definite upward turn and crossed the previous high point on December 28, has been 3.30, with the quotation now midway between the early high point of the year 1909 and the price at which the remarkably short lived new year boom may be said to have started. The showing of the industrials is equally vague. They have not approached within a point of the last high figure of November 13, 1908. They are below the figures shown when the railroad stocks began to move on December 28, and altogether make a discouraging showing.

From this one can derive at least the definite information that the prices did not boom after the new year, as they had been expected to do. They did not show anything like the life and activity displayed after the election. Million share days, which were the rule at that time, have become the exception. The tendency also is to develop some activity on declines and a most tedious dullness on rallies. As the range in each case is about 3 points, taken over a period of twenty trading days, it is not unfair to infer that there has been some distribution, restrained by the limited capacity of a narrowing market.

On a strictly technical study of the average price movement over many years, there is a fairly clear inference to be drawn. It is that the market is waiting for a new impulse, and that at the present level the impulse will have to be more powerful than those which preceded it in the long advance of 1908. The economical steaming capacity, on 100 tons of coal a day, of a 2,000-ton steamer may be 12 knots. It takes 130 tons to get her up to 13 knots, and possibly 200 tons to make 15 under forced draught.

The parallel with the movement of the stock market is obvious. In a rising market, everything looks bullish and in defiance of all previous experience, the trader who is making money cannot see why prices should ever go down. Even when the movement begins to labor, he is still convinced that the pause is only to gather fresh strength. This view has previously been confirmed as after the occasional set-backs of the long advance of 1907-8. It may be taken as a natural rule that when the market's "economical steaming capacity" has been reached, there are at least some engineers who are expending a great deal more fuel for a very small gain in speed.

Even at this date, the market would look like a further resumption of bullish activity with an advance of some four points in the average price of industrials and two points or so in the railroad stocks. The bull point, however, would by no means be so convincing as it was on such occasions in 1908. It was only at the very end of that year that the bull point given in this way was taken back by a disconcerting reaction in the average price; and it is the occurrence of this reaction since the new year which has given an uncertain note to the trading. It cannot be said that the averages are definitely bearish, but they might be so with a very moderate recession, while a marked increase of activity and strength in stocks would be necessary to make the averages a good argument for bulling the general market.

The Wall Street Journal: February 12, 1909

TENDENCIES OF THE MARKET

The action of the market since this year's highest price of the twenty active railroad stocks was touched on January 2 has been exasperating to the trader, but ought to have intelligible lessons to the student. Since that date, we have had thirty-four trading days in which the extreme fluctuation in the average price has been 3.04 points or between 116.93 and 119.97. And after this long period of uncertainty we are still balancing midway, like Mahomet's coffin.

The twelve industrial stocks did not reach the high point of the present year until Jan. 7, but their fluctuation has been even less, having been confined to a range of 2.84 points with 86.95 for the high and 84.09 for the low. The present price in this case is still almost equidistant from these points.

The present is plainly a period of rest. . . . Nevertheless the market looks healthy enough and unless serious and unexpected trouble develops, a long period of dullness, especially early in the year, often in the past has developed into a broad and healthy market with a higher tendency.

The Wall Street Journal: February 26, 1909

STOCK PRICE MOVEMENTS

On Tuesday, Feb. 23, the twenty active railroad stocks used for purposes of comparison in *The Wall Street Journal* averages suddenly broke below a very well defined line, extending as far back as Nov. 24, 1908. In seventy-one trading days, with a single exception, the average price had not been below 116 or above 121. The movement after the election had amounted to about six points, or from 110 to 116, and had virtually culminated on Nov. 24.

It must be obvious that in this three-month period a very large interchange of stocks has occurred. As a matter of fact, the sales daily never ran below 380,000 shares, and exceeded 1,500,000 shares at times. What seems to be implied now is a move following this most prolonged resting period, and the market is liable to make a radical change. It has been frequently pointed out in these columns that there are three movements always in progress in stock prices. These are the broad market movement, upwards or downwards, which may continue for years and is seldom shorter than a year at the least; then there is the short market swing, which may take anything from one month to three months. These two movements are in operation together and, obviously, may contradict each other. They are still further complicated by the daily movement, which is the third current to be considered by the navigator in these difficult waters.

Anybody will admit that while manipulation is possible in the day-to-day market movement, and the short swing is subject to such an influence in a more limited degree, the great market movement must be beyond the manipulation of the combined financial interests of the world. No combination could possibly succeed in influencing the market over such a movement, for instance, as that between the semi-panic of October, 1907, and the high price touched on Jan. 2 of the present year. The period is too extensive for artificial influence, and the reasons for an independent advance are manifest.

In the same way it would have been impossible to manipulate any such decline as took place between the high price of December, 1906 and the low figure recorded in November of the following year. This movement, moreover, is remarkable for the fact that the main decline lasted less than a year, although the highest price in the active railroad stocks ever touched was in January, 1906. That figure was 138.36 on January 22, but on September 17, 1906, 137.84 was reached, and after a six-point reaction, 137.56 was touched on December 11 of the same year. It is fair, therefore, to say that the main decline was from the latter figure.

It has often happened that the averages have given their best indications on the arrest of a movement rather than in the advance or the sharp break. What is really indicated is a period of distribution, where the constantly floating balance of stocks finds new ownership. It

can easily be imagined, for instance, that a number of people thought that the rally from the panic had gone far enough. Against this may be placed the invincible American optimism, which makes many believe that prices will run further and discount the inexhaustible possibilities of this continent. The new bulls of stocks obviously have not the capital or accumulated profits of the old, and consequently were more liable to be frightened into selling as Tuesday's decline shows.

The price movement at present certainly seems to indicate that after an exceptionally long pause for distribution, new conditions have forced the new holders of stocks to sell. On the surface, the indications of the averages are rather bearish, but sharp advances would easily change them.

The Wall Street Journal: March 17, 1909

THE PRICE MOVEMENT

There is an interesting fluctuation in the average price of twenty active railroad stocks as shown in the figures of the past ten days. The price has in fact alternately declined and advanced from day to day with the regularity of a pendulum. The extreme daily fluctuation was .55 and the smallest change in that time was .19. The net variation between March 3 and March 13 inclusive was less than ⅜ of 1%.

This curious seesaw movement occurs only very occasionally and quite often precedes a broad change in the general market swing. It is perhaps a little significant that after the regular daily fluctuation up and down alluded to, the sequence should have been broken by a further small decline on March 15. The movement itself, however, is altogether too small to draw broad inferences from.

It cannot too often be said that the road to ruin lies in dogmatizing on charts, systems and generalizations. Trading on any such basis is gambling as distinguished from legitimate speculation. It is no more defensible than an attempt to break the bank at Monte Carlo with one of the innumerable systems which have tempted weak human beings since the prehistoric ages when man first learned to count beyond the number of his fingers and toes.

Premising this it may be said that the

showing of the averages since the first of the year has been decidedly discouraging to the speculator for the rise. The fluctuation has been within narrow limits, as in the case of the well defined line between 117 and 121 from which the market broke over three points suddenly on February 23. Part of that decline was recovered soon afterwards but the rally did not hold well and stocks have been for sale on any recovery.

No doubt a very little would change the entire current of the market. A rapid rally of no great extent would put an entirely different complexion upon prices generally. The public likes to buy in a rising market. It is, in fact, upon advancing prices that the small speculator makes his futile plunges in a market which does not really need him and could do very well without him, and complains for ever afterwards about the wickedness of Wall Street.

Such a bull market on the present showing of the averages would be easily possible in the summer or the early fall. Against this it may be said that commission houses are borrowing from two to three times as much money as they were at this time last year when the market movement was very definitely upward. This is not altogether a good sign in a dull market. It indicates something of a stale bull account and tempts the professional to operate for a reaction. On the showing of the averages at present, the market is in a position to respond to bad news more readily than to good.

The Wall Street Journal: March 30, 1909

MOVEMENT OF THE AVERAGES

Not for a long time has the average price of twenty active railroad stocks and twelve industrials, as recorded in these columns for the past twenty-five years for the purposes of comparison, made a more hopeful showing than at present. The high point of the year was touched on January 2, but after that date the market lost strength and direction, and toward the end of February the indication was decidedly bearish.

The real change appears to have come about in the past seven trading days. On Monday, March 22, there was a sharp advance and the active railroad stocks made the most vigorous move out of their rut since the beginning of the year. The

movement looked hopeful, but on the following day the market receded and the technical bull point was in a sense taken back. On the following day, however, the market again developed real strength and is now selling at a higher figure than at any time since the beginning of the year, passing the high price level prevailing about the middle of February.

What has been shown is that after a period of fluctuation within very narrow limits, the market has made a definite movement out of that range on the upward side. Taking the averages merely as the mathematical analysis of the market movements, to a certain extent beyond the possibility of manipulation, the indifference of Wall Street to bear news on industrial matters is emphasized. On March 15 the averages for a day looked bearish, but rallied quickly and although chances then rather favored a decline on technical conditions, stocks nevertheless gradually developed strength and are now five points on the average above the figure of a fortnight ago.

One good sign also for the student of the market from such records as this, ignoring supposed outside factors such as tariff revision and industrial conditions, is that the volume of business has steadily improved during the advance. This is usually a good indication, as there is plainly not much stock in the market. A market which has been overbought shows it very plainly by becoming dull on small rallies and developing activity on declines.

On the closing figures of Monday night indications would seem to point to some continuance of bullish activity. This will be especially emphasized if the high point of the year 120.93 for the railroad stocks, is crossed in the present movement.

The Wall Street Journal: April 22, 1909

THE PRICE MOVEMENT

When, on March 31 the average price of twenty active railroad stocks crossed the high point of January 2, it was pointed out that on all previous experience of the average the market gave indications of broadening and advancing further. This was in face of the fact that there had already been an average recovery of six points or so from the low point of February. The deductions proved legitimate. New high records for the movement were recorded on Monday and Tuesday, while the volume of trading has been broad enough to give importance to the movement.

The bullish indication given by the advance of the end of March was intensified by previous experience. It will be remembered that from the time the market began to rally in November, 1907, each successive crossing of the previous high figure, following a moderate reaction, added strength to the upward movement. How strong that movement has been can be gathered from the fact that from December, 1906, to November, 1907, the average of twenty active railroad stocks declined 55 points, or from 136 to 81. Since that low point was reached the recovery has been no less than 42 points in the face of the depression in general business.

There does not seem to be much stock in the Street. No doubt some of the larger operators are carrying fairly heavy lines, but they are helped by the cheapest of cheap money and not incommoded by any public selling in unmanageable volume. The investor who bought stocks in the months succeeding the panic has a handsome profit but it cannot be said that he seems at all anxious to sell. Such stock, in fact, has gone out of the market and has not come back.

Prices are now not far from the best they ever touched. An advance of 14 points in the average price of the railroad stocks would pass the high figure of January, 1906, the best price ever recorded. It can hardly be contended that business has improved in a corresponding degree, but it must be remembered that the stock market looks a long way ahead.

Indications on the showing of the averages are for a further advance and quite possibly something in the nature of an inflation market, helped by large gold production, cheap money, superabundant bank note circulation, and the absence of definite commercial enterprise to take up surplus financial energy.

The Wall Street Journal: May 21, 1909

THE PRICE MOVEMENT

When the average price of twenty active railroad stocks on March 31 crossed the previous high point of this year established January 2, it was pointed out in these columns that on all previous history of the average movement of stocks a further advance of considerable importance was indicated, even though the total rally from Feb. 23 had then been 7.74 points. The deduction proved entirely correct, and since March 31 a new high point has been made at 126.13, while the present price is not far from that figure. On the recession the market has become dull and narrower.

Various meanings are ascribed to reductions in the volume of trading. One of the platitudes most constantly quoted in Wall Street is to the effect that one should never sell a dull market short. That advice is probably right oftener than it is wrong, but it is always wrong in an extended bear swing. In such a swing the tendency is to become dull on rallies and active on declines. The professionals on the floor of the Stock Exchange, than whom there are no shrewder judges of the market movement, took the short side of the market on every rally throughout 1907 and did not abandon that position until the real recovery had started.

The highest point the average price of the railroad stocks ever touched was on January 22, 1906, at 138.36. It is true that that figure was closely approached twice in the course of that year. The market came within a point of it once on September 17 and once on December 11. It was from the latter point that the severe decline set in.

That decline carried the market down in a little under a year over 56 points, or to 81.41 on November 21, 1907. It will be remembered that it was not until nearly a month after the October crisis that the big rally started. That rally may be said to be in operation continuously ever since. The recovery to date has been nearly 45 points or 78% of the decline from the highest point of the average to the low point touched in November, 1907. During that recovery the most considerable reaction was in January and February, 1908, and was under 10 points. There have been nine definite reactions in the course of this most important upward swing and they have averaged barely 5 points apiece.

What is very clearly indicated in these figures is that the upward swing does not give as yet, any signs of culminating. For all indications in the technical condition of the market, prices, in spite of dull times and contingent uncertainties, may be well on their way to a new high record. The present figure for railroad stocks, in fact, is less than 13 points below the record of 1906, while the industrial average has recovered over 38 points of a fifty-point decline, and is now less than 12 points below the high figure of January, 1906.

The Wall Street Journal: June 5, 1909

PRICE MOVEMENT

On May 11 the average price of twelve industrial stocks made a new high figure for the year at 91.25, and two days afterwards the average price of twenty active railroad stocks followed that example, reaching 126.13. The industrials soon crossed the high figure of May 11, but the active railroad stocks did not make a new high point until June 3, when they reached 127.14. In the interval they had reacted a trifle under a point and a quarter.

Both averages, therefore, were on June 3, at the high point of the year.

It was pointed out in these columns on May 20, soon after the last high point was made, that the long upward swing in prices which has been in operation since November, 1907, gave no signs of culminating. The same remark may be repeated now with entire consciousness that a number of securities may be selling above their real value. The average price of 12 industrial stocks is, in fact, within nine points of the highest figure ever touched, on January 19, 1906; and the twenty active railroad stocks are less than eleven points away from their record figure reached two days afterwards.

The Wall Street Journal: June 24, 1909

PRICE MOVEMENT

Since the average price of twenty active railroad stocks touched 128.28 on June 11, and that of the twelve industrials 94.19 three days afterwards, there has been a reaction of over 4 points in the latter, and of almost as much in the former. This is the first considerable reaction since the market started to advance in February. The rise from the low figure of 113.90 on February 23 in the railroads and 79.91 in the industrials has been continuous, and the gain recorded since those dates amounted roughly to 15 points in each case.

This is a long upward swing, and on all technical conditions the market was overdue for a reaction. There were five measurable set-backs since the low figures following the semi-panic of October, 1907, were recorded, and that of the past ten days makes the sixth. According to precedent it ought to run further, although there are modifying conditions which would probably prevent the intelligent trader from following the decline far, however bearish he might be on general conditions.

At 128.28 the average price of the active railroad stocks was only 10 points away from the highest figure ever touched, in January, 1906; while the industrials reached within less than 9 points of their record. This is undoubtedly a high range of prices, and one which even to the most sanguine indicates that a great deal of possible improvement in general business conditions, together with the best conceivable agricultural results for the year, have been discounted.

It will hardly be contended that values as indicated by stock prices have so nearly attained to the high level of 1906 within eighteen months of a world-wide crisis. It is impossible to avoid the conclusion that cheap money and an abundant supply of new gold, which, thanks to our preposterous currency system, our neighbors secure, have together produced an inflated range of prices. The remark is equally true of commodities of all kinds, as the various index numbers conclusively show. The index number of the London Economist, in fact, at the end of May was the highest since March, 1908.

All this by no means conclusively proves that the advance in prices is over. The stock market was undoubtedly overbought, and public interest instead of increasing on the advance diminished; while large speculators had increased their lines and were pyramiding at the top, as the rapid increase in the loans in the bank statement showed. A healthier condition was undoubtedly produced when those loans were reduced $37,000,-000 last week, and a similar curtailment has been shown in London at the settlement now in progress. The day to day course of the market is pure guesswork. A recovery might set in at any time with the account sufficiently liquidated, and if the average price crossed the last high figure of ten days ago, the indication would still be bullish, all other conditions notwithstanding.

The Wall Street Journal: July 16, 1909

THE PRICE MOVEMENT

In the present condition of the market study of the average price of the active stocks is fruitful and should give some instructive indication on the possibilities of the market. The previous high point of the average price of 20 active railroad stocks was 128.28 and was recorded on June 11 of this year. A few days before the industrials taken for purpose of comparison in *The Wall Street Journal's* averages touched 94.46. The railroads, therefore, were only 10 points away from the best figure ever reached, that of January, 1906, while the industrial stocks were within less than nine points of the record.

Since June 11 there has been a reaction in each instance of between three and four points followed by a period of considerable dullness, in which nevertheless the market has rallied, showing the principal strength in the railroad department in spite of some individual activity in United States Steel common stock. Without crossing the last high point the railroad average on five days in the recent past has risen to 128 or over. It would almost seem as if the market were fighting to make a new high level. Such a movement has some striking parallels in the past and on previous experience of the average, extending over a sufficient number of years to indicate something like a law in the matter, such movements have been highly significant.

The broad advance in the stock market has experienced half a dozen appreciable recessions of from four to ten points in a period of twenty months. This is a very long upward movement and may be said to be more than what is technically known as a "swing," which really means a movement of, at most, a very few months duration. We are plainly still in a bull market and it may be said that each new high point has meant a subsequent further advance.

The indication is always stronger when both the industrials and the railroads make such a new high level about the same time, and the industrial group is still measurably below the last high of June 5.

On the other hand, the repeated approach to an old high point without that high point being definitely crossed has before now indicated the end of a bull market. This was noticeably the case in September and December of 1906, when the high point of the previous January was approached but not crossed. What followed was a very severe break in the market, extending over eleven months.

From the averages it may be said that the indications are distinctly bullish. It is obvious that there are no factors working in the present cheap money market to cause any such decline as that of 1907. A very little would establish a new high record, and with the cheapest of cheap money to finance stocks the market could be carried materially higher, although any conservative judge would admit that the present range of prices is decidedly high.

The Wall Street Journal: August 21, 1909

MOVEMENT OF AVERAGES

Average prices of the score of railway stocks represented in the daily movement are back to a point midway between the average reached on July 31 and that of August 2, the next business day following. Whatever gain had been made thus far this month is now lost. On Monday, August 2, the railway average stood at 131.55. The maximum of advance was reached on Saturday, August 14, 134.46, so that a full gain of 2.91 occurred. Meanwhile there has been a total decline of 3.49 points on three out of four days, offset by an advance of .44 points, leaving a net loss for the period ending with Thursday of 3.05, and placing the average at 131.41. The high point on previous record was 138.36, in January, 1906, so that the current level is 6.95 points below the maximum.

In the industrial group the average of the twelve stocks at 97.71, after two days' decline, had still a small margin left above that of 97.52, at which the group entered the month of August. The largest decline of industrial averages this month occurred in the fourth business day after the opening on August 5, when a loss of .93 was recorded. Since the opening of August there have been seven days of decline, representing a net loss of 3.55 points, and eight days of advances, representing a gain of 4.47 points, with one day unchanged. This brings the two groups within ten days of September 1, with industrials within 5.27 points of their maximum of record.

Looking back to the low point of record reached in the middle of November, 1907, when panic level was struck, the average of the twenty railway stocks has gone from 81.41 to 50 units higher, or an advance of almost 60% in average prices. Between the previous maximum of 1906 and the panic level of 1907 there was a drop of 43% in railways.

These records apparently indicate that the movement of averages is not yet at the turning point. After a long low swing, terminating in a crisis, the period has elapsed during which advances moved up toward the beginning of a high continuous level. The immediate question is whether the level thus anticipated is to be extended from the present points of averages or whether a further upward drift is to be awaited. If the records of the past ten years are to be relied upon, the weight of probability would seem to require that the advance should go to a point not below 140 for the railway group of averages. The maximums of 1905–06 and 1906–07 stood for seven different months between 135 and 140. Then, values had no such slack rope of prosperity to take up as exists now. There was no such abundance of funds and corresponding low rates of interest, nor was there the elasticity in the demand for commodities such as characterizes the present commercial situation. The effect of these upon security values should ultimately be to make for higher prices, provided counteracting influences such as the large issue of new stocks or unforeseen checks to prices do not intervene. Of course, the tendency of prices to advance, as a result of increase in the gold supply, affects security averages as well as commodity averages.

The Wall Street Journal: August 24, 1909

INFERENCES FROM THE PRICE MOVEMENT

Last week the average price of twelve industrial stocks and also that of twenty active railroad stocks, kept for a number of years by this newspaper for comparison, touched the highest figures recorded since 1906. In both cases they were less than four points from the highest point ever reached by the averages. There was a break of some three points in the average price of the railroad stocks, followed by a substantial recovery last Saturday. The situation is interesting and some useful inferences may reasonably be drawn from it.

During the long advance which began in November, 1907, and has not yet culminated, the stock market, judged by the average price of the railroad stocks, has had six reactions, none of them extending to ten points and with one exception with none much larger than the setback of last week. This is a remarkably small reaction when the extent of the advance is considered. A week ago the twenty active railroad stocks had recovered no less than fifty-three points from the low figure of twenty-one months ago. A more considerable reaction than any the market has furnished would seemingly have been in order, but it has so far failed to develop.

It is evident that we are still in a bull market, and it is useless to ignore that the indications of the average are still bullish, in spite of the remarkably high range of prices. A year ago the bull of stocks could see a prolonged period of cheap money before him, while he could buy securities obviously cheap on their merits. Many of the favorable factors upon which he based his optimism then have now been discounted, but on all previous experience a substantial further advance would be indicated if the twenty active railroad stocks advanced above 134.46 and the industrials above 99.26, the last high points recorded August 14.

Here is where the conservative adviser of the public must not allow popular sentiment to run away with him. Prices are high and even inflated, and given an already tangible tightening in the money market, they may become dangerously high at a critical time in the financial year. Money is unquestionably hardening and the bank statement does not indicate that there has really been any drastic liquidation in an extended speculative position. What has happened, in fact, has been a transfer of loans from the banks, who want to oblige their country customers over the crop-moving period, to the trust companies, who are willing enough to lend on call at anything over 2%. Loans of this character are quickly called and we have no very extended resources abroad to depend upon as we have had in previous years.

The buyer of stocks on margin must remember, therefore, that he is taking a greatly more serious risk than he did a year ago. Higher prices mean larger margins, and they also mean a capacity for reaction which may make the average margin look like a very feeble protection. It must never be forgotten that however great the prosperity of the country, advances in prices do not go on forever, and that a movement at least partly inflated which establishes record high prices is apt to show something out of the common in the inevitable reaction when a top-heavy market breaks.

The Wall Street Journal: September 11, 1909

CHANGE IN THE PRICE MOVE-
MENT

In the face of Friday's sensational recovery there are indications in the movement of averages which the conservative observer cannot afford to ignore. They should be very carefully considered by anybody tempted to believe that E. H. Harriman's death ought to be the signal for the resumption of the bull movement.

Thursday saw the most important change in the price movement, considered from the point of view of the average price of stocks, that has occurred since the great bull market started in November, 1907. The high point of the year and of the man upward movement was reached on Aug. 14, when the twenty active railroad stocks taken for purposes of comparison touched 134.46, and twelve industrials 99.26, or both within four points of the best figures ever recorded. From that point there was a reaction which carried the railroad stocks down nearly six points to 128.71. The market then turned and part of this was recovered in a little more than a week.

On that rally it was pointed out that if the last high point were crossed it would be a bull argument independent of all other considerations. The averages gave such a lead with absolute uniformity after each reaction for nearly two years past. The new feature of the market, therefore, is that the recovery failed to hold, and on Thursday the last low point of 128.71 had been crossed, while there was a smaller movement in the industrial stocks.

One such movement as this does not make a bear market, but it can very easily mark the end of a great bull movement. An advance of nearly two years is by no means unprecedented, but is sufficient to indicate the great primary movement of the market, defined in what is called Dow's theory of price movements. The others are the secondary swing in the opposite direction, and the day to day fluctuation. In the bull market which may or may not have terminated now, we have had notably few secondary swings of any great extent, and only one exceeding six points on the average.

Throughout the great bear market of 1907, after a rally from the low point, the crossing of that low figure in a further reaction was invariably a trustworthy bearish indication on the market. This was even the case after the October crisis. It was not until late in November that the movement in the opposite direction definitely set in. The movement of the average on Thursday's break was one which has often marked the commencement of a downward swing. The indication as yet is not very authoritative, but whatever we may think about a resumption of the bull movement "now that all the bad news is out" the averages undoubtedly look more bearish than they have done in a long period.

Pessimism has never been the policy of this paper, but it published an earnest plea for conservatism when the market was at the top. Nothing has occurred since which has not emphasized the position taken.

The Wall Street Journal: October 28, 1909

THE PRICE MOVEMENT

There has been an interesting change in the complexion of the stock averages since the middle of August, when twenty active railroad stocks reached the high figure of the year. On August 14 the railroads recorded 134.46, or less than four points below the best figure ever touched, in January, 1906. The August high point has not been reached since. On the same day the industrials made a new high for the year; but both groups receded, and on September 9 the railroad stocks had fallen below the last low point, giving what would ordinarily be a rather bearish indication.

This fact was recognized in the last criticism of the price movement published in these columns, but it must be admitted that the industrial stocks did not give the same bear point, in spite of a reaction of over four points, and subsequently, at 100.36 on October 1, made a new high for the year, less than three points below the best figure ever reached. When that new high was made the railroad stocks had recovered five points of their seven point reaction, and at 132.64 looked like crossing the previous high figure. Had such further advance occurred it would have been reasonable to say, on all previous experience of a bull movement extending over nearly two years, that a further general advance in the market was indicated.

From that point, however, the average prices of the industrials and the railroads moved together again, and moved downwards. On October 23 the railroad stocks sold below the low figure of September 9 and the industrials gave a similar indication. On the reasoning which has made students of the averages bullish on each new hight point for the past two years the present indication may be called decidedly bearish. The market as unquestionably been running up and running off again, but the declines have exceeded the advances in a way to indicate a heavy distribution of stock, and a speculative position in weaker hands than it had been during the main upward movement. The failure to hold rallies in the past three weeks was especially marked, and is well worthy of the attention of those students of the market who draw inferences from the average price of these 32 stocks, the manipulation of all of which at one time would be beyond the power of any single financial interest.

Against this argument it must be admitted that the market on this reasoning gave a bear indication on September 9, which was belied by the subsequent action of stocks. This is not an uncommon indication where a market shows signs of turning; but upon the whole the movement's indications for lower prices are more impressive than those pointing to a resumption of the main bull movement. The railroad stocks would need to rally upwards of seven points and the industrial stocks five before we could confidently assert that the broad bull movement had been re-established.

There is no pretense here to pass an opinion upon the market from any other point of view than a purely technical one, based upon the experience of the price movements as shown in the average record of many years, but the depression in the barometer here evidenced is well worthy of the consideration of thoughtful traders.

The Wall Street Journal: December 18, 1909

THE PRICE MOVEMENT

A Massachusetts correspondent, who is a close student of the stock market through the movement of the averages, writes as follows:

"Probably the railroad magnates want strikes for a horrible example, and I am inclined to think that probably a few points may be achieved towards a lower quotation; but an eventual result will be, in six months, a running away of judgment, based on expectation of future values."

It is curious how widely this idea of a bull market in the coming year is held. Such bears as there are seem to take the view of a temporary fluctuation, giving them an opportunity to buy some cheap stock for an ultimate advance of the character here described. A good many of the professionals sell the market short on bulges, but they are almost unanimous in the opinion that stocks have not yet seen their high point.

There seems to be no use in trying to

run counter to an opinion so universally held. The averages give no indication whatever. For many weeks they have fluctuated within a space of a few points, vacillating between the high of October and the low point at the beginning of the present month. The volume of business shows a tendency to decrease, while speculation has been confined to a limited number of stocks.

This does not tell much, but it does indicate to some extent a market approaching to equilibrium, where a new impulse is necessary to set the pendulum swinging again. Which way the big swing may be no one can surmise from technical conditions alone. The public is not in the market. Stocks are probably concentrated in fewer hands than they have been since the panic of 1907. The big men do not seem to want to sell, although one would suspect that they have expended a good deal of ammunition on trying to stimulate a public interest. Dividends have been increased or restored on half a dozen of the big roads, while valuable rights have been distributed on as many more. All this "meloncutting" has so far failed to awaken public enthusiasm.

There are serious possibilities before the market, both in the matter of the labor situation and threatened legislation at Washington. Nobody ever made much money selling the market short on a strike, but these lavish distributions to stockholders were bound sooner or later to stimulate a demand that labor should share in the good things. Underlying other factors is one which is so all-pervading that it is scarcely recognized. This is the high cost of living. Something has got to break sooner or later, and in similar circumstances in past times, we know that something did break when the toleration point was passed.

This is not to express any bearish opinion upon the market, but it is only reasonable to point out that in Wall Street it is not the majority which is usually right.

The Wall Street Journal: December 20, 1909

By all accounts we are to have a great bull market in the next six months when the public is to take stocks at the top. So far the judicious distribution of

ground bait has not attracted fish in any great numbers.

The Wall Street Journal: January 18, 1910

THE PRICE MOVEMENT

In a study of the price movement published in these columns on December 18, it was pointed out that the stock market, as reflected in the average price of stocks, tended to approach equilibrium, and that a new impulse seemed necessary to set the pendulum swinging again. No explicitly bearish opinion was expressed, but the possibilities of the labor situation and threatened legislation at Washington were pointed out. It was said then that an overwhelming public opinion anticipated a January boom, and that in Wall street the majority was seldom right.

So far from any boom developing at the new year, the averages show that the market is not only out of its rut, but is beginning to give definite indications of the possibility of a further downward movement. From the time the high point of the year was reached in the railroad stocks on September 20, and in the industrials on October 1, the market, instead of making new high records, has reacted and rallied again and again, so that throughout the fall the range of fluctuation tended to become narrower. There was a rally whenever the low point of the beginning of December was approached; the market became dull and reactionary before a really convincing recovery could be established, and even at the new year the same appearances prevailed, although in the first week of January it was already plain enough that technical conditions were changing.

Heavy liquidation has filled the market with stocks, and on Jan. 14 the market price broke through the old low points of six weeks ago in a very definite manner, both in the industrials and the railroads. In the long advance which may be said to have culminated in September and the beginning of October, the market for nearly two years had given a plain and profitable bull indication every time the previous high point had been passed in the averages after a moderate recession. Indications on the bear side were of a vague and inconclusive character afterwards. Reactions were not of sufficient extent to make new low points convincing. The indication is a little clearer now, and with a reaction from the high of 1909 of over six points in the industrials, and over eight points in the railroads, it is fair to assume that a radical change has taken place in technical conditions.

It is at least clear that the back of the big bull movement has been broken and that time will be required to build up a new one. We cannot grumble. We enjoyed as a main movement, one of the longest and most profitable upward swings in the history of the averages. The range of prices so established was so high as to be entirely unattractive to the speculative public. This is not to say that a higher level cannot ultimately be established, but on usual and fairly reasonable methods of reading the averages the indication given is distinctly bearish.

The Wall Street Journal: January 24, 1910

It is a usual course for stocks, after vigorous pressure following a prolonged upward movement, to rally sharply. Recoveries in a bear market are always brisk when once stocks begin to get sold out, but are very usually followed by a period of dullness and uncertainty consequent upon the necessity for distribution of stocks bought to support the market. Something of this kind may be expected in the present week, and the true test will lie in the capacity of the market to absorb such stock.

The Wall Street Journal: February 19, 1910

PRICE MOVEMENT

In a study of the price movement on January 18, it was pointed out that for the first time since the long advance of 1908 and 1909 set in, the average prices of the railroad stocks and industrials gave a distinctly bearish indication. For two months the market had fluctuated within a narrow range as if, to use a well worn simile, the pendulum was slowing down to equilibrium and the market was waiting for a new impulse. Stocks broke through the low point recorded in December; a new low was established,

and although prices were then several points from the high of last October, a further downward movement was indicated.

This movement came in due course, and it was not until February 8 that the bear swing, which had then extended for some weeks, culminated. From the high figures of 1909, the average decline in the industrial stocks had been 15.50 points, and that in the railroads 13.93. Since Fedbruary 8, there has been a significantly sharp rally, amounting in each instance to 30% of the decline. Discarding outside influences, and reasoning on the indication of the averages alone, what is the inference from technical conditions?

It will be generally admitted that we were in a definite and well-developed bear movement. The bull market was dead last October, although it was some time before we realized it. Does the week's rally indicate that a new bull market has started, or is it merely one of those sharp recoveries which are typical of an extended bear swing? Past experience certainly points rather to the latter inference.

In a broad bull movement, sharp reactions are in order. The reason is obvious. The market suffers from too much company on the bull side. Commission houses are over-extended. Large operators who bought much lower down perceive the weakness of the position, and a market which has advanced 25 points on the average in seven months easily loses 20% of its gains in seven days. In the same way, rallies in a bear market are always sharp, and there is nothing in the least abnormal in the substantial recovery shown in little more than a week. After a prolonged decline, exactly such a recovery was in order.

A rally of 30% of the decline is considerable enough to wipe out much of the invaluable support afforded by an extended bear position. Sentiment changes, and there is once more a bull party confident and even aggressive. Results may or may not justify such confidence. So far as the averages are concerned, they have not given any really bullish indications, and any reactionary movement now would look bearish, especially if lower prices than those of Feb. 8 were established.

The Wall Street Journal: March 19, 1910

A month ago we discussed in these columns the price movement as shown in the average fluctuation of twelve industrials and twenty railroad stocks. It was pointed out then that after the decline from the high prices of September and November, 1909, of 15.50 points for the industrials and 13.93 points for the railroad stocks, there had been a rally of approximately 30%, extending over eight trading days. The two averages since that time have not kept as closely together as they usually do. The railroad stocks are slightly below and the industrials somewhat above the figures of a month ago.

Following this sharp rally we have had a month of fluctuations within a range of less than four points for the industrials and considerably less than three points for the railroad stocks. In other words, the sharp recovery did not continue, although there was something which at the time looked like a resumption on March 7. This, however, was the high point of the month, and since then the old uncertainty has reasserted itself. Judging from technical conditions alone, what seems to be indicated is a market held up and supported in order to distribute stocks.

Long experience, which can be verified from the averages, teaches that in a broad bull movement, of a kind that lasts over a year or more, the advance looks slow compared to the sharpness of the occasional reactions. In the same way, in a bear market, sharp recoveries are in order. After the decline from the high prices of last autumn, we can see that stocks recovered far faster than they went down. Active traders on the floor will explain this readily enough. The market becomes temporarily sold out. Prices become attractive to people who pay for their stock outright. A large and vulnerable short interest develops, and these causes together make it easy, when once the rally is started, to run prices up rapidly.

The buying movement thus engendered seems usually to possess a rallying power of from 30 to 50 per cent, of the previous decline before it becomes exhausted, and prices reach something like equilibrium. By that time the market has generally been supplied with stocks bought to protect it on the way down, profit-taking sales, realizing by holders who distrust the recovery, and the development of a new bear party powerful enough to take care of itself, and intrenched in the knowledge that a genuine and broad new impulse would be necessary to resume the recovery with the old vigor. Prices, therefore, begin to hesitate, and we are now at one of those critical and interesting periods.

To judge by the absence of public interest, there can hardly be any broadly extended bull position. There must be plenty of large professional operators long of the market, as distinguished from the absolute amateur who trades, when he does trade, in small lots but in large aggregate volume. Against this there is doubtless an influential party which does not believe in the market at its present level. From the showing of the averages, in spite of the strength of the past day or two, the tendency seems lower, but no very clear indication beyond the exhaustion of the rallying impulse is yet given.

The Wall Street Journal: April 16, 1910

A month ago the condition of the stock market as a technical proposition was considered here. It was then pointed out that if any tendency were indicated at all, it was downwards. The average price of twenty active railroad stocks was then 123.66, and that of the twelve representative industrials in *The Wall Street Journal's* averages was 92.33. From these figures there was a decline of 2.44 in the railroads and of 2.97 in the industrials, followed by a rally which has carried the averages to within a point or less of where they were a month ago.

When the market is waiting for a new impulse, as this one seems to have been doing, the movements of the day become important. It will be remembered that after reaching the high point of last year in August, the market worked downwards, with a decline culminating in February more considerable than any reaction during the long advance which followed the crisis of October, 1907. Following this relatively sharp break in the market, there was the usual rally of about 50% of the decline. This was followed by what may fairly be called the secondary decline (which is practically a constant feature of such market swings) and then business became extremely dull with no deciding movement anywhere.

We may use once more the well worked simile of the pendulum because it fits this method of studying market movements as nothing else does. Each recurring swing, as the figures quoted show, took in a smaller segment of the arc until the pendulum reached equilibrium. Obviously the market waited for a new impulse.

What follows also is that such a market becomes thoroughly sold out. As the traders say, it has not "bulled easily," and consequently the professionals sell it short, feeling safe in the absence of any aggressive bull leadership. In the same way, inactivity tires out the bulls. No broker likes "sleeping accounts," and finally the market gets in such a position that a very little impetus will start it one way or the other. The sharp rally from last Monday, when it was known that the Standard Oil and American Tobacco decisions would, at least, not be hanging over the market for an indefinite time to come, seems to indicate that prices are now out of their rut, and for the moment at least are working in the upward direction.

There is nothing to show that the bear market which may be said to have set in somewhere about last September, has culminated; but on technical considerations, an upward swing is indicated. It need not run very fast or very far, but bearish considerations are now sufficiently remote to leave room for an upward movement, especially if the public shows a disposition to get back into the market. The showing of the average after such a secondary swing is over, is likely to be highly interesting.

The Wall Street Journal: June 16, 1910

THE PRICE MOVEMENT

Less than a month ago, in discussing the price movements in these columns, it was found that, while technical conditions were not particularly encouraging, the market seemed in the humor to rally a little further, and that, in view of the uncertainties of the autumn, a bull campaign to have much chance of success, if taken in hand at all, might be expected early. There was some further advance after those lines were written and on May 21 the average price of both the industrials and the railroad stocks touched the best figures since March 8.

The new level of prices was barely maintained, but no real pressure developed until May 25, when there were signs of weakness in both the market groups. In spite of a rally on the following day, these indications had developed into vigorous liquidation, ostensibly arising out of the attitude of the Administration toward the railroads, which culminated in a severe break, with the industrials selling at 82.05, and the railroads at 114.59, new low points for the year and respectively 7.61 and 8.73 below the previous high of May 21.

On the treaty of peace between the administration and the railroads a moderate rally developed, amounting to 35% of the break in the railroads, and 37% in the industrials. One inference which might be reasonably drawn from this fluctuation is that if the decline had been solely on the spectacular action of the Attorney General against the western roads, the recovery ought to have been faster and carried further. For the present we are studying merely technical market conditions, as disclosed by the average movement of prices which experience has taught us is governed by definite laws, even if long periods of time are necessary to demonstrate their truth. It is not necessary here to go into the question of the real as distinguished from the ostensible causes for the decline.

Students of the price movement will notice that the rally ought to run further, and a development of dullness after about 50% of the sudden decline had been recovered would be in keeping with the normal action of a market which has broken on the unexpected. Whether there is sufficient driving power to carry prices higher, remains extremely doubtful, in a market restricted to a few large financial interests and the active professional element, to the almost total exclusion of the speculative public.

Cautious traders would take a conservatively bullish view, and would be apt to detect a new bull influence in the market if prices recovered more than 50% of the decline from May 21 to June 6.

The Wall Street Journal: July 19, 1910

THE PRICE MOVEMENT

When the price movement was last discussed in these columns on June 16, the market was in the middle of a rally, following the severe break of the beginning of the month when the Administration made its sudden attack upon the western roads. The rally had then extended to about 30% of the sudden and severe decline on the unexpected news. It was shown that by past experience the recovery should run further or to the extent of at least half the break. This is exactly what happened. The recovery continued to June 22, when the market again developed weakness.

What had happened technically was that the shorts had covered, and the stock bought to protect the market had come out in sufficient quantity to exhaust its absorbing capacity. Any trader operating on technical conditions must have sold short on June 22 and 23 with absolute confidence. There was a further sharp decline, brief in duration, but serious in extent, establishing new low records for the year, both in the industrials and railroad stocks. These on July 5, or in nine trading days had lost 6.05 points and 8.77 points respectively.

Students of the averages know that as soon as the low point of the June break had been crossed on the new reaction, the indications were distinctly bearish. They made good to the extent of 2 points in the industrials and nearly 4 in the railroad stocks before prices began to make something of a line at the low level. From there, the recovery has not carried the market above the low figures of June, and in spite of the recovery it may, therefore, be said that the market has not yet taken back its bear point.

It is always promised in these studies that only technical indications are taken, and the general conditions upon which the miscellaneous public buys and sells stocks are not under discussion.

There is in Wall Street a small but very useful section of traders which is oftener right than wrong, and its methods, often unconsciously, are strictly technical, bearing very little reference to conjectures based upon crop prospects or politics. This class, on the indications of the average today,

would probably be trading for a further rally, but in a position to run quickly. Any check in the recovery, or indication that the market, as the traders say, "bulled hard" would mean a switch to the short side. It can at least be said that there is no indication whatever that the broad bear market has culminated, but a very small further recovery might initiate one of those secondary bull swings of a month or so which are a feature of any broad decline.

The Wall Street Journal: July 29, 1910

RALLIES IN THE STOCK MARKET

After the last and most serious break on Tuesday, the stock market has rallied, and on previous experience the recovery should carry further. We have been experiencing a broad downward movement virtually since last October, even if the real decline did not set in earlier, at least we have had, in fact, a bear market extending over some eight months without any very aggressive rally, and a recovery was due, especially after the drive of last Tuesday.

It has often been pointed out in these columns that the rally in a bear market is apt to be sharp and relatively short. Stocks seem to recover faster than they went down and not infrequently from 30 to 40 per cent of a decline extending over four months is recovered in as many weeks. This is the secondary movement of the market. The first is, of course, the main movement usually running upwards some two years or more, or the bear movement not often much exceeding twelve months. In a broad advance, we are liable to sudden and rapid reactions, and in a broad decline to parallel recoveries. These often last for thirty days, constituting the secondary movement as distinguished from the daily fluctuations. Generally, it may be said that the shorter the movement, the more difficult it is to forecast.

One indication which is sometimes useful to the trader, who believes that the ticker tells all the story if we are only shrewd enough to interpret it, is the recovery from the last severe break of a long decline. We may take it that the recent decline in the market culminated in a downward movement over ten trading days, with a net loss on the average of 8.06 points in the railroad stocks and of 7.79 in the industrials. On its normal movement in such a rally as seems now to have set in about 40% of the last break should be rapidly recovered. Should the market become dull after such a rally most professionals would sell stocks, on the theory that enough buying power had not been generated to warrant the assumption of a real thirty-day bull swing.

If, on the other hand, stocks continue strong, with a more gradual improvement after such a recovery, the professional tape reader would follow the market up. He would not assume at once that the great bear movement had concluded. The technical indications do not yet point that way, nor would they even if the market indulged in one of those August rises which have, it must be confessed, been very consistent in recent years.

It is probable that the professional trader would attach more importance to the present rally if the market had remained dull and inactive near the low level, with an appreciable time before recovering. The conditions which make for a big upward or a big downward movement of the primary class practically never change themselves overnight, however encouraging the first recovery may seem.

The Wall Street Journal: August 30, 1910

In writing of the price movement, as shown by the average price of the active railroad stocks and industrials, from day to day and over a period of years, it was said in this paper on July 19 that there was no indication whatever that the broad bear market had culminated. The inference was so accurately justified that the average price of twenty railroads, which was then 112.64, sold down to 105.59, the low point of the year, within seven trading days; while there was an accompanying 8 point further decline in the industrial stocks.

This decline over a short period following a long bear movement was too violent not to encourage a sharp recovery. This recovery set in on July 27,

and by August 17 the railroad stocks had regained 9.88 points, and the industrials 7.79 points. This movement extended over three weeks and may fairly be taken as representing the short, or secondary, bull swing in a bear market. It will be noticed that the usual characteristics of such a swing were in evidence. It was short and sharp, comparing in that respect with the occasional breaks so often observed in a prolonged upward movement.

When everybody had decided that the market was in line to fulfill all predictions founded on desire, the upward movement was arrested, and since August 17, or in nine trading days, there has been a definite reaction. This indicates at least that the secondary movement of the market, the short bull swing in a bear market, has culminated. To offer any hopes of a genuine change in the broad current, it would be necessary for the average prices to advance above the high figure recorded on August 17. There is certain encouragement about the daily fluctuation occasionally, but there is no present indication of any such recovery.

It should be repeated, as it is our custom to do in these studies, that they take into account only the technical position of the market, and do not consider the outside influences. It has been the experience of twenty-five years of market averages used for comparison that these outside influences are recorded in the price movement before they have become the subject of popular discussion; and that the only exceptions are events beyond human foresight, such as the San Francisco disaster. Even in the interruption caused by such a calamity, it will be found that the subsequent rapid recovery tends to restore the broad market condition on which these discussions are based.

As the averages stand at present, it would appear that we have had a typical recovery and have resumed the general movement. The inference would be that the broad decline has not culminated, although in the process of time it must obviously be approaching its completion. The record shows that such movements do not as a rule enjoy more than a year's duration.

The Wall Street Journal: September 20, 1910

THE PRICE MOVEMENT

When the average price of stocks shows merely nominal fluctuations, it is still possible to draw useful inferences from the condition. In such a case "they also serve who only stand and wait." The fluctuation in the average price of twelve industrial stocks since, and including, August 22 is no more than 1.36 points, and that of twenty active railroads only 2.31 points. The market obviously has settled down to wait for a new impulse following the short-lived rally which culminated on August 17.

In deceptively parallel instances it has been found that a market after a severe break, followed successively by a rally of 40% or better, a slower subsequent reaction, and minor fluctuations either way, acts like a pendulum running down until it reaches equilibrium. This is not unusually a condition following a panic break in the market. It is because of the deceptive parallel of this panic break that the difference is worth demonstrating.

In the crisis of 1907 we never had a real stock market panic. Stocks were made very weak both in March and October of that year, but they never got quite out of hand, which is the essence of a panic break. People who trade on these technical evidences were misled for this reason and bought stocks after the crisis of October, 1907, only to be squeezed out at the still lower level in November, reached before the bear market turned.

In the present bear market the average prices rallied rapidly up to Aug. 17, but having exhausted the secondary or upward swing, the strength evaporated, both in respect of market movement and the volume of trading, and we have been hopelessly in the doldrums ever since. There is no serviceable parallel here to the bear market of 1907. Sooner or later the market must break out of the narrow rut which at present constrains it. What would be the technical value of such a change, upward or down?

If the market advanced to the above figures of the rally which culminated Aug. 17, 115.47 and 81.41 for the railroads and industrials respectively, the sign would be moderately bullish. It would not indicate, of itself, a broad general change in the current until further price movement in the same direction emphasized the change. If, on the other hand, the market broke out of its rut on the down side, crossing 105.59 and 73.62, the low prices of the year recorded July 26, the effect would be extremely bearish. It would indicate a further violent fall which might even carry the averages down to figures not very far from those of the latter part of 1907.

We are plainly not out of the bear market yet, and such a market not infrequently culminates with a last violent decline. That we are approaching the end of the broad movement seems indicated by technical conditions, even if we assume that the main downward market movement was not really established until December, 1909.

The Wall Street Journal: October 18, 1910

THE PRICE MOVEMENT

In discussing the stock market on the indications given in the average price of twelve industrials and twenty active railroads a month ago, it was said that an advance above 81.41 and 115.47 respectively, the high points of August, would be moderately bullish. At that time the market was in a rut, where for a month or more the extreme fluctuation was only about two points or so. On October 3 and 4 the averages closely approached the previous high of the year, and on October 10 both groups were selling well above the August figures.

The forecast might have been made with a good deal of confidence in view of the record of the averages in the past. Prices advanced with redoubled assurance, making further gains of from two to four points. There is a dangerous temptation about a market which has accurately fulfilled predictions. It was relatively easy to say that strength would be developed in whatever direction the market broke out of the rut of a month ago. There is no such guide for what prices may do after the advance has been established. Fortunately, it is no part of the business of this newspaper to encourage day to day speculation on philosophical deductions drawn from comparisons of history.

Unquestionably we have developed at least a strong secondary bull swing in a bear market. That the main current has changed and that the broad tendency of prices for a long period of time is likely to be upward, the averages certainly do not show. The rally from the low of July has been twelve points in the railroad stocks, after an extreme decline of some thirty points to that date. A further advance extending over a longer period of time than has been covered by the present rally would be necessary to establish a reasonable presumption that the major movement of the market was upwards. On the other hand, the market would have to show a substantial decline to re-establish the general downward tendency which has been comparatively easy to forecast in the past year.

It looks as if it would be necessary for the price of the active railroad stocks to recede to 112, and that of the industrials to 78, to establish the secondary character of tne present bull swing. To give a really alarming bear point the reaction would, according to precedent, require to be more considerable than this. Anything which carried the average prices below the figures of July would indicate a further break, in which the range of prices might be expected to reach the low figures of 1903, if not those of 1907.

One strong feature of the advance is that the volume of trading has increased with each successive daily gain in price. Such a movement is apt to culminate in one or two days of noticeably heavy trading, but the essence of the analysis of averages is that they are taken as reflecting these and all other factors.

The Wall Street Journal: November 29, 1910

THE PRICE MOVEMENT

Soon after our discussion on October 18th of the condition of the stock market, judged by the average price movement alone, both the railroads and the industrial stocks established high points for the year, subsequently receding to the extent of three points or so, and becoming conspicuously dull on the recession. In these discussions the idea is to accept the average as the sum of all the influences either way, and to discuss the price movement purely on previous experience as shown by the figures over a long period of years.

Before the high point was reached the stock market had risen through a long line of quotations within a narrow range, establishing a bull argument which was justified by the continuance of what was at least a bull swing of most respectable proportions in a long bear market. Since that time there has been a recession, with the establishment of another "line" of trading within a narrow range, about on the level of the place from which the final spurt of the bull swing started. One thing which will strike the experienced observer is the essential difference between these two lines.

A period of accumulation seemed to be indicated in the remarkable steadiness in the market before the final advance which culminated October 20. Since that culmination the market has closely approached the old high, but failed to cross it. That high point was 118.43 in the railroad stocks. On Nov. 11, 115.09 was touched with some subsequent rally, but all within the same narrow range. This line on the recession of the average prices bears considerable evidence of well-handled distribution of the stocks.

We are aware that there are good arguments in favor of simultaneously considering the volume of business with the average price movement, but there are practical objections to that method. To give such a comparison any value, it would be necessary to establish the volume of business day by day over a quarter of a century, when we should probably find that the averages themselves had made allowance sooner or later for this influence, as well as for all others. In the same way there are effects traceable to special causes at present operating.

Following our custom month by month, we prefer to neglect these factors.

Judged by past experience of the market, a decline of the active railroad stocks below 115.09, the reaction point established November 10, and of the industrials below the 83.50 of the same date, would be distinctly bearish, and a further recession would point to more definite indications that the main bear movement, operative for a year past, was still in active effect.

The Wall Street Journal: January 5, 1911

THE PRICE MOVEMENT

There has not been such inducement to discuss the price movement, as shown in the fluctuations of the average price of industrials and railroad stocks, since our last editorial on the subject on Nov. 29. At that time we said that the averages, and particularly the railroad average, were making what looked like a line of distribution; and that a break below 115.09, the reaction point of Nov. 10, would be bearish, although not necessarily indicating specifically a return to the main bear movement of 1910.

The inference was fully justified by the action of the market when it broke through the level of Nov. 10; an average decline of four points in the industrials and of nearly five points in the railroads followed, culminating on Dec. 6. There was a subsequent rally, which has seemed to carry the railroad stocks above 115 and the industrials above 82. The break below the November level was not sufficient to carry us back into the prices ruling during the same bear market, while the most that can be said of the rally in the past month is that it would have to carry the railroads above the October high of 118.43 to justify any positively bullish inference.

We prefer to neglect volume and the character of the trading in these studies, believing that the average itself, being absolutely impartial, makes allowances for these factors as well as for the chapter of accidents, the conditions of trade, the tone of the money market, and the temper of the speculating public and even the character of the investment demand. There is nothing in the averages to dogmatize about. They are an immensely valuable guide when studied over long periods in the past. They frequently give useful indications of the tendency of the market's short swing. For day-to-day trading they are not only valueless but would probably be dangerous as well.

The man who played the stock market on the averages from day to day, ranking his occupation no higher than that of the punter at Monte Carlo, would be no better than the gambler with a system, whether he based his conclusions on the averages or not, and would meet a like fate sooner or later.

Drawing broad but legitimate inferences, it may be fairly inferred from the present level that an advance in the railroad stocks above 118.43 would be decidedly bullish; while a definite bear inference might be drawn from a decline below 111.33, especially if these movements were accompanied by corresponding fluctuations in the average price of the industrial stocks. Which of these movements is the more probable is a matter of opinion. The averages do not say.

The Wall Street Journal: February 1, 1911

THE PRICE MOVEMENT

In a discussion of the market indications given by the movement of the average price of stocks on Jan. 5, it was shown that an advance above the last high price of Oct. 18, 1910, would give a more definitely bullish indication than any fluctuation since the bear movement of last year set in. The latest movement, although the industrials are still some distance from the last high point, is of considerable importance.

Since the rally which culminated last October the market has fluctuated in such a manner as to leave the averages of very little worth to the student of market movements, to say nothing of the speculative investor who bases broad conclusions upon them. Scrutiny of the price movement, however, discloses that each recent reaction terminated at a figure above the point previously touched, while the recoveries tended to establish new high levels. This has proved a decidedly bullish intimation on former occasions when uncertainty existed following one of the larger swings of the market.

To give the maximum of comfort to the bull it would be necessary for the industrial stocks to make a further advance of 2 points or so in order to confirm the indications given by the railroad stocks. The two groups tend to move together, but either can develop greater strength or weakness than the other, and in spite of the volume of trading in United States Steel common the main movement since the beginning of the year has been in the railroad issues. With so much railroad financing in sight, this is not at all surprising, especially as new financing seems to be received with more public favor than it was at any time last year.

The present movement may fairly be said to date back to the December low figures, some five points under the present level in the industrials, and seven points in the railroads. It is still entirely possible that the movement is a vigorous secondary bull swing, in a bear market broader than we have been accustomed to since 1896. This secondary movement, however, has unquestionably gained considerable strength. It is easy to say that the public is not in the market, but the advance shows in the aggregate a large volume of sound distribution, and estimates of the general volume of business in Wall Street are constantly based on what the informant is doing himself.

Without talking about a runaway bull market, or a return to "boom" times, it may still be said that, on analysis of the averages, the market looks like going higher.

The Wall Street Journal: February 6, 1911

Last week saw an almost continuous advance in the stock market, slightly checked on Friday. The average price of the active railroad stocks crossed the high point of last October on Tuesday, to the gratification of students of price movements, and those who base their opinions in part upon statistical analysis. There seems to have been a large distribution of stock on the advance, but such stock has been well absorbed, as the technical market movement shows. The market became dull on small reactions, showing increasing activity on any resumption of the advance. As any professional knows, this is a good indication that the strength is still on the buying side. Realizing toward the end of the week had left the market sufficiently full of stocks to justify a moderate recession; but it must be admitted that the bears are chiefly those who have sold their stocks too soon, and want to get them back, or those who distrusted the rise from the

beginning, and want Fate to give them another chance. The latter class usually concludes by loading up at the top, and would probably be more bearish than ever with a reaction sufficient to bring in a renewal of good buying.

The Wall Street Journal: February 13, 1911

Last week the price of stocks fluctuated within a narrow range, not extending to a full point in the average price of either the industrials or the railroad stocks. A plan for establishing the advance of the past month or so on a firm basis seemed to be an execution. Traders generally reported an absence of stocks on a moderate recession, with a substantial volume of distribution on advances, unusually well absorbed. This is what the professionals call getting the public accustomed to higher prices. After a certain time a very small recession makes stocks look cheap, while prices become easier to advance. The market, in fact, takes care of itself, and is in a good strategic position for any kind of news. It would hardly be inferred from the surface evidence that stocks have lost their original impulse. Most experienced judges would conclude that prices were steadying themselves preparatory to a further advance.

The Wall Street Journal: March 6, 1911

THE PRICE MOVEMENT

Since we last discussed the movement of the stock market, as shown by the fluctuations in the average price of stocks, a bull point so clear that we were obliged to draw a distinctly bullish inference from it has justified itself. Since that further advance, however, a change of considerable moment has taken place. Its most interesting feature is the long line made from Feb. 1, where in twelve trading days the average price of twenty active railroad stocks did not go below 119 or above 120.

After a downward fluctuation of about a point there was a return to this level, which was successfully held for four days more. The first serious break followed the railway rates decision, and since that time it has been apparent that there was stock pressing for sale. It is plain that there must have been a large distribution in the early part of February, and the market for a time looked as if it could absorb such stock and yet be in a position to resume its advance. This is the view we should have taken a month ago; but the developments of the past week or two so closely resemble a definite interruption of a secondary upward swing that it is necessary to point out the more conservative indication of the averages.

Previous experience teaches us that after a line at the top of the movement has been broken through on the downward side, as in the case both of the industrials and the railroads, it would be necessary for the last high point to be reached again before we could assume anything like a bullish indication in the average. It would be necessary for the price of the industrials to advance well above 86, and that of the railroads to 120 to indicate that the recent fairly extended bull swing had been resumed.

On the other hand, a downward fluctuation as considerable in extent would be necessary before the averages really began to talk bearish. We may take it that the secondary bull movement dates from the low point of Dec. 6, 1910, when the industrial price was 79.68, and that of the railroads 111.33. A decline below these figures would represent a fluctuation of over four points in the railroad stocks and three points in the industrials from the present level. Crossing the last low would be definitely bearish.

It will be seen, therefore, that there is nothing much to dogmatize about. It rather looks as if the secondary bull swing were over; or, at any rate, as if serious doubt had been cast on the possible existence of a broad bull market, of which the upward movement from Dec. 6, 1910, and the high point of the nary spurt.

The Wall Street Journal: April 5, 1911
1911

Throughout last week stocks marked time, with trifling changes and an insignificant volume of business. On Thursday, in fact, the average price of twenty active railroad stocks did not change on the day, and that of the twelve industrials declined .01. This is the nearest thing to absolute equilibrium the averages have ever shown. It is in a sense merely a coincidence, but it is a fair illustration of the stagnation prevailing in the stock market. Such inactivity is in itself a symptom. The superficial observer is constantly startled to find that the stock market fails to respond to sudden and important developments; while it seems to be guided by impulses too obscure to be traceable. Consciously or unconsciously, the movement of prices reflects not the past but the future. When coming events cast their shadows before, the shadow falls on the New York Stock Exchange.

The market now is not merely saying that general business is dull. If our reasoning is worth anything at all, it is predicting a period of stagnaticn for some time to come. There is, however, another way of looking at it. It may be that a new stimulant is needed. A good deal might happen with the Trust decisions out of the way, and this irrespective of the character of the decisions. The Northern Securities decision, it will be remembered, was technically unfavorable to Wall Street and marked the beginning of one of the best bull markets we ever had.

THE PRICE MOVEMENT

The Wall Street Journal: March 27,

When the price movement of the stock market. as shown by the fluctuations in the averages of twenty railroad stocks and twelve industrials, was discussed in these columns on March 6, the price was then hanging in each instance midway between the low point of Dec. 6 to Feb. 1 was only the preliminary-present year, recorded on Feb. 4. It was argued that an advance above the last high point would be decidedly bullish, while a decline below last December's figure would go a long way towards indicating a return to the bear market of last year.

Since the last study was made the movements of prices have been interesting, if not conclusive. Neither of the conditions postulated has come about. The industrials did not even approximate the low of 79.62, although they came within 2.02 points of the high of 86.02. In like manner the railroad stocks showed no tendency whatever in the past month to a downward movement of any sort, much less one which would carry them below the low of 111.33. They have approached as close to the high of 119.97 as 118.73; but since that figure, recorded a week ago, have backed and filled with some net recession on the week.

This is certainly inconclusive, although it will be noticed that the prices in each case have been almost uniformly above those obtaining at the time of our last analysis. The averages have looked as if they wanted to go up, although some students might argue that the small volume of business detracted from the importance of such changes as there were. Nevertheless the tendency has been distinctly bullish. So far as volume is concerned we prefer to neglect it in these studies, arguing that this, as well as all other considerations, may be eliminated in the comparison of extended price movements over any considerable period of time. Such volume of trading, like even the chapter of accidents itself, tends in such periods to average itself. Dullness and activity have alternated in stock markets throughout their existence.

There is no positively bullish indication, but the inference drawn in our last study still seems to obtain. An advance from the present level of the railroad stocks to 120, a little more than 2 points, would be a strongly bullish indication for the market of the spring and early summer; and a corresponding movement of the industrials to anywhere over 86, or less than three points, would tend to confirm the indication given by the railroad average.

The Wall Street Journal: April 24, 1911

Stocks lost ground last week, showing their solitary rally on Wedensday and failing altogether to develop the spurt not unusual after a holiday. There was a relatively sharp break on Tuesday, with a little more activity than has been shown for some time past. Perhaps the weakest feature of the market was that it tended to become more active on declines. Superficially, there is no speculative bull account, but stocks are being carried on margins in each case and have to be kept good, pressure beyond

a certain point dislodges long stock, even when its existence is not apparent from the previous transactions on the floor. The average price of the active railroad stocks is now about midway between the high of last February and the low of last December, while the industrials are rather nearer the low figure.

The purely technical indications would be bearish on a break below 111.33 in the one case and 79.68 in the other, which would make a number of professionals aggressive and would probably bring realizing sales as well. The market, however, is not out of its rut, and chances either way are still evenly divided.

The Wall Street Journal: May 4, 1911

THE PRICE MOVEMENT

For the third month in succession the average prices of the industrial and railroad stocks have not crossed the low point of December 6 on the one hand or the high of last February on the other. When we discussed the price movement a month ago the market was in something of a rut, from which it seemed towards the middle of April inclined to emerge on the downward side. For a few days at least the aggressive traders found activity on declines with dullness on rallies, and consequently took the short side of the market.

Last week a material change in the character of the trading took place, although it cannot be claimed that the volume of business was much more impressive than it had been. Prices rallied with considerable confidence, and at the close on Wednesday the average price of twenty active railroad stocks was within 0.74 of the last high figure; while the industrials were slightly over two points from their best of the year, recorded on Feb. 4.

For purposes of scientific study the averages in these discussions are taken as representing the sum of all the varying influences on the market, even including the volume of business. It is of secondary consequence, therefore, that news has had little or no market influence. If trading was dull a month ago because tariff uncertainty prevailed and the Supreme Court's decisions were still held back, the same influences are felt to-day. We are inclined to think that such influences are overrated, for history shows that when certainty on such matters is reached the market deceives the most experienced judges of the value of news.

There are certain well-worn rules, perhaps more honored in the breach than the observance, for market movements throughout the year. A normal market is the kind that never really happens. Otherwise we might say that on an average over a period of years the tendency in March and April is to advance, and in May and June to decline. This is consonant with the volume of general business, but would be following it too closely to give much barometrical value to the price movement.

It is with these facts considered that, on previous experiences of the averages, an advance above 120 for the railroad stocks and 86 for the industrials, or from 1 to 2 points from the present level, may be pronounced decidedly bullish; and would, indeed, indicate a tendency which might be prolonged well into the summer.

The Wall Street Journal: June 1, 1911

THE PRICE MOVEMENT

In a discussion of the price movement published in these columns on May 4 it was pointed out that the average prices of the twenty railroads and the twelve industrials, taken for purposes of comparison over many years, were closely approaching the high point recorded early in February, and that to cross that point would give a bullish indication. These prices for three months had hung somewhere about midway between the low point of last December and the high point of last February. On previous experience a movement out of such a rut either way would mean ultimately a change of considerable importance.

On May 22 the average price of twenty railroad stocks made a new high point for the year, while the industrial issues did the same on May 29. The former crossed the February high on May 16 and the latter on May 18. Since that time considerable strength has been shown, although the market has hesitated and industrials have even

occasionally relapsed below the February high point.

Allowing for this, however, and the dullness and occasional reaction of the market, it may still be said that the averages gave a bull point when they made a new high figure for the year, and have not taken that point back. Leaving everything but the purely technical aspect of the question, taking, as we always do in these studies, the averages as reflecting over a period of years all considerations, including even the volume of business, it may even be said that the indication at present is emphatically bullish.

To take back that bullish indication, an average decline in the railroad stocks of at least five points, or below the low point of the year, 115.75, made on March 2, and of the same extent in the industrials, to 81.32, made on April 22, would be necessary on all comparison with former movements of the averages. It is not a bad trading point on the face of it, and the trader who is guided by such considerations would probably take the long side of the market, with a stop-loss order a point or two below the present level.

The Wall Street Journal: July 14, 1911

THE PRICE MOVEMENT

Since we last discussed the price movement as shown by the averages on June 1, a condition of inaction has supervened which, however, must not be construed into a meaningless fluctuation within narrow limits. In studies of the price movement inertia has its value as well as activity, and not infrequently gives an important indication of future changes of a more radical character.

Since June 1, or in a period of six weeks, the average price of twenty active railroad stocks has not been above 123.31 or below 121.09; while that of the twelve industrials taken for comparison shows a still smaller fluctuation, between 87.06 and 85.28. The low figure in each case was made on the same day, and since that time there has been a recovery of a point or more, bringing both averages about midway or rather above the middle of the fluctuation in this period of waiting.

Prior to its entry upon an era of such

striking steadiness the market had made a new high figure for the year in both averages, giving what would unquestionably be called a bull point by students of the market movement from this point of view. This point has certainly not been taken back; and at the worst recessions have not amounted to more than what the French call "reculer pour mieux sauter"—stepping back to jump better.

A long line, such as the averages have described in the past six weeks, may even, with a limited volume of business, be taken as indicating one or two things. Either stocks have been successfully distributed at the new high level, or an accumulation has been in progress sufficient in the aggregate to warrant the assumption that a strong section of opinion believes prices should work higher. We prefer in these studies to ignore the volume of general business, the state of trade, the condition of crops, the political outlook, and the other possibilities which are influences in the daily movement, but not often seriously apparent in the short swings, to say nothing of the main broad movement of the market. Analysis of the averages over a long period of years shows that the averages discount all these things and are more trustworthy as a guide if transitory influences are ignored.

It may be repeated that no one should speculate on average indications. The daily fluctuation of an active market must make such operations hazardous. But, as a guide to future movements of the stock market—which is after all our best barometer of trade—the averages are invaluable. They gave a bullish indication more than six weeks ago, which they have not taken back, and technically, the long rest within narrow limits seems to have added strength.

The Wall Street Journal: August 10, 1911

THE PRICE MOVEMENT

A somewhat belated study of the price movement as shown by the average industrial and railroad stock prices appeared on July 14. The most that could be inferred then was that the six weeks' halt between limits of about two points meant a condition becoming significant when prices broke out of the rut either way. It was plain at that time that the bull point given by the averages, when the new high point for the year was established in the latter part of June, had not been taken back; but the indications were insufficient to warrant any broad inferences.

A change of importance took place last week when the averages declined five points in all, touching a low figure not seen since May 15. The reaction is significant when viewed broadly. It can be said, from previous records of the market movement as reflected in this way for over a quarter of a century, that the bull point was definitely cancelled by the decline. Opinions will differ as to whether any trustworthy bear indication has been established. To look really bullish again the averages would have to advance above the price of July 21, 123.86 in the case of the railroads, and above the price of June 19, 87.06 in the case of the industrials.

Viewed more broadly the position becomes interesting. The market definitely turned after July 26, 1910, and since that time, with reactions of from four to seven points in four different movements we were in what was unquestionably a bull market, if it was not one in which the traders for the rise made much money. The net advance, looked at in this way, was from 105.59 for the railroad stocks on July 26, 1910, to 123.86 on July 21, 1911, almost exactly a year afterwards.

If there is one thing shown more clearly than another in the averages, it is that in times of prosperity extending over periods of several years the bull markets last longer than the bear markets; while in times of retrenchment and recuperation accompanied by depression and severe contraction of trade, bear markets tend to last longer than bull markets. The top of the averages was reached in 1906 after a period of prosperity which had lasted, with interruptions, a full nine years. It will not be pretended that we returned to boom times at any period since that market culminated, even allowing for the substantial recovery in stock prices and general business in 1908–1909.

This is not to say that we are at the inception of a great bear market. That inception, however, is a possibility on the showing of the averages, and it need hardly be said that nothing is taken here but the bare comparison of price movements with those of times past, without reference to the general condition of business in Wall Street and out of it.

Whether the indications at present are positively bearish is a matter of individual opinion, but the movement no longer points upwards.

The Wall Street Journal: September 9, 1911

THE PRICE MOVEMENT

A month ago, in discussing the technical condition of the stock market as shown by the prices of the industrial and railroad stocks in The Wall Street Journal averages, it was pointed out that, while opinions might differ as to the positive bearishness of the indications, the averages had at least taken back all the bull points offered early in the summer. At the time that analysis was written the 20 active railroad stocks were upward of 4 points above the figure touched at the end of August and the 12 industrials 3 points.

From the low point of 112.60, made by the railroads on August 30, there was a recovery to 114.11, in four consecutive days of moderate advance, followed by a single day's reaction, which wiped out nearly all the improvement. The rally in the industrials was more irregular and less considerable. Trading on the recovery showed a tendency to stagnate, and the market only became active on declines which, to the professional, is fairly good indication of a continued bear movement.

It will be remembered that after fluctuating narrowly for several weeks within less than a 3 point range about 120, the railroads broke out of the rut in the downward direction, while virtually the same movement occurred in the other group, showing a fairly broad market tendency, as each average tended to confirm the other. Many followers of the averages would have considered the evidence quite good enough to warrant selling short on the first break, and it need hardly be said that the price movement would have fully justified them.

On the technical showing, taking the averages in our usual manner as discounting in themselves crops, general business conditions, volume of trading and all the other factors, it may be said that the indications are bearish, and becoming more so with the average price of the railroads now below 112.60, recorded on Aug. 30, and that of the industrials nearing 78.93, which was the low of the decline on Aug. 26. To make anything like a bull point most students would consider it necessary that the averages should first make a "line," and after a period of what might reasonably be taken as accumulation within a narrow range should advance sharply to the levels of last July.

There has been no time so far to make such a "line," and it must be confessed that, on the average showing at any rate, the market looks like anything but a good purchase.

The Wall Street Journal: October 9, 1911

A glance at the average price of the railroad and industrial stocks show a narrow fluctuation on the week without considerable changes. Movements of a point or more in half a dozen active stocks marked the trading from day to day. But the market was at no time broadly affected, becoming dull on small rallies and equally dull on declines. The theory of what may be called the semi-professional element of Wall Street, with whom for the most part the wish is father to the thought, is that this represents a steady condition where all liquidation has been absorbed. There might be something in this were it not that the leading stocks have had a considerable rally, and on a number of announcements expected to advance them have altogether failed to respond.

It is true the technical analysis of the averages does not show much, but even there industrial stocks have rallied four points from the lowest and railroad stocks two, after each had shown a decline of eleven points. On theory, the rally should have been proportionately larger at least in the railroad stocks. But the so-called "line," that prices are making at this level may indicate that stocks, as far as manipulation is possible, are being held to distribute. If this is the case, the market should reach the saturation point within a few days, and precipitation should follow. If there is really any powerful accumulation, it should show in the near future in a scarcity of stocks not at present indicated.

The Wall Street Journal: November 3, 1911

THE PRICE MOVEMENT

From and including October 10, the average price of twenty active railroad stocks fluctuated from day to day within a range of almost exactly two points or the difference between 112.08 and 114.13. From Sept. 30 to Oct. 26 the twelve industrial stocks, taken for the purpose of an average price, did not sell below 76.15 or above 78.11. It is important to note that on Oct. 27 the average broke through this remarkably close line of the industrials.

On the usual theory of the averages any movement above or below such a line as this would be strongly indicative of the market's course for some time to come. The industrials gave a bear point when they broke through on the downward side. But the lead was by no means as good as it looked, as there was no simultaneous change in the railroad stocks. The industrial decline, moreover, was all recovered in four trading days, bringing the average price of the twelve industrial stocks to well within a point of the high figure of the rally.

Simultaneously with this recovery, the twenty active railroad stocks made a new high point for the rally which had followed the decline beginning at the end of July. For a short swing, at any rate, a new high point on the rally by the industrials, confirming the movement already made by the railroad stocks would look definitely bullish. During a period of fluctuation within narrow limits such as we have seen in the recent past, one of two inferences may fairly be made, provided the market is not absolutely stagnant. Either stocks are being held, so far as manipulation will allow, to facilitate accumulation, or they are being supported in order to make a market for distribution.

If the latter had been the case the Street would have been overloaded with stocks, and saturation point, with its inevitable precipitation, would have been reached sooner or later. When United States Steel Common broke six

points in one day it would, had the market been carrying too much stock, have precipitated a sympathetic decline in the railroad group. This decline did not take place; and, as soon as the market had recovered from an influence which unexpectedly proved to be of a most temporary character, the railroads took the lead on the upward side.

So far as the greater movement of the market is concerned, that which lasts for a year or more, nothing of a really satisfactory character can be deduced from the averages. Fairly balanced, it looks as if a bear market set in at the end of July, already interrupted once by a fair rally, and now not unlikely to be interrupted again by another typical secondary swing in the upward direction. Ignoring outside influences, like the averages themselves, the operator on technical conditions only would probably now be trading with an eye to higher prices.

The Wall Street Journal: December 6, 1911

THE PRICE MOVEMENT

A month ago the average price of both the industrials and the railroad stocks gave a bull point, and in a study of the price movement on November 3 it was said in this place that the trader on technical conditions only would be operating for a further rally. His judgment would have proved correct, for on November 23 the average price of twenty active railroad stocks showed a gain of 3.49 points and that of the twelve industrials of 3.79 points.

This was the high point of the present rally, and since that time the railroad stocks have reacted, and for the past nine days have been making another line, with a restricted range of about 2 points but with no marked tendency to seek new high levels, on the one hand, or to return to the bear market which culminated at the end of September on the other.

Students of the averages would say the bull point indicated when last the topic was discussed had not been taken back, in spite of a moderate recession. From the present level, in fact, an advance of less than three points in the railroad stocks and less than two in the industrials, carrying the average prices above the level of November 23, would renew and emphasize the last bull point. To look bearish, for a short turn at any rate, prices would become interesting if they broke through the line to which we have alluded.

A formal resumption of the principal bear movement of the year, that which may be said to have started at the end of July, would require a decline from the present level of something like seven points, or below 109.80, in the railroad stocks; and one of as much or more, to 72.94, in the industrials. This is manifestly a large order, and the professionals would still be more inclined to buy on reactions than to sell the market short on bulges, on the theory that to resume a confident bull movement prices would have to move less than half the distance to give an authoritative bear point.

It must be confessed that technically the main bull market, if it were established, would disturb some well-worn and workable theories. On November 23 stocks had recovered eight points of a thirteen-point decline. This was decidedly above what is customary after a severe break like that which culminated in September. It still looks as if we would not make a new high point for the year; and it is difficult to see what there is to make it on; but stocks are hesitating in a peculiar way at the moment, and forecasts are unusually difficult.

Perhaps a conservatively bullish attitude is still indicated, but the inference is drawn with considerably less confidence than when the subject was discussed on November 3.

The Wall Street Journal: January 1, 1912

DEVELOPMENTS OF THE WEEK

Stocks last week ran off after the Christmas holidays and rallied on Friday, showing a small net loss on the week on the comparison of average prices. The movements were not important, nor did the technical indications offer much real light on the market situation. Prices would certainly have to advance above the high figure of the recent rally to make professionals bullish for the new year; and to establish anything that looked convincingly like a broad bull market the average price of both the industrials and railroad stocks

would have to advance above the high figure of last year, made towards the end of July. On the other hand, average prices do not indicate any bear movement, or that the rally, which may be said to have set in at the end of September, is exhausted. The market, in fact, is backing and filling, looking rather full of stock at times, and as if there had been a heavy distribution on any recent activity, but recovering also rather quickly on the appearance of the somewhat superficial "short interest" made up for the most part by traders on the floor. The least attractive feature of the market in Friday's price recovery was in fact the dullness which supervened when the shorts had been induced to cover. Whatever the public may do in the new year, it is certain that there is no broad interest in the market at present. It would be difficult to name a stock which could be sold in quantity at the moment without breaking not only its own price but that of other active issues. So far as forecasting the future of general business is concerned, all the market is saying is that there is dullness ahead for as far as it can see.

The Wall Street Journal: January 17, 1912

THE PRICE MOVEMENT

In writing of the price movement of stocks six weeks ago, it was said in this place that indications were less bullish and that, while the averages of the twenty active railroad stocks and twelve industrials taken for comparison did not look bearish, there was not enough in them to stimulate optimistic sentiment on the market. It is remarkable that in that period the average price of twenty active railroad stocks has not touched 115 on the one hand or 118 on the other; and the industrial price shows a maximum of 82.48 and a minimum of 79.19 in the same period.

This is a striking continuance of what may be called a "line" of accumulation or distribution, established more than a week before our previous price movement discussion was printed. Such a narrow fluctuation, to the experienced student of the averages, may be as significant as a sharp movement in either direction. If the long pause in the price movement has been made in order to accumulate stock without advancing prices, the result ought to show soon, when the price in both averages crosses the limit of the line in the upward direction. Let it be observed that the word "line" is here used in the market sense, and does not mean strictly "length without breadth." It means length with very little breadth—less than three points in the railroad stocks and a little more than that in the industrials.

This would mean then that 118 for the railroads and 83 for the industrials would look distinctly bullish. The converse is true, if we may assume the possible bull point. If the industrials sold at 79 and the railroad stocks at 115, traders who base their general positions on the barometer of the averages would go short of the market, protecting themselves, as usual, against the day-to-day fluctuations which constitute in practice the most confusing element in charting the currents of the broad market movement.

If this condition of stability, which has existed for some seven weeks, does not represent accumulation for a possible future advance, its only other explanation would seem to be a careful and well-managed distribution of stock. The inference would be that there was plenty of stock for sale from people who could afford to take their time in selling it. The large holders of stocks by no means act together in the way the public supposes; but there are psychological influences which are apt to affect them simultaneously. The market shows it in time, because, however carefully it is supported, there must come a moment when it reaches saturation point; and all the banking powers in Wall Street, or the world over, for that matter, could not prevent precipitation.

In the last discussion of the averages it was necessary to modify bullish inferences previously, and justifiably, drawn. At the moment it may be said that, on the averages, the market looks like working lower, and that a decline of 2½ points in the industrials and less than a point in the railroad stocks would look definitely bearish.

The Wall Street Journal: January 29, 1912

Stocks last week fluctuated on the average within a range of less than three-quarters of a point, losing a little ground but failing to establish anything different from a long continued rut which has obtained for something like three months. Fluctuations either way of less than 4 points in the price movement of the averages in both the industrials and the railroad stocks have ruled the market since November. There have, of course, been individual instances of changes more considerable, as for instance, the advance of the new American Tobacco common stock last week. But one swallow does not make a summer, and a single active specialty does not make an active market. It is not improbable that this fact has dawned upon the speculators who have been active in Lehigh Valley. Instead of increasing public interest, as such manipulation is presumably intended to do, the result in that and other coal stocks has been to drive the public out of the market altogether. The opportunities for the small trader in such conditions are certainly not enticing, and it can hardly surprise anybody, that he declines a contest with better players than himself, where he thinks he is not getting a fair deal. The quality of the market in this respect has greatly deteriorated, and there seems to be small chance of improvement until it breaks out of its present rut.

In the industrials the average would look bullish at 83 and bearish at 79, and in the railroads 118, on technical grounds alone, would point to higher prices, while 115, especially if accompanied by a similar retrograde movement, in the industrials, would be taken as justifying professional short selling.

The Wall Street Journal: February 1 1912

OUT OF THE GROOVE

Inferences may be drawn from an inactive market often more weighty than those open to anybody following an active movement up or down. Allowing for all sorts of movements in specialties, the stock market has made an astonishing exhibition of steadiness, when analyzed from the point of view of the averages. The average price of twenty active railroads, for instance, has not been above 118 since November 28; and between that price and 115 is the low limit for the trading days of more than two months.

So far as the industrials are concerned, there has been an identically similar price movement there. The last time the industrial average was so low as 79 was on November 6; and during the nearly three months elapsed since then the price has never once reached 83. This is a strikingly uniform movement, and should be full of meaning; in the industrials we even have the remarkable coincidence of the average price of twelve stocks remaining unchanged for three days in succession. There is no parallel to this in *The Wall Street Journal's* averages for a quarter of a century past.

To students of the price movement what is indicated in a market so steady as this is either the carefully organized accumulation of stocks for a future advance or an equally well-managed distribution, each facilitated by a fairly even distribution of bull or bear sentiment making itself felt in the market. During the period indicated the railroads have three times fluctuated more than a point in the day's trading, and two of these fluctuations represent advances. In spite of such gains, however, the railroad stocks look more bearish than the industrials, where a daily change of over a point has not been recorded since the advance of December 13.

On the method of reading the averages which has best stood the test of experience, it may be said that the outlook for railroad stocks would look bearish at 115 or below; while the industrials would have to decline to 79 to give a similar indication. The former, at any rate, seem trembling on the brink of the line; and both averages would require a most substantial advance in order to give a moderately bullish indication.

The Wall Street Journal: March 7, 1912

THE PRICE MOVEMENT

Since November 9 the average price of the twelve industrial stocks has not been as low as 79, or touched 83; while the twenty active railroad stocks taken for comparison have, with one day's exception, not been below 115, or above 119, since November 23. This is nearly four months of remarkable steadiness, and the fact that a few individual issues have been occasionally active does not detract from the significance of the general condition.

On one occasion the railroads, but not the industrials, looked like getting out of the groove and sold below 115. Had this occurred simultaneously with a downward movement of the industrials people who judge the market by the record of the averages, compared over a long period of years, would have said that the signal had been given for a broad general decline. The industrials, however, gave no confirmation to the movement. The railroad stocks almost instantly rallied, and since that date both averages have been well within the old range, giving little indication of future tendencies.

It will be observed that the average price of the industrials is closely approaching the limit of the groove on the upper side. If, for instance, their position was firmly established above 83, while the railroad stocks confirmed by moving above 119, unquestionably the advent of a further upward movement broadly affecting the whole market would be indicated. Periods of rest in the stock market may be as significant as periods of activity. If stocks hang for a long time around the same level two inferences are allowable and subsequent movements will confirm one or the other of them. It may be that prices are being sustained by a strong combination in order to distribute stock. Or it may be that the market is being held in check to discourage weak holders and to facilitate the accumulation of a cheap line preparatory to a general advance.

It is always taken in the periodical discussions of the average price movement appearing in this place that the average discounts everything—volume, general conditions, dividends, interest rates, politics—and just because it is an average it is the impartial summing up of every possible market influence. Looked at in this way, the averages for the moment do not tell us much. The railroad stocks gave a false bear point when they sold for the moment below 115; the industrials might equally give a deceptive bull point if they sold above

83 without a corresponding movement of the railroad issues.

It is a rather blind outlook, but the indications are certainly not disquieting, and are, in fact, more bullish than they were when the subject was discussed a month ago.

The Wall Street Journal: March 25, 1912

In the past week the stock market broadened remarkably and developed a strength which was consistently sustained throughout the trading. For many months past business seems to have been confined, speculatively at least, to three stocks, Union Pacific, Reading and U. S. Steel common. Last week, however, there were at least a score of issues showing transactions in sufficient volume to indicate a public interest in the market. In both the industrials and the railroad stocks, as shown by the averages, the net advance of the week was better than in any similar period since the end of October. So far as the averages are concerned, the action of the market has been bullish by comparison with previous recorded movements. The industrial stocks, since they emerged from the rut between 79 and 83, have advanced nearly five points, and in the case of the railroads the rise above 118 in a more modified degree indicates a similar advance, which would become still more marked at 119. This is of course on the dry assumption that the averages represent everything and discount everything, which in the long run they may be honestly said to do, as any comparison between the state of general business and the average price of stocks over a period of years will clearly show. What seems to be indicated, in fact, is that the period of nearly four months, in which the market worked within a narrow groove, exhausted the floating supply of stocks. The market moves along the line of least resistance, and obviously in such condition the easiest movement is upwards. There are no present signs of an interruption, and this may be said with full comprehension of all the possibilities of labor, politics and crops.

The Wall Street Journal: April 1, 1912

In spite of some irregularity in the daily fluctuations, the stock market last week saw a further advance in the railroad group, while the industrials maintained their ground in the face of heavy realizing sales. It is a commonplace of Wall Street that there is no news in a bull market; and it is true that the publication of the reason for a rise in a stock quite frequently marks the termination of the movement. A better sentiment towards speculative securities, however, is not confined to this market, but has made itself felt in London and on the Continental Bourses. After a period of nervousness and distrust the speculative investor is beginning to pick up his courage again. On the technical conditions as disclosed by the average prices of stocks, comparison with previous statistical records points to a further advance. It will be remembered that for something like four months the industrial average did not go below 79 or above 83, while the railroads remained in a similar rut between 115 on the one side and 119 on the other. On March 8 the industrials emerged on the upward side, indicating that there had been accumulation of stocks between the two low levels, and that the floating supply had been so reduced as to force an advance. The railroad average lagged behind, but on Friday crossed 119, thereby confirming the bull indication given by the industrials. Since the industrials made that significant movement, the average price has gained over five points.

The Wall Street Journal: April 5, 1912

THE PRICE MOVEMENT

It was pointed out in a discussion of the average prices of the industrial stocks and railroad issues in these columns a month ago, when the twelve industrials were selling below 83 and the twenty railroads taken for comparison only a little above 116, that the stock market was in a groove, and that any movement out of the groove, upward or downward, should give a good indication of its course for some time ahead. At that time the industrial stocks for some four months had not sold below 79 or above 83, while the railroads between the date when the analysis was published (March 7) and November 28, of last year, had not been materially below 115 or above 118.

From these facts the inference was drawn that stocks were making what the specialists call a "line," indicating either accumulation or well organized distribution. The result, sooner or later, must necessarily have shown itself, either in such a condition as that when the atmosphere becomes overcharged with moisture and precipitation follows; or where the floating supply of stocks has been unduly depleted, and prices must consequently advance, to meet the irreducible minimum of demand underlying the market in good times and bad.

Curiously enough, on the day that the last price movement analysis was published in these columns the industrial stocks crossed 83. This was decidedly bullish as regards that group, but only moderately so as concerns the railroads, because when that average for one day sold below 115 no resulting bear movement followed, and the figure itself was virtually accidental. The bull point on the industrials, however, proceeded to make good, and there has now been an advance of more than six points on the average since its significance was pointed out in these columns.

In the case of the railroads it was not until a fortnight afterward, on March 20, that the upward tendency of the industrials was confirmed by an advance above 118, the first time that figure had been recorded since November 28, 1911, nearly four months previously. The inference drawn from such developments in the past held good; and both industrials and railroads have advanced steadily, with small reactions when the market for the moment became too full of stocks.

Whatever the general outlook of business may be, the stock market averages look bullish. They indicate a rising market so definitely that only the trader on the floor would be justified in selling short, and then only for a quick market turn. It would, moreover, take not merely an important movement, but a considerable time for the averages to take back their bull point. If the railroads, for instance, merely went back to 118, or the industrials to 83, nothing more than an ordinary reaction would be indicated.

It should be thoroughly understood that these discussions are not intended for the speculator who proposes to make a quick profit in transactions from day to day. It is assumed that the average eliminates every individual consideration; politics, money, crops—everything but the chapter of accidents, and ultimately that; a rising market seems indicated, while the averages would not give a bear point, unless a period of suspense should develop at the higher level, like that between November and the beginning of March, followed by a sharp decline.

The Wall Street Journal: May 2, 1912

THE PRICE MOVEMENT

In a discussion of the price movement published in these columns on April 5 last it was said:

"A rising market seems indicated, while the averages would not give a bear point, unless a period of suspense should develop at the higher level, like that between November and the beginning of March, followed by a sharp decline."

It is curious that the average price of the twelve industrials taken for comparison in these discussions began to make just such a line on the day that criticism was written. From Thursday, April 4, to date the industrial stocks have, with only one day's exception, fluctuated within a range of less than two points failing to reach 91, or to sell below 89, except at the close on April 22. The railroad stocks, also, between March 29 and April 24, with a single exception, did not sell below 119, or above 121.

Both averages in the course of this period of suspense gave a false lead. The break in the industrials below 89 on April 22 looked bearish; while the advance in the railroads above 121 on April 9 looked bullish. In each case the market withdrew its forecast and returned to the old rut. In the case of the railroad stocks, however, there seems to have been a genuine bull point on April 23, when the average touched 121, and this was followed by the sort of rise which students of the averages have become accustomed to expect after prices have hung for any appreciable period at about the same level.

It seems fairly clear that the market

h'as been tested by a month of distribution, and it remains to be seen whether the new hands into which stocks have gone are as strong as the old ones. On such a point the averages do not commit themselves. They discount alike activity and dullness, good news and bad, crop forecasts and political possibilities, and the net result is, in fact, the average. It is this which makes them so valuable for study, and makes it possible to get light on the future market movement not obtainable in any other way.

It is fair to assume that a genuine upward movement of the market set in early in February, and last month evidently saw the first large volume of realizing. This by no means indicates the end of a bull movement, and it is quite conceivable that a secondary rise may be impending. The averages should give the signal for such a movement if the industrial stocks sold above 91. The railroad stocks have already given the same signal at 121; and an agreement between the two averages would indicate that the floating supply of stocks had been absorbed, and that the normal demand was operating to establish a higher range of prices without adventitious aid.

On the present showing the averages look bullish, and a decline of more than two points in the railroad stocks, with a figure below 89 in the industrials, would be necessary to give a bearish indication of any real consequence.

The Wall Street Journal: May 27, 1912

Last week saw no important changes in stocks, and the extreme fluctuation did not amount to a point on the average in the railroads, or much more than half of that in the industrials. Upon the whole there was a tendency to sag, but the market was not under pressure, and acted in an entirely normal way, without any evidence of manipulation.

Trading was largely professional, varied by an occasional spurt of activity in minor specialties, each with its own strictly limited popularity. Operators for the rise reported an unsatisfactory week, and on the short side only the traders on the floor could have made any money. The market, indeed, is marking time, and the averages cast about as

intelligible a light upon it as any outside influence.

Last week, in fact, saw no news calculated to move stocks out of their rut, in spite of ingenious attempts to connect some trifling fluctuation with politics, money or the weather. From the averages it is plain that the condition has not been changed specially since a week ago. Both the railroad stocks and the industrials continue to fluctuate within a narrow range, and both average prices would require to make a definite move in either direction simultaneously to give any trustworthy lead on the future movement of the market.

Certainly there is nothing to take back the conclusion that the main tendency of the stock market is still upward, with long pauses and occasional setbacks. The main swing has now run for a year or more, and in the general condition of business is subject to change without notice.

The Wall Street Journal: June 3, 1912

Last week the tendency of stock prices was downward, culminating in a severe break on Friday. Apparently, the liquidation of a stale bull position has been in progress, and the operators who lately occupied the leadership in the market left stocks to take care of themselves, with disastrous results for the trader on small margin.

Taken as a whole the speculation has exhibited little wisdom. One prominent operator was credited by the public with a degree of intelligence and power such as no stock market leader has ever shown before. It was inferred that, after the successful gamble in American Can, other stocks affected by the same operator would be advanced, with the result that the small trader hooked up with Rock Island Common at 30 and over, only to see it sell below 23 on Friday.

Looked at from the point of view of the averages, the market does not offer much encouragement. The break on Friday carried the average price of both the industrials and the railroad stocks below the groove in which they have been vacillating so long, within the limits of 89 to 91 for the industrials and 119 to 121 for the railroads.

What appears to be indicated, therefore, is that the market had been filled up with stocks until precipitation followed after it had reached saturation point. Most professionals would be inclined to take a conservative and even bearish attitude pending some genuine encouragement on the bull side.

The Wall Street Journal: July 8, 1912

After showing considerable strength last week the stock market sold off after the holiday, losing practically all the week's advance, and in the case of the industrials, a little more. Stocks acted as if they wanted to go up, but were obviously hampered by the indifference of the trading public, and in these circumstances professionals did not hesitate to attack. The better tone at the beginning of the week may reasonably be ascribed to the satisfaction felt at having the party conventions out of the way, with a straightforward and representative nomination on both sides; and also with the knowledge that politics would be much less strenuous for 2 or 3 months at least.

From the purely technical point of view of the averages, not much information is to be gained. The industrials made a new high point in the present movement on Tuesday; but the railroad group failed to follow, and no specific lead was therefore indicated.

The most that can be said to the student of the price movement is that the averages have not taken back their bull points or given any trustworthy bearish indications.

Prices, in fact, are in the same rut that has confined them for three months or more, and an advance above 92 for the industrials and 123 for the railroad stocks (the latter three points above the present figure) would constitute the nearest bull point, on the accepted method of reading the averages.

The Wall Street Journal: July 10, 1912

THE PRICE MOVEMENT

In writing of the price movement on June 4 it was pointed out that the average prices of both industrial and railroad stocks had on May 31 simultaneously broken through a line which they had established within narrow limits in a period of close on three months, on the customary method of reading the averages, and the one which has best stood the test of experience, this looked bearish, although prices rallied to the old line again within a few days. It was said at that time that the bear point had been given which has not been taken back, in spite of the recovery.

On the same reasoning, if that were true then, it is true today. The small rally then in progress merely brought the industrial average from 88.1 to 90.67 and that of the railroads from 118.37 to 120.66. The latter figure has not been touched since. The industrials have shown some independent strength, giving a doubtful bull point at 91.69 on July 2, almost immediately taken back; with a subsequent decline, bringing both averages within little more than a point of the low level of the past four months.

In spite of the deceptive bear point on May 31, the net result is a condition which still indicates the maintainance of the old groove representing in the sales for so long a period a large volume of trading, which may be taken as organized distribution or accumulation, in a market which has been to a great extent natural and unmanipulated, even if a substantial part of the transactions was made up of professional trading. It may even be allowable to concede more elasticity to the line of distribution, representing the low limits of industrials and railroad stocks, respectively, at 88 and 118; while it would be necessary to establish, simultaneously, or virtually so, 92 and 123, before anything looking like a bull point, and upward movement out of the rut, would be foreshadowed.

At the present level the industrials are nearly three points away from the high line, and not much more than a point from the low one; while the railroads are considerably more than three points below a bullish figure, and within a point or so of a price which would confirm the bearish indication given on May 31. The price movement is becoming increasingly interesting, and ought soon to give more definite information, after a period of narrow fluctuations highly suggestive in itself. Looked at from the purely technical point of view, the averages are anything but bullish, although there has been no positive bear point since they were last discussed.

The Wall Street Journal: July 15, 1912

DEVELOPMENTS OF THE WEEK

A REACTIONARY STOCK MARKET

With encouraging reports from many sections, and an essentially sound condition indicated in steel, transportation and other basic industries, the stock market last week was noticeably and significantly depressed. The downward movement was uniform, and the most sinister feature was the dullness on small rallies and the markedly increased activity on declines.

Professionals have taken a somewhat bearish point of view of the market for several weeks past, acting more or less on the theory that if stocks could not be advanced on good news and prospects, and the removal of disturbing factors, like the political conventions, there must necessarily be a stale bull account, which would sooner or later prove itself vulnerable to well organized attack.

From the technical point of view of the averages, there is a good deal to be said for the professional theory. Within the relatively narrow range of 88–92 for the industrials, and of 118–123 for the railroad stock averages, the market has been in a rut for months past, having given a bear point by a simultaneous break in the two averages on May 31, which was not subsequently confirmed but not taken back. Both averages on Friday broke below 88 and 118 respectively.

This is, of course, in line with the professional idea. The long period of fluctuation within a narrow range is assumed to have represented the cautious distribution of stock. No market will hold more than a manageable floating supply, and when this is exceeded, something which may be called saturation point is reached and precipitation follows.

The Wall Street Journal: August 19, 1912

Stocks were strong in the early part of last week and inclined to hesitate in the last three days. The net improvements on the week was, however, substantial, and the market has at least broadened sufficiently to stand up under a heavy volume of profit taking and re-tain most of its not inconsiderable advance.

Although the professionals, especially in the latter part of the week, made up most of the market, it is fair to say that the public interest is wider than it was, and the disposition to buy stocks on good news is greater than for a good many weeks past.

Whether the banks and other lenders of money will care to encourage an extended speculative position in stocks on the eve of the outward movement of money for the crops is another question. It is satisfactory to notice, however, that the foreign interest in our market was more active last week, both through London and the continent.

From the point of view of the averages, the outlook is more bullish than it was a week ago. The twenty active railroad, stocks are still well above 123 which previously had been for months the high limit of their narrow fluctuation; while the industrials have closely approached 92, which also represents the upper limit. The technical inference from these facts is that accumulation for an advance had been in progress since the early spring, and prices should improve on the absorption of the floating supply of stock.

The Wall Street Journal: September 23, 1912

It will be noticed that the averages show substantial advances on the week, and the industrials have crossed the high price recorded in August and are now at the top for the year.

The railroad stocks are still a point below the August high; but an advance there would give a general bullish aspect to the market, on the accepted method of reading the averages, in spite of the financial difficulties tending to restrict operations for the rise.

The Wall Street Journal: September 30, 1912

From the point of view of the averages, the outlook is decidedly bullish; both the industrials and the railroads have emerged from the prolonged rut of the spring and summer, and have exceeded the prices made on the first bulge afterwards. Eliminating all other considerations, the student of the price movement would consider that the advance had by no means exhausted its strength.

The Wall Street Journal: December 9, 1912

The averages begin to look interesting again, and at Friday's (Dec. 6) level gave something like a bear point, although only one of the averages made a new low. The market, however, seems to have dropped out of its groove and technically, the argument is for lower prices, although it may be that the market is, as the French proverb says, running back to jump better.

The Wall Street Journal: December 16, 1912

It was pointed out in this paper a week ago that the averages had broken through the lower line of their groove, and gave a genuinely bearish indication. Events fully justified this conclusion; but there is nothing in the averages to show how far the December decline might go; while the indications of the usual January rally are not likely to be explicit.

The Wall Street Journal: December 23, 1912

Looked at from the purely technical point of view of the averages, the stock market acts as if it had seen the customary December break, and was now rallying for a substantial upward movement in the new year, possibly extending into the early spring. The December decline in both averages was nearly nine points, which is heavier than usual. The two-point rally from the low looks bullish, according to the usual method of reading the averages.

The Wall Street Journal: January 20, 1913

When Wall Street gets a fit of the blues in the face of a continued large volume of business, in the aggregate, it means that it is discounting a position as far ahead as it can see. The market does not trade upon what everybody

knows, but upon what those with the best information can foresee. There is an explanation for every stock market movement somewhere in the future, and the much talked of manipulation is a trifling factor.

After making an interesting line within a narrow range in a period extending over a month the averages of the railroad and industrial prices broke through the line at the beginning of the last week, giving a bear point which was sufficiently confirmed by the subsequent movement of the market. The movement is the more noteworthy as not more than ten days ago the indications were rather the other way, but for the fact that the industrials did not confirm the somewhat bullish indications of the railroads. There is nothing in the averages to say that the bear movement is over.

The Wall Street Journal: February 3, 1913

On the averages, the bear point given when the break began in the middle of January has by no means been taken back. Stocks, however, are beginning to form a new line at the lower level, and the averages do not look as bearish as they did a week ago. The technical inference, in fact, would be that some further rally is indicated.

The Wall Street Journal: February 10, 1913

Looked at from the view of the averages, the stock market gave a somewhat bearish indication. The active railroad stocks on Thursday were within a quarter of a point of the low of Jan. 20, and the industrials were less than a point and a half away from their figure then. A decline below these points would look decidedly bearish, on the most satisfactory method of reading the averages.

The Wall Street Journal: February 17, 1913

Both averages made a new low point during the week and this in itself would be decidedly bearish on the accepted method of reading the market movement by this means. Certainly the previous bear indications have justified themselves since prices began to go back, and the failure of the rally which culminated about the end of January is another bearish indication.

The Wall Street Journal: March 3, 1913

There are always special reasons offered at the moment, to explain why a market goes up and down, but they do not really explain, for the cause of market movements are absolutely unexpected and unforeseen, they are discounted in the price of stocks long before the public begins to take cognizance of them. Nowhere is it true that coming events cast their shadow before, as in the stock market.

Of outside influences, those which can be definitely traced are rather in the direction of discouraging speculative activity, and have not yet developed into an active reason for selling investment holdings of stocks. The principal legislation at Albany, for the report of the Pujo Committee, alike in Wall Street and in Congress, is treated with well-merited contempt.

On the technical position by the averages the outlook is not for any marked change in the meantime. A strong bear point was given when prices broke out of the groove which obtained up to the middle of January, and it must be admitted that the hint so given has not been taken back, although if the market made something of a line at the present level, a rally in both averages would look bullish.

The Wall Street Journal: March 17, 1913

Indications from the averages are of a somewhat negative character. No genuine turn in the market is shown, but a somewht narrow fluctuation after a severe decline indicates something of a line, and a movement out of that range would be bullish or bearish, as the case might be.

The bear indications given in January have not been taken back, but the downward swing has stopped, for the moment at least, and the market is waiting for a new impulse to develop.

The Wall Street Journal: March 29, 1913

THE PRICE MOVEMENT

On the best tested theory of the market, judged from the impartial standpoint of the average movement of prices, the stock market may have seen a secondary downward swing, culminating about March 20. Broadly speaking "Dow's Theory" was that a secondary movement lasted a few weeks. The third movement was that from day to day, and the primary movement was, of course, that great tendency which may easily take two years to exhaust itself, and has in times past taken even longer.

There is an interesting situation in the market today, judged by the averages. Stocks have had a severe decline, but since the low figures of March 20 have rallied, and seem disposed to make something of a line between 78.25 and 80.20 in the industrials; and between 108.94 and 110.79 for the railroad stocks. After a decline so substantial as that since the high price of the year was recorded in January, it is quite possible that the downward swing of the market has exhausted itself, whatever the broad general tendency may be. Let it always be remembered that the averages are assumed to discount everything— dullness or activity, boom or panic— and that the study of the market tendency is in some sense academic, although in the past this method has been of the greatest utility.

At the end of September and the beginning of October the industrial stocks were selling sixteen points above the figure of a week ago, and an almost identical decline has been recorded in the railroad stocks. This is something more considerable than Dow's so-called short, or secondary, swing. It indicates something which may prove before the end of the year to have been the initiation of a bear maarket in the autumn of last year. This is not to say, however, that the outlook for the moment, or even for some considerable time ahead, is necessarily bearish, even on the most rigid construction of the averages.

In a primary bear market the rallies are apt to be violent and erratic, and always occupy less time than the decline which they partially recover. In a bull market the reverse is the case. The market goes ahead, as it did after the second election of McKinley, suffers an apparent disaster in the Northern Pacific panic of May, 1901, and then continues its true direction, with an upward movement which only culminated in the late autumn of 1902. Declines in that period were severe but of brief duration.

If, as the averages seem to indicate, the broad tendency of prices is downwards, a sharp rally, carrying prices on the average several points higher, would be very much in order at this time. It would be deceptive, as such rallies always are, but to the student of the averages, familiar with their history, it would be almost proof positive of the deeper general tendency of stock prices.

The Wall Street Journal: April 7, 1913

The market may be said to have established two claims for confidence, in the ability to take care of itself both on the death of Mr. Morgan and on the disastrous floods in the Middle West.

There is some confirmation of this in the averages, which, to use a sporting phrase, are running remarkably true to form. They made a line within a limit of two points in both the industrials and the railroad stocks during March, and it has been pointed out in these columns that the advance above that level more than a week ago was bullish. The gain since that time has been three points on the average, and nearly five points from the low of March 20. Technically a further recovery is indicated.

The Wall Street Journal: April 14, 1913

On the averages, eliminating all outside influences as having been discounted in the price, the showing for the week is not bearish, and a two point rally to the last previous high point, made April 4 for both industrials and railroads, would be bullish, and would not take much of an advance; while a decline below the low point recorded about March 20 would be necessary to give the student of the averages a bear point.

The Wall Street Journal: April 28, 1913

On the averages the indication is bearish. Prices have steadily receded from the high point of April 4, and a further decline of less than a point in the railroads, and of not much more in the industrials would break through the low point of March 20, giving, on the customary method of reading the averages, a positive bear indication.

The Wall Street Journal: May 5, 1913

DEVELOPMENTS OF THE WEEK

A MODERATE RALLY IN STOCKS

Showing renewed weakness in the early part of last week, particularly on Tuesday, the stock market steadied itself on Wednesday, and on the following day made the best rally since the beginning of April. The recovery was rather technical, in the respect that stocks were sold out; but the relief from pressure restored confidence in the general outlook.

It could hardly be said that stocks moved upon specific news. A great deal of the pressure looked altogether too good to be true, as, for instance, in New Haven stock, which has never hitherto been a speculative security. The frightening of weak holders of that issue was manifest, and, of course, something of the kind was essential in creating a bear market in an investment stock where there must be a floating supply to borrow.

Stocks did not move on broad news considerations, and so far from suffering from the European situation, London, and presumably the Continent, bought substantially on balance. Without seeming unpatriotic, it may fairly be said that London buys staples and securities on their merits when they look intrinsically cheap, without concerning herself about the possibility of their looking cheaper; while our disposition is to buy whenever everybody else is buying, as, for instance, when the English spinners get all their cotton below ten cents, while our own manufacturers pay top prices for the worst of the crop.

It looked on Wednsday as if the averages might give a definite lead by making a new low point for the industrials where one had already been made for the railroad stocks. This failed to materialize, and while the showing of the averages is bearish, it still lacks that simultaneous movement in the railroads and the industrials which would be, according to the experience of price movements over a long period of time, a significant danger signal.

The Wall Street Journal: May 12, 1913

Looked at from the point of view of the averages, the market gives decidedly bearish indications, which would be still more marked with a small fractional decline in the railroad stocks, and one of less than a point in the industrials. This would establish a new low point for the year, and, on previous experience of the averages, it would indicate a market full of stocks liquidated at or about the present level.

The Wall Street Journal: June 4, 1913

THE PRICE MOVEMENT

On Monday the average prices of twenty active railroad stocks and twelve industrials made a simultaneous movement which may conceivably throw considerable light upon the future course of the stock market. After the railroads had fluctuated for more than a month within a range of less than two points and the industrials had moved within limits still narrower, both together broke through the line of dullness so established, and made a new low point for the year.

The Wall Street Journal: June 4, 1913

To those who have not read previous discussions of the price movement as diagnosed from the averages, it snould be said that the price average by its very nature discounts everything. Dullness and inactivity are but symptoms, and for these the average allows, as it does likewise for activity, unexpected news, dividends and everything else contributing to make up the fluctuating market price. This is why the volume of trading is ignored in these studies. In the quarter of a century of the price movement recorded in the Dow, Jones & Company averages, the volume of business has borne little perceptible relation to the tendency of prices.

Stress should be especially laid upon the fact that the two averages made their new low point simultaneously. A new low or a new high made by the one but not confirmed by the other is almost invariably deceptive. The reason is not far to seek. One group of securities acts upon the other; and if the market for railroad stocks is sold out it cannot lift the whole list with it if there is a super-abundant supply of the industrials.

To use a simile which has done good service in this place before, it may be said that the market, when the average prices break through a long line, as they did on Monday, has reached saturation point, and that precipitation is consequently indicated. It is easy to say that brokers are not carrying much stock. Stock is carried somewhere; and the averages show quite plainly that enough of it is being supplied to force a lower level as a protection to the market.

In fact, the averages look decidedly bearish. They do not pretend to tell the reason for the decline they seem to predict, and indeed, reasons for declines or advances are only fully disclosed long after such movements have occurred. The aggregate knowledge of coming events, as reflected in the impartial movement of the averages, is greater than any single individual can possess. It is not here suggested that stocks are dear, or that some of them are not genuinely cheap. But the price movement, on the exeprience of twenty-five years of the most conservative and impartial record yet devised, points to lower prices irrespective of values.

The Wall Street Journal: June 16, 1913

Looked at from the averages, the market may be said to have developed an incipient secondary movement, which may run further. If it holds its present rally, fluctuating for a week or so within a small distance of the higher level, and then advancing above that line, it looks safe to assume a secondary bull swing in what has unquestionably been a bear market since last autumn.

If the advance were lost, however, and a new low point established in both the industrial and railroad stocks, the averages would again look decidedly bearish. On past experience they are now running, to use a sporting expression, remarkably true to form.

The Wall Street Journal: June 23, 1913

It would be difficult to lay the movement of the market either way to any specific influence and whenever Congress is sitting the vagaries of our politicians may safely be quoted to the unfortunate investor for the erratic movements of his stocks.

General trade conditions and the promise of the crops might also be quoted, but probably the technical condition of the market, due to over-selling, and the more thorough absorption of liquidated stocks, would constitute sufficient explanation of price movements.

This holds good when the impartial test of the averages is applied. Starting on June 12, the twelve industrial stocks had rallied 3.74 points, and the twenty active railroads 4.55 by June 18. This is a substantial recovery, and was only to be expected after the long and severe decline.

The averages are giving a good deal of light at present. Prices seem to be in the secondary upward swing characteristic of such a bear market as we have had since early last autumn. The rally might easily run further, and on past experience, if stocks continued to make a "line," fluctuating within narrow limits as they did last week, and then advancing above that line, it might fairly be argued that the bull swing would run further. If, however, the averages went back to the low points of June 11, the indication would be decidedly bearish.

The Wall Street Journal: June 30, 1913

On the averages stocks do not give any definite suggestion yet, but they would offer an important lead with a most moderate change in price, provided it occurred simultaneously in the industrial and railroad stocks. A decline of from two to three points (in both averages would break the last low point of June 11, and this would mean a resumption of the main bear movement.

If, however, the averages rallied from one to two points, to figures above the high point of June 18, it would look as though the secondary rally in what has been a bear market since Last October had not exhausted its impetus.

The Wall Street Journal: July 14, 1913

There is not much information to be gleaned from the averages, but their showing is by no means bearish. An advance of less than two points in the railroad stocks, and of a bare half point in the industrials would look decidedly bullish, especially if the two advances were recorded simultaneously. To give an indication of the resumption of the broader bear movement which set in last autumn, both averages would need to decline more than three points. Students of the price movement will be inclined to think that chances favor a further rally on the technical position.

The Wall Street Journal: July 21, 1913

From the point of view of the averages, the indications are decidedly bullish. This is not to say that they show a primary bull market. But on Friday the average price of twelve industrial stocks and twenty railroad stocks crossed the previous high price of the present rally recorded a month ago. This would seem to indicate that the bull swings in the bear market which set in in last October, had by no means exhausted itself. In other words, the averages ring the bell for the usual August advance in stocks.

The Wall Street Journal: August 11, 1913

The market seems to indicate a further improvement. It was pointed out in this place more than a month ago that the average prices, after making a line within a narrow range, had advanced above that range, indicating clearly enough that the floating supply of stocks had been absorbed and more would be forthcoming only at higher prices. The bull point made good and it may be said that the averages have not taken it back so far.

The Wall Street Journal: August 25, 1913

From the averages not much is to be gleaned. Prices are making something of a line, which may be instructive later. On August 13 industrials touched 80.93, and the railroads 107.76. No reaction since that time has carried the average price of the former a point and a half below the last high, and the same is true of the railroad stocks.

This represents the fluctuations of nine trading days, and, continued for a little longer, would indicate either distribution or accumulation for a further advance. An advance beyond the high of August 13 would be bullish, but a definite break through the line might easily indicate the end of the present highly typical secondary bull swing in what since last October was a primary bear market.

The Wall Street Journal: September 8, 1913

Looked at from the point of view of the averages, the outlook is by no means as bullish as it was, although positive bear indications are lacking. For nearly a month in the case of each of the averages, prices have fluctuated within little more than two points range. On Aug. 28, the industrials advanced above this line, but the railroad stocks did not confirm.

On Sept. 3, the railroad stocks broke through on the down side, but the industrials held their own. To readers of the averages this constitutes a standoff, especially as both averages are now well within the old range. A simultaneous movement in either direction, but especially downwards, would, on previous experience, give an important lead on further movements.

The Wall Street Journal: September 15, 1913

Regarded from the point of view of the averages, the stock market looks as if it were working higher. The prices made a long line during the month of August and early in September. The railroad stocks sold below the line on Sept. 3, after the industrials had advanced above it on August 28. The latter average advanced above the upper side of its line, which may be taken as 81, on Sept. 5, but the industrials hung back.

These independent movements, on previous experience, are usually deceptive, but when both averages advance or decline together the indication of a uniform market movement is good. This simultaneous advance on Friday may be reasonably taken as an indication that the floating supply of stocks has been absorbed, and that a higher level will have to be established before any quantity comes out.

The Wall Street Journal: September 24, 1913

THE PRICE MOVEMENT

On Sept. 13 the averages of both the twelve industrials and the twenty active railroad stocks, taken for purposes of comparison over a number of years by this newspaper, recorded the high figures for a movement which set in after the low point of the year had been reached on June 12. The net advance had been something over eleven points in the industrials and rather less than nine in the railroad stocks.

Preceding this advance the market had declined, with only the briefest rallies, since the beginning of October, 1912. In that nine months' decline the industrial stocks lost over twenty-two points and the railroads twenty-four. As is frequently the case in the main or primary movement, the decline occurred after a long period of indeterminate fluctuations following a bull market. Assuming that the current of the market radically changed last October, is the rally which has been in progress since last June a primary change in the market movement, or a secondary swing in what is still a bear market?

In lapse of time the recovery has not taken more than has often been consumed by a bear swing in a bull market or a bull swing in a bear market, during the history of the averages. On the other hand, the nine months consumed by the previous decline is much too long for any secondary market movement; while it is not long enough for one of those great and radical market changes indicating broad modifications in general conditions, which it may be assumed the stock market reflects, and in a large measure predicts.

It seems, on all previous experience of the averages, reasonable to assume that the recent upward swing was the periodic secondary movement against the main current, rather than a broad change of direction. It does not follow, however, that the minor movement has exhausted itself, and on really useful trustworthy methods of testing the averages the inference would be that it has not. Between Aug. 5 and Aug. 31, inclusive, the industrials did not fall below 79 or rise above 81. Between August 4 and Sept. 2 the railroads did not sell below 106 or above 108. This indicated a "line"—that is, a period either of distribution or accumulation, to be interpreted by the subsequent movement above or below those limits.

Both averages gave deceptive indications. The industrials sold above the line in the last two trading days of August, but did not carry the railroads with them. The railroads sold below the line on Sept. 3 and 4, but without a similar movement by the industrials. On Sept. 12, however, the two averages simultaneously made a new high point. That indicated reasonably that the floating supply of stock had been absorbed, and that an advance to a higher level would be in order before a new supply checked the movement or reversed it.

Stocks have been marking time within a comparative narrow range since the high point was made, but if the reasoning submitted is sound, the bull point of Sept. 12 has not been taken back.

The Wall Street Journal: October 13, 1913

It must be confessed that the averages look decidedly bearish. With the industrials below 79 and the railroads below 106 there is a practically simultaneous decline below the line established throughout September and maintained up to the present. The bull point, given when stocks advanced above the line on Sept. 12, did not make good for any length of time; and the movement of the market since indicates that heavy distribution of stock has been made.

The market seems at saturation point, and precipitation might be expected, carrying prices lower, and not improbably resuming the primary bear swing which set in a year ago. The secondary bull movement which began early in June and culminated Sept. 13, would be entirely in line with this assumption.

The Wall Street Journal: October 27, 1913

Regarded from the point of view of the averages, the market may be said to have given an authoritative bear point on Oct. 11, which has not been taken back, and justified itself in a sharp decline. There has been a rally to about the figures prevailing then, but a very much broader and more impressive movement would be necessary to indicate the real resumption of the secondary bull swing in a bear market which started in June and culminated about Sept. 13.

It is as well to repeat the occasional caution given in this column, that the averages make a good barometer, viewed from a disinterested point, but are calculated to ruin anybody if treated as a "system" for playing the market.

The Wall Street Journal: December 8, 1913

From the point of view of the averages, nothing very striking is to be gleaned. Industrial and railroad stocks are one and two points respectively, above the low figure of the present movement; but the low point of last June, before the substantial autumn rally set in, has not been touched again; while the recovery since the broad bear market has not been particularly convincing to students of the averages.

If the prices were to make a line about the present level, which would mean a long series of fluctuations within a narrow range irrespective of volume, an advance above those limits might look rather bullish. There has not been time to make a convincing line of the sort; and students of the average price movement who have been bearish would hardly see cause for changing their position.

The Wall Street Journal: January 5, 1914

Not much information could be derived from fluctuations of the averages last week. On the usual movement in a market which ought to be approaching the latter part of a long primary downward movement, some further rally seems indicated, although deductions to be drawn from the averages are more applicable to the secondary swing than the broad underlying current of the price movement.

The Wall Street Journal: January 12, 1914

There was nothing in the averages to stimulate speculative activity. Since the last low point was made in the middle of December there has been a substantial advance, extending to four points in the industrials. A new high point was established by that group last week; but the railroad stocks did not follow suit. On comparisons with the averages in the past the conservative inference would be that the secondary bull swing in what is primarily a bear market is still in operation.

The Wall Street Journal: January 19, 1914

On the movement of the averages both the industrial and the railroad stocks continued to give a typical example of a secondary bull swing in a primary bear market. Such movements rarely develop into greater ones. But as the main bear market has been in operation since October, 1912, it is fair in the nature of things to assume that its final turn downwards is not far off, and that a reversal of the primary movement is due some time this year. Perhaps this is what the market is discounting now.

The Wall Street Journal: January 26, 1914

The present rally has the vigorous appearance of a secondary bull swing in the (primary) bear market, and there has been only one other such movement in its progress. Whether the present rally represents a radical change in the general direction, is a matter of opinion. In some important respects students of the averages will recognize that the market still lacks that endorsement.

The Wall Street Journal: February 2, 1914

The averages still fail to show whether the present movement is merely a secondary bull swing in a bear market, which has not concluded its primary movement, or whether conditions are reversed and the present advance is a change in the main current. Both averages give some signs of making a "line" around present levels.

This may indicate well-organized distribution, or accumulation for another advance, as the case might be. The next fortnight or so ought to decide, when an advance above the line of both averages, or a decline below, would be equally significant.

The Wall Street Journal: February 9, 1914

Students of the averages should find them interesting. During the present rally they have several times come within a fraction of making higher points than those of the recovery which culminated last autumn. Both the industrial and railroad averages have done this independently, but not simultaneously.

For four weeks past the extreme fluctuation in either average was considerably less than three points. This gives every indication of a "line" which should throw light on the future movements of the market, as it clearly discloses either distribution or accumulation in large volume.

If the two averages went below 80 and 106 respectively, simultaneously, or above 84 and 110, the one would indicate the close of a secondary bull swing in a primary bear market; while the other would impel students to consider whether the main current had not changed when the present rally set in.

The Wall Street Journal: February 12, 1914

PRICE MOVEMENT

For twenty-four trading days the average prices of twenty active railroad stocks and of twelve industrials have been making what is called a "line." The industrials, for instance, in that time have not sold below 80.77, or above

83.19; while the railroads have moved between 106.52 and 109.43. During that time there has been a relatively large volume of transactions.

On all previous experience of the averages this indicates either heavy distribution in a market receiving organized support, or a large accumulation with a view to a further advance. The only difficulty for the student of the averages, in fact, is to say whether the rally which set in on Dec. 16, 1913, was a secondary bull swing in a bear market, or whether there had been a radical change in the primary movement.

At the beginning of October, 1912, when the industrials were selling at 94.12 and the railroads at 124.35, a primary bear market set in which, by the middle of the following June, had reduced the industrial average to 72.11 and the railroad average to 100.50. Following this there was a typical secondary bull swing, which carried into the following September, with a net recovery of nearly eleven points in the industrials and something more than eight points in the railroads. This represented less than half the previous decline.

A resumption of the bear movement carried the industrial average back to within three points of the June low, and the railroad average within less than two points. Since then the market has had a substantial recovery, and at the beginning of February had regained nearly eight points in the industrials, and about as much in the railroads.

Students of the averages may take their choice as to whether the bull movement which set in two months ago has spent its force. On previous experience of the averages a simultaneous movement to about 80.50 and 106.50 respectively, would indicate rather clearly that the primary bear market had resumed. On the other hand, an advance above 83.19 in the industrials and 109.43 in the railroads might indicate a radical change in the primary movement. If the bear market were resumed, the chances would point to figures below those of last December, and, less probably, under those of the previous June. But according to precedent, the main bear market should exhaust itself some time this year.

The Wall Street Journal: March 2, 1914

To be convincing, both averages must move together. If the stationary market of the past month has been a result of well-organized distribution, the saturation point will show itself in a decline in the industrials corresponding to that already shown in railroads. On past experience vigorous precipitation might follow.

The Wall Street Journal: March 9, 1914

On the averages, the market at the end of the week gave indications which would point to a definite resumption of the main bear movement, which began in October, 1912. Both averages had made a striking "line," and the movement below that line is a sufficiently clear indication of organized distribution which has left the market saturated with stocks, which the short interest is not large enough to absorb.

The Wall Street Journal: March 16, 1914

It has been said that the stock market is a good barometer of trade, and this is largely true when it is clearly understood that it is prophesying as far ahead as it can see. It is seldom, however, that the movement in prices coincides with the immediate movements of trade. It is the more curious therefore, that the present condition in the stock market should so exactly reflect the general showing of business all over the country.

Stocks rallied in December, and ran up during January and part of February, coincidently with an ordinary and seasonal revival of business. Then there was a halt, followed by fluctuations within narrow limits, about corresponding to the general business movement of the country.

A week ago the market seemed to be full of stocks, and broke through its supports in some cases, again following the conditions of general trade. In like manner it seems to be hanging on the edge of a considerable contraction; while a broad change of the most radical character would be necessary to restore a basis for the precipitate assumption of returning prosperity which was so popular a month ago.

This seems to be about the reflection of the market in the averages. They made in the case of both the industrials and the railroads what is called a "line," in which their fluctuations were confined for a month's trading within less than three points. The railroads broke through the lower limits of the line; while the industrials approached close to it. With a further break in the railroads, the industrials still held on by their teeth. This is the one bull indication of the averages, which otherwise would be interpreted as saying, with considerable emphasis, that the bear market which started in October, 1912, had resumed its sway.

The Wall Street Journal: March 23, 1914

Little can be gathered from the averages. They may be said to have taken back the bear point partially given when the railroads broke so far below the line, and the industrials hovered on the edge of it. They would have in each case some distance to go to give a bullish indication, while they would have to repeat the decline at the beginning of the month simultaneously to indicate that the market was too full of stocks to liquidate except at lower levels. This figure would be approximately 80.5 for the industrials and 103 for the railroads.

The Wall Street Journal: March 30, 1914

Both the industrial and the railroad averages had a substantial setback, and are now within less than two points of a low figure, which would indicate a definite resumption of the main bear movement. To do this, and to indicate fully that the stock market had reached saturation point, a simultaneous movement of the two averages would be necessary. The significant figures would be 103 for the railroads and 80.5 for the industrials. A much more considerable advance would be necessary to indicate an independent bull movement.

The Wall Street Journal: April 16, 1914

PRICE MOVEMENT

For seventy trading days previous to April 14, the average price of the twelve industrial stocks did not go above 84, or below 81. For forty days before that date, the average price of twenty active railroads never went above 106 or below 103. Here is a range of three points for the two averages kept for comparison by *The Wall Street Journal,* and they simultaneously broke through the "line," on the lower side, on April 14.

On all previous experience of the averages, the indication is so bearish as to point to a resumption of the primary bear market which set in early in October, 1912. Both averages, in fact, made a "line," and the fact that they broke through indicates exceptional support for the distribution of stock to a point where the market became so full that it could carry no more; and, like the humidity in the atmosphere, precipitation had to follow.

It may be explained again that the "theory" of Charles H. Dow, confirmed by many years of observation, was that the market had three simultaneous movements. The first of these is the great primary movement lasting for a year or more. The second is the occasional rally in a bear market, or the break in a bull market. The third represents the daily fluctuations, which for present purposes of discussions may be discarded.

There were two well defined secondary bull swings in the main bear market now apparently in operation. The industrials from the end of September, 1912, when they sold at 94.15, declined to 72.11 in the following June. The railroads in that time sold down from 124.35 to 100.50. The secondary bull swing then carried them up to 83.43 and 109.17 respectively. On the resumption of the bear market, in September of last year, the decline extended to 75.27 and 101.87. The second upward swing at the beginning of this year carried the industrials to 83.43 and the railroad stocks to 107.26.

At these figures it was an open question whether the primary movement had changed. The recent decline indicates that it had not, unless the averages falsify themselves for the first time in like conditions. They are frequently misleading where one group breaks through the line and the other does not. When, however, the movement is simultaneous there is a uniform body of experience to indicate the market trend.

Opinions would vary as to the probable extent of the bear movement before a radical change takes place. It would be in line with previous movements if something under the low of June, 1913, were established in the coming summer.

The Wall Street Journal: June 8, 1914

There is an interesting situation in the averages. Since April 30, or for thirty-two trading days, the price of the twelve industrial stocks has not been below 79 or above 82; while twenty active railroad stocks in that period have not been below 101 or above 104. This is a very well marked and typical line, which can only indicate one of two things —a period of accumulation or a period of well managed distribution.

If the railroad stocks sold at 101 and the industrials, simultaneously, at 79, the indication would be most positively bearish, and would point to an active resumption of the main bear movement which developed in October, 1912. An advance together to 82 and 104 respectively, however, would be definitely bullish, and might easily indicate a primary change in the market movement, pointing to a bull market of a year or more duration.

The Wall Street Journal: June 15, 1914

There is an interesting situation in the averages, which may have large significance in the near future. Since the beginning of May the industrials have not been as low as 79, nor as high as 82 while the railroads have not touched 101 or 104 respectively. Here is an extreme fluctuation in each case of considerably less than three points over a period of thirty-seven trading days. Even allowing for the narrowness of the market, this seems to indicate successful accumulation or distribution. A simultaneous advance of both averages to 82 and 104 respectively would mean a gain of less than a point in each instance, and would be decidedly bullish, as indicating the complete absorption of the floating supply of stocks. Such a movement would be acting strictly according to prece-

dent if it inaugurated a primary bull market, such as culminated in June, 1912.

The Wall Street Journal: June 22, 1914

Stock market movements have a significance over and above the mere effect on the market value of securities. But it is not so generally realized, that stock market stagnation is a symptom in itself, from which useful lessons may be drawn. The net fluctuation in the industrials and railroad stocks last week was in each instance less than a point, on the average.

If the volume of sales precludes the idea that any large accumulation is in progress at the amount of steadiness of the market and the absence of any need or organized support are valuable, in respect of the light they cast upon the future. Price movements, indeed, have the invaluable quality of reflecting the business of the country far ahead as the combined intelligence and information of the country's financial center can see.

On a major premise such as this, virtually amounting to an axiom, it can be said that the stock barometer indicates that, for some distance ahead, business cannot get worse, and may become better, and this view is curiously borne out in the remarkable showing of the averages for seven weeks past.

During that time the price of the industrials has not touched 79 on the one side, or 82 on the other; while there has been an identical restriction in the movement of the railroads, where the price has not been down to 101 or up to 104. Granting spells of inactivity for days together, there must yet in that time have been either remarkably well handled liquidation, which will ultimately leave the market at saturation point with precipitation to follow or an orderly absorption of stocks, which will lead to a sharp advance in prices, when it is realized how small is the floating supply.

In other words, a simultaneous advance of the two averages above 82 and 104 respectively, would indicate a broad and significant bull movement, while there would be an equivalently bearish influence on a simultaneous break through 79 and 101. Conditions pointing to the former outcome seem to gain in volume.

The Wall Street Journal: July 14, 1914

PRICE MOVEMENT

On April 16 the price movement, as shown by the two stock averages, was discussed in these columns. It was possible to say that, after the twelve industrial stocks had not for 70 days been above 84 or below 81; while the railroads for 40 days had not been above 106 or below 103, a line of distribution had been demonstrated. The simultaneous break below the line of the two averages carried the railroads down to 99.24, and the industrials to 76.97, reached April 25.

It is fair to assume that this break indicated the resumption of the main or primary bear market which set in at the end of September, 1912, when the railroads were selling at 124.35 and the industrials at 94.15. There were two secondary bull swings, but the movement downwards, when these had spent their force, was consistent.

In the past 61 days a line similar to that described last April has been made. The industrials in that time have not been below 79 or above 82; while the railroads in the same period have not been below 101 or above 104, with a single exception in the case of the latter, which proved nothing. The small "warning" below 101, in fact, was immediately taken back.

With a primary bear market which has undoubtedly been running for less than three months short of two years, a change in the main movement cannot be far off. Such a change comes not from a quick rally after a severe decline, but following a prolonged period of narrow fluctuations within a well recognized range. Such a period is now in progress. If the averages simultaneously break below the respective low points of the line of 79 and 101, the inference is that the main bear market has not spent its force.

If, however, the averages advanced simultaneously above 82 and 104 respectively, the inference would be bullish, and might even indicate the beginning of a primary bull market only to be interrupted by occasional secondary bear swings. It would then be clear that there had been a line of sound accumulation, and that the stocks so absorbed would not come on the market again except in eventualities sufficiently far ahead as to warrant the assumption of rising prices for a year or more.

At no time have the averages been more interesting than they are now. It is assumed in these studies that they are impartial, and allow for everything. They cover too many issues to make manipulation possible, and in the past have discounted all contingencies, including the volume of business.

The Wall Street Journal: July 20, 1914

There is certainly not much comfort in the averages. The twenty active railroad stocks, fluctuating so long between 101 and 104, broke through the lower line on Thursday. The industrials did not follow, and are still between the limits of 79 and 82, which have obtained for an unusually long period. If, however, the average broke through this line a resumption of the main bear market in operation since October, 1912, would be clearly indicated.

The Wall Street Journal: February 10, 1915

PRICE MOVEMENT

Since the price movement, as shown by *The Wall Street Journal* averages of twelve industrials and twenty active railroad stocks, was discussed on July 14, 1914, two unprecedented conditions have supervened. One was the closing of the Stock Exchange for a period of eighteen weeks; the other was the fixing of arbitrary low prices on the reopening of the Exchange.

Nevertheless, even these conditions are not sufficient to induce a change in the accepted method of analyzing the averages. Undoubtedly, the war has produced a continuance of the bear market, which at the closing of the Exchange had lasted within three months of two years. It might almost be said that a semi-panic break had taken place in the last four days previous to the close of the market, and on its reopening a duplication of previous panic markets might be expected. To some extent this was what took place. The industrial stocks on July 30 closed at 71.42, and the railroads at 89.41. A rally, with a reaction, carrying prices down to the old panic level, or near it, would be in order. The movement was not uniform in both averages, where the industrials only sold down 2.54 points from the best of the rally to 73.48 on Dec. 24; while the industrials lost 4.89 points at the same date, and at 87.40 were two points below the July close.

Still this was fairly typical, and represented a return to normal conditions, where the averages might be expected to give fairly trustworthy indications in the future, as they have done in the past. There was a real recovery after the inevitable realizing which follows a postpanic rally. This carried the railroad stocks up 6.55 points to 94.05, and the industrials up 4.93 points to 78.41, both recording their maximum on January 21.

Since that date the market has sagged, losing not quite three points in each average. There are signs that it might make something of a "line" around the present level; and it is to be noticed that the movement of the two averages holds remarkably well together, which is always an interesting sign, because when one breaks through an old low level without the other, or when one establishes a new high for the short swing, unsupported, the inference is almost invariably deceptive.

Indications are obviously anything but clear. But the tendency of the averages to discount everything, and resume their well-tried functions as a barometer of the market movement, is in itself encouraging.

The Wall Street Journal: April 6, 1915

PRICE MOVEMENT

Is this a primary bull market? After the reopening of the Stock Exchange there was a recovery of an irregular character, which was unable, in the case of the railroad average of stocks, to prevent a decline in the price to 87.40, which was two points below the somewhat disastrous close of July 30, when the Stock Exchange shut down. The low point of the reaction in the industrials, however, after the first recovery, did not reach within two points of the Stock Exchange's closing price. The market bal-

anced then, and it was a question of what it would do. There was a vital point involved, because a bear market which had been operating since the autumn of 1912, was possibly on the turn.

In December both averages steadied, the industrials advanced on Jan. 4 above 75, with the railroads above 89. They maintained this minimum, with one break in the industrials to a trifle below 75, until Feb. 5. They had less than a two-point recovery until Feb. 24, when the railroads touched a small decimal below the reopening low level, and the industrials at 73.81 had not reached the low point since the Stock Exchange resumed business.

It will be observed this was in effect the natural advance and reaction after what really constituted a panic, resulting from the closing of the Stock Exchange, moving in very much the same way that a panic recovery does. The tendency is to recover a part of the severe decline, say from the price of July 18, which meant some thirteen points in the railroads, and seven points in the industrials.

From that figure the indications became an open question. If the two averages made a line, it would indicate accumulation or distribution of stocks. From subsequent developments it looks as if there had been genuine aaccumulation by investors.

Industrial stocks from Feb. 25 up to March 20 did not go below 74 or above 78, representing twenty-four trading days; while in the same period the railroad stocks were not below 87.91, or above 90. This is clearly a "line," from which subsequent movements of the market have shown genuine evidence of accumulation. The railroads, in fact, have approached closely to the ephemeral rally following the panic decline; while the industrials are above the abnormally high figures of the middle of July, and, indeed, above those of the averages since the period when the war was a factor in the market.

This is a movement of the highest importance. It is fair to say that there has been a bear market in stocks, as reflected by both averages, since the autumn of 1912. This represents more than two and a half years, which is long for a primary swing, as a glance at a quarter of a century's averages will show.

The time seems ripe for a bull market; and if this is the case, the advance since the average made a line of accumulation—as it most evidently has—is highly significant, and indicates an upward trend which may easily be of a primary character. This is not to suggest there will be no secondaary downward swings, as the market becomes over-bought; or that there will not be the usual tertiary fluctuations from day to day.

But there is a strong indication in the movement of the averages that there has been a distinct turn for the better in the averages, something like that in the early summer of 1904, holding to January, if not August, of 1906.

The Wall Street Journal: June 9, 1915

THE PRICE MOVEMENT

There is a remarkable confirmation in the movement of the stock market averages, kept for many years by this newspaper, of the inference drawn on April 6 of this year, that there was a primary change in the market. It was said then that both averages had been making what is called a "line," either of distribution or accumulation of stocks; and that they had started to advance in a way to indicate that the bear market of over two years preceding had given way to a primary upward movement.

It will be remembered that, on what all students of the law apparently governing stock market price movements know as Dow's theory (which is the standard), the primary movement in one direction might last for anything from one to three years; while the secondary movement, the quick recovery in a bear market, or the rapid liquidation after an advance, could interrupt, but not arrest, the main movement; while the third influence, that of the day-to-day trading, need not be seriously considered in an extensive view.

After the inference drawn on April 6 had justified itself, the stock market had what looks like one of these secondary reactions. The industrial stocks had sold close to 91, and the railroads above 98, but both experienced a decline amounting, at the low figures of the reaction to nearly ten points in the industrials and nine points in the railroads.

But after this severe decline, which should be classified as coming under the secondary price movement mentioned, the industrials for twenty-one days fluctuated between 79.83 and 84.89, without touching the old high of the previous "line," upon which the bull market inference was formed. At the same time the railroads made an even more convincing line, for they did not sell below 90.75 or approach 94 in twenty-eight trading days. They are, in fact, still in this groove.

Once more it is worth while to emphasize that the movement of these two averages is deceptive unless they act together. The railroads are still in what might be fairly called a secondary line of accumulation, and at this point it does not matter whether there has been distribution or not, because when somebody sells somebody else buys. An advance by the industrial stocks above the old high of April 30, 90.91, followed at a brief interval by an advance in the railroads above the April 20 high of 98.75, would almost give proof positive of the primary tendency of the market, as inferred in the study of the price movement published in these columns early in April.

The Wall Street Journal: June 26, 1915

THE PRICE MARKET

During a time when the industrial average as shown in *The Wall Street Journal's* tabulation of twelve such stocks, has made a net upward movement of more than ten points, in thirty-four trading days from May 15, the railroads have fluctuated within a close range of 2.49 points, and are about where they were when the independent industrial movement started.

Premising that conclusions drawn from one average but not confirmed by the other, are sometimes misleading, and should always be treated with caution, the remarkable stability of the railroad stocks has significance, and may fairly be treated on its merits. It does not often happen that one average will make an important movement while the other remains stationary. This has happened on the present occasion, and it is necessary to go back eleven years to find a similar movement. Then, the conditions were exactly reversed. It was the railroads that advanced and the industrials that stood still.

Early in the year it was inferred in this place, correctly as subsequent events demonstrated, that there had been a fundamental change in the price movement, and that a primary bull market was well under way. When the twenty active railroad stocks over thirty-four trading days fluctuate within a range of 2.49 points, one of two conditions may, on all previous experience of the averages, be assumed to exist. Either these stocks are being accumulated for an important upward movement, or well organized distribution is in progress.

In view of a "line," so clear and definite, the more probable inference would be that the railroads are preparing for an upward movement corresponding to that already registered by the industrials. An advance of the railroad averages above 94.17 would be a strong indication that the floating supply of stocks had been absorbed. It would necessarily mean a substantial general advance before new supplies of stocks were tapped.

On the other hand, a reaction below 91.68, the low limit of the present line, need not be particularly bearish. There is no way in which the industrials could by a similar movement give such a decline special significance. The situation is well worth watching. The upward movement indicated would be a remarkably strong and convincing forecast of the market in the summer and autumn.

The Wall Street Journal: March 20, 1916

THE AVERAGES

Many subscribers have asked why there is not more frequent discussion in these columns of the price movement, from the point of view of the stock averages. The answer is that the averages are not enlightening at present. They are not indicating anything more positive than the obvious fact that the bull movement which set in after the reopening of the Stock Exchange has not spent its force.

To this primary movement there can hardly be said to have been an interruption sufficiently impressive to be called a secondary swing. The industrial stocks have presented the most striking advance in an abnormal time, due of course to the inclusion of one of the most active "war" stocks, General Motors. It begins to look as if this were merely a transitory phenomenon, and that the average would reassert itself.

It will be noticed that the railroad stocks have not made an advance corresponding to that of the industrials. After the new year there was something of a line between 100 and 103, which may or may not have had significance, although it should be remembered that all past experience of the average has shown that unless such a line is made simultaneously by both the industrials and the railroads it is more apt to be deceptive than not.

It would seem, however, a fair inference from the subsequent action of the railroad stock average, that there had been a pause for accumulation followed by fair evidence that the floating supply of stock had been absorbed, and that prices consequently were trending to a higher level. This would be entirely in keeping with the rest of the market, and would in fact be complementary to the extensive advance in the primary movement of the industrials.

It is well to remember, however, that the main movement has now lasted fifteen months, and would tend in the natural course of things to exhaust itself, on all past experience of the averages. Such a movement, however, might easily last some months longer, although the material for drawing inferences is singularly scanty.

Any sign of the two averages making a simultaneous line would have considerable significance in these circumstances. It would almost certainly indicate the coming interruption of the main movement by a secondary swing, and it might even indicate a radical change in the whole market. This is a matter for future consideration upon which no light can be shed at present.

The Wall Street Journal: August 6, 1910

HAS THE BULL MARKET CULMINATED?

Does the sharp reaction in the bull market, which between February 8 of this year and July 14 showed an advance in the average of twenty industrials from 79.15 to 112.23 or 33.08, and in twenty railroads between January 21 and May 26 a gain of nearly 11 points, indicate a culmination of the main upward movement? Any student of the price movement whose deductions are based upon comparisons of the averages over a period of twenty-four years would answer, No.

Such a reaction, in fact, is itself typical of a bull market, in which experience shows that the breaks, other than negligible fluctuations, are short and sharp, and are exactly paralleled by the quick rallies in a bear market. Something much more convincing in this typical sharp break would be necessary to persuade students of the price movement that the bull market has run its course.

An examination of the averages since the hundred-day suspension of the Stock Exchange following the original declaration of war should make the point sufficiently clear. After the Stock Exchange reopened there was a period during which, with the fluctuation of a few points extending over the end of 1914 and the early winter months of 1915, the market showed a line of accumulation within relatively narrow limits, followed by a strong bull movement which with characteristic sharp declines continued up to the end of the year 1915.

There was again a relatively narrow fluctuation, followed by a decline indicating that distribution had been in progress, although this decline did not carry prices down to the old low level of the previous year. There was then a characteristic advance, where the railroads and industrials both reached new high levels. This was followed, rather sharply, by a decline, and in the early part of 1917 by a period proved by events to have been one of distribution. The market became loaded with stocks to saturation point and a true bear market set in which continued almost to the end of the year, and in the case of the industrials into 1918.

In the beginning of that year another line was made which proved to be one of accumulation, and there was a sharp advance representing a bull market of moderate force which continued to the following autumn. There was then a decline previous to the armistice, which was followed by a period again proving to be one of accumulation, emerging early in the current year into the present bull market.

These movements are typical, and it may be said that the intention and effect of the averages taken over a long period of years is to discount all considerations—labor, threats, government ownership or even the great war itself. If on the present reaction the market should in both averages make a line simultaneously over an appreciable period of time, say a month or more, and should then break through that line on the downward side, substantially lower prices might be looked for.

If, however, the line proved to be one of accumulation, an advance over its narrow limits would on all precedent indicate that the floating supply of stock had been absorbed and that the bull market was once more in full swing. There is nothing at present to show that this is not the more probable development from the reaction.

The Wall Street Journal: August 8, 1919

STOCK MARKET ANALYSIS

A sympathetic reader asks if the method of estimating the trend of the stock market by analysis of previous movements as shown in the industrial and railroad price averages is not empirical? Of course it is, but not entirely so, and the method is far removed from quackery. Any conclusion reached from a number of recorded instances is open to that charge. It depends on the scientific accuracy of the method of indication.

Medical diagnosis is empirical where symptoms are merely compared to similar symptoms observed in the past. But when diagnosis is reinforced by tests of blood pressure, blood and other analysis, nervous reaction, bacteriological examination, pulse, temperature and other aids, it approaches to an exact science, with the usual human deductions. It is still true that there is no way of forecasting the future except by the record of the past, and given accuracy and impartiality in the record, much can be learned.

Study of the averages is based on "Dow's Theory," propounded by the late Charles H. Dow, the founder of this newspaper. The books which published that theory seem to be out of print; but briefly it was this: Simultaneously in any broad stock market there are—acting, reacting and interacting—three definite movements. That on the surface is the daily fluctuation; the second is a briefer movement typified by the reaction in a bull market or the sharp recovery in a bear market which has been oversold; the third and main movement is, that which decides the trend over a period of many months, or the main true movement of the market.

It is with these facts well in mind that the student approaches analysis of the averages, premising that broad conclusions are valueless on the daily fluctuation and deceptive on the secondary movement, but possible and helpful on the main movement of the market, and of real barometrical value to general business. It may be said as a matter of record that studies in the price movement, with these facts well in view, published in these columns from time to time and especially in the years before the war, were far oftener right than wrong, and were wrong for the most part when they departed from Dow's sound and scientific rule.

This is why it was possible last Wednesday to say that the sharp reaction in the market from the beginning of the week was a typical secondary movement, and did not invalidate the bull market which set in from the period of accumulation of stocks around the beginning of this year. No wise man would dream of trading upon such generalization; but the conclusions are sufficiently useful and definite to have secured the confidence of thoughtful and intelligent observers.

The Wall Street Journal: October 9, 1919

STOCK MARKET AVERAGES

Daily averages as compiled by Dow, Jones & Co. for twenty industrial and twenty railroad stocks have reached a point of interesting comparison with their course in the present past. At Tuesday's and again at Wednesday's close the industrial average had just overtopped the level of mid July, when it stood at 112.23. It was fifteen points lower in August. The rails at 82.04 are still nine points below the high point of the year, made May 26, and only four points above the intervening low level of 78.60, made August 20. In both cases the reaction following the mid-year high was less than half the advance subsequent to the first week in February.

On August 6 The Wall Street Journal said editorially that the averages did not then indicate that the bull market had culminated. They have not yet given any definite reason for qualifying that conclusion or even supplementing it, since the August decline, in the light of the subsequent recovery, may well be regarded as a secondary movement, that is, a sharp reaction characteristic of a bull market. In the same editorial it was said that if the averages should make a line below the mid-year high and then break through downward they would indicate the approach of a true bear market. What actually followed was a succession of sharp fluctuations in the industrial average and a lower level on August 20 than earlier in the month, succeeded by a rapid and continuous recovery to above 108 on September 3, ten points from the August low. Around that level the industrial average made a fair line for two weeks, then rose sharply during the latter part of September and the first few days of October. It has now passed a point above the July high.

The rail average has made a line since early in August, the only important deviation from which has been the upward turn of the past three or four market days. There would be less reason on outside considerations to regard this as meaning distribution than in the case of the industrials.

Chart followers, who are perhaps too disposed to look for such oracular manifestations as "double tops," assert that the industrial average must now either give one of those infallible warnings of a bear market or break through extensively into higher ground, in which latter case the conclusion would be that the true main movement was still that of a bull market. Neither inference would be compelling, since if the extraordinary violence of the secondary movement in the industrials during the whole war period is considered it might be assumed that a decline from the present level was marking the second half of a double bottom, the first half of which was made in August. Such a theory might have, and would need, the support of continued strength in the rails. Nevertheless, any extended decline in the industrial average now would be a matter for serious thought.

It cannot be too much reiterated that the averages are not to be regarded by themselves as conclusively presaging future markets. They are only one of many indices of the financial position and should not be overweighted.

The Wall Street Journal: June 7, 1920

DEVELOPMENTS OF THE WEEK

Last week's stock market was typ-*ically narrow, upon the whole tending to work better, after some pressure following the holiday at the beginning of the week. It is plain from the averages that there has now been a recovery, over a period of a fortnight or so, of rather more than 4 points in the industrials and less than 3 in the railroads, from a low figure of last May which carried the industrials 32 points below the culmination of the bull movement in November and the railroads some 15 points down. On well tested theories of reading the market by the averages this looks like a secondary upward swing in a market the primary movement of which is downwards and cannot be said to have culminated. On all experience the rally ought to carry further, as the Street is bare of stocks and commission houses report little of the active issues carried for customers.

The Wall Street Journal: June 21, 1920

A STUDY IN THE PRICE MOVEMENT

There seems a perennial interest in methods of reading the movement of the stock market, as represented in the average prices recorded at the close of the market daily for industrial and railroad stocks. A number of readers have written to inquire about the well-known system upon which the present tendency of the market was described

in the weekly review of conditions published on a recent Monday, called "Developments of the Week."

Dow's "theory" on the market movement, formulated nearly twenty years ago, has borne the test of experience, although in his day the value of the stock market as a relatively accurate barometer of general business conditions was little recognized. He had perhaps fifteen years' record of the market movement to guide him, and we have more than twice that now. But there is little to doubt that his theory is sound, although, of course, it is not advanced as a "martingale" or system for "breaking" the Wall Street bank.

Dow's theory was that the market had three movements, two of them, and sometimes three, simultaneous. The primary underlying movement disclosed a "bear" or a "bull" market, upward or downward as the case might be, over a period of seldom less than a year and sometimes much longer. The secondary movement was represented by a reaction in a bull market, relatively short and severe, or a recovery, equally abrupt, in a bear market. Experience shows that this secondary movement may continue from three weeks to as many months before its force is spent and the main movement is resumed.

The third movement, simultaneous with either or both of the others, is the daily fluctuation, which may in this case be ignored. The averages have run true to form, discounting even extraordinary events, and the war has been no exception. A glance at the averages will show that a primary bull market, interrupted by occasional secondary relapses, culminated last October. A bear market then set in and was interrupted by a characteristic secondary rally beginning in the latter part of May. There is no evidence at present either that the main downward movement will not be resumed before the broad course of the market radically changes, or that the secondary rally has exhausted itself.

It may be that the decline between October and May represented the whole of the primary movement, and the low prices of stocks, on values, might seem to create a new precedent. The volume of transactions is against this theory, and so short a movement is contrary to all experience. There would need to be evidence of accumulation in great volume. The market itself should soon test this theory. If it shows signs of what may be called saturation point after the present rally, the indications are for considerably lower prices when the main downward swing is resumed, as it would be, on this theory, in the late Summer or early fall.

The Wall Street Journal: March 30, 1921

STOCKS UNATTRACTIVELY CHEAP

There are plenty of wise saws and modern instances to show that the investor seldom buys at the bottom and rarely or never sells at the top. Cheap stocks are never attractive. This is no Chestertonian paradox but a matter of market record. If cheap stocks were attractive there would be an active market today, with an interested and even excited public. The further inference is obvious that stocks would not be cheap for long. It is easy to tell the man who can pay for his stock and forget about it that the market is full of attractive possibilities. There are not enough such customers to go around.

One might point him to the United States Steel report, and show him that Steel common is selling at less than a third of its book value, on a plain statement of the assets. He may be able to pay for the stocks, but he cannot forget about it; he thinks he must read the price list every morning. Your customer sees Steel common down five points a share. He forgets all that you told him about book value. He says he will take his loss and remember the lesson. He is entirely mistaken about the lesson, and what he is forgetting is not his loss but the reason why he bought the stock.

In a market unsettled by long liquidation, with high money rates, it is easy to forget that good stocks are often more vulnerable than bad ones. The market for the good stocks is real and that for the bad ones is nominal. It follows that on any pressure involving the calling of loans, it is the good stocks—United States Steel common

and the rest of them—which suffer. The people who have to meet the loans liquidate what can be sold at some price because they hold other things which cannot be sold at any price.

Is there a foundation for a bull market? On Dow's theory of the averages there may well be an excellent basis upon which a primary bull movement may set in. The present primary bear market developed in October, 1919. Since the beginning of this year the averages of both the industrials and the railroad stocks have been making "a line," within a range of several points but relatively close compared to the extent of the decline. The speculative investor for a long pull may well ask himself if this does not indicate accumulation.

It will be noticed that the industrials marked the upper range of this line on February 16 at 77.14, then reacted nearly five points, and touched 77.78 again on March 23; while the railroad stocks, after a recovery to 77.56 on January 15, followed by a reaction of more than eight points and a recovery of 2.52 points to March 16, are well within their line, but still six points away from what may be called the upper limits. The typical secondary rallies in a primary bear market have been well marked. The old rule for reading the averages would hold good. If both of them established 78 the indication would be remarkably like the beginning of a primary bull market. That figure for the industrials alone might easily be deceptive.

The Wall Street Journal: May 10, 1921

THE PRICE MOVEMENT

In the financial page of The New York American there is an attempted study of the charted price movement from the average price of stocks over a period of years. The chart itself is adopted, and the figures were taken bodily without acknowledgment, from the well-known Dow-Jones averages, which have been the standard of comparison for much more than a quarter of a century. Altruists who believe that ill-gotten gains do not prosper will hear with relief that the author of the Hearst article did not even understand the meaning of what he appropriated.

His deductions are pretentious guessing.

With entire ignorance of the principle upon which the averages are read he announces a bull movement for the industrial stocks, even prescribing its limits, while the railroads "mark time." If any such movement develops it will be absolutely unprecedented in the stock market, on the record of the averages or of any representative price list. At times one group has moved more quickly than the other. Momentarily, the railroad and industrial averages have crossed each other. But invariably any major movement has been one of both averages together. Indeed it may be said that a new high or a new low by one of the averages unconfirmed by the other has been invariably deceptive. New high or low points for both have preceded every major movement since the averages were established.

On March 30, under the caption "STOCKS UNATTRACTIVELY CHEAP" it was said in this place:

(The entire editorial under date of March 30, 1921, was quoted, and which may be referred to above, is here omitted.)

Not knowing, or, more probably, not understanding the tested theory of the averages, this tipster was misled by the advance of the industrials above 78. But the most encouraging feature, which, of course, he missed, was the rally of the railroads to within four points of 78 on May 5, 6, and 7. It is the latter rally which is important. If it is continued four points further, while the position of the industrials is only maintained, there will be strong evidence of the completed accumulation preceding a fundamental or primary bull market.

But according to Dow's closely reasoned theory there are no indications of a sustained independent industrial rise. Industrials are likely to relapse into another period of dullness if the railroads do not respond. Yet it may be said conservatively that the present indications are anything but bearish and may easily become generally bullish, with the railroad average leading.

The Wall Street Journal: June 16, 1921

A STUDY IN THE AVERAGES

For a period extending from the beginning of the year the stock market averages, both industrial and railroad, showed remarkable power of resistance when either of them approached the low limit of 72. It is noteworthy as substantiating the best theory of reading the averages that the industrials broke through in December, making a new low of 66.75, without sufficient confirmation from the railroad averages; while the latter sold down to 67.86 in April without the necessary confirmation from the industrials. A bull point on the upper side of the line, above 78, with a high of 80.03, was given by the industrials in May but was not confirmed by the railroads.

Both averages have now broken through the obstinate line of resistance at 72. The indications would be most bearish if these had been new low figures in the primary bear movement which has now been running since October, 1919. The inference is sufficiently bearish, but it would certainly be more so if the industrials were below the figure of December and the railroads below that of April. It is correctly expressed by a modest but competent student of the averages, who says:

"Granting that it may be a small thing to cling to, nevertheless I have frequently found that the sanctity of previous Dow-Jones average lows was a consolation in a time like this. Say what we will, the industrial average is still three points higher than it was in December and the rails, even with the disheartening break in Northern Pacific, are still a point above this year's lows."

The consolation is not very exhilarating, but it is a whole lot better than none. Both averages have shown a distinct and obstinately held line, and by breaking through it have indicated that it was a line of distribution and not one of accumulation for the long deferred rally. Naturally there are no signs yet of a new line forming, but it might very well be that a convincing bull point will be given at a much lower figure than 78. The averages are remorseless. They represent all everybody knows or foresees about conditions. The grimmest bear argument today is Congress. For all it cares the railroads may totter over the brink of bankruptcy, so far as ninety per cent. of them are concerned, in the next few months or even weeks. The necessity for tax revision is desperate and Congress is fooling away its time on plans to spend more money—a veritable arteriotomy on the taxpayer's lifeblood, like the soldiers' bonus and the $500,-000,000 appropriation for the battleships which may be obsolete before they are launched.

This is no place to sum up the general view of the market, but clearly it cannot see its way and the averages are saying so. Their indication may not be as bearish as it seems, but they have long taken back any bull point they may have given.

The Wall Street Journal: June 23, 1921

INDICATIONS OF THE AVERAGES

After making a line of resistance above 72 the stock market averages broke through, giving a bearish indication below that figure which was amply confirmed, for the industrials on June 20 had declined 7 points from the line and the railroads a bare half point less. The "line" had been one not of accumulation, as seemed not impossible for a time, but of distribution. The Street was full of stocks. Saturation point was reached and precipitation followed almost automatically.

It is noteworthy, moreover, that in the decline the consolatory low points of December for the industrials and April for the railroads were also canceled. New low figures for the main movement were established. The primary bear market which set in early in October, 1919, resumed its sway. After such a punishing break it is natural that traders should ask about indications, judged by experience of the past.

To clear misunderstanding it should be said that there is no precedent which demands that the market should make another line before it rallies. On Dow's old theory of the averages the secondary breaks in a primary bull market and the secondary rallies in a bear market are sudden and rapid, conspicuously so in the recovery after an ac-

tual panic break. The test is not at the bottom but in what the market does after a rally in a condition like the present where stocks could easily become sold out or oversold. Sentiment is always superbearish at the bottom, and professionals begin to "copper" public sentiment when the elevator boy talks of his "short position."

A secondary rally in a bear market, as the averages for many years past show with curious uniformity, is followed by the making of a line which thoroughly tests the public absorption power. On a serious break such as the market has just experienced there is always heavy buying in support, to protect weak accounts too large to be liquidated, and this stock is fed out on a recovery. It is largely offset by the covering of shorts and bargain buying, but if the absorption power is still lacking there is a further and slower decline, usually establishing new low points.

Speaking merely of probabilities and not of scientific deductions from the averages, a sharp secondary rally would be as likely a development as anything at the present stage. The averages merely say that the primary bear market is not over, although it has had a long lease of life. The rest is an open question, where you pay your money and take your choice, or where you even pay your money and get little choice.

The Wall Street Journal: August 25, 1921

A STUDY IN THE PRICE MOVEMENT

From letters received it would seem that readers who study the stock market averages for barometrical indications attach more importance to the weakness in the stock market now than it seems to deserve, although it has unquestionable significance. At Tuesday's close the twenty active industrials broke the previous low of June 20, 1921. The low of the railroad stocks, recorded on the same date, and the low for the primary bear market which has been the governing influence since October, 1919, was 65.52, and it will be seen that the railroad average is still well above that figure.

It cannot be too often repeated that the two averages must confirm each other to provide the basis for any confident prediction. The railroads are still four points above the June low; and while the indication there is bearish they have some distance to fall before the indication would be positive. They have made a significant line in the recent past. For sixteen trading days the average price did not rise to 73, or fall to 70. On Tuesday it broke 71, giving a preliminary indication that distribution had been in progress, confirmed by Wednesday's close at 69.87.

In all the applications of Dow's theory of the price movement the best of all, as proved by experience, is this line of distribution or accumulation. One of two things, as experience shows, must be happening when normal trading continues within such a range. If the railroad stocks break through the line it is evident that the market has taken all it can absorb at that level, and that a new level must be found before new buyers can handle the oversupply pressing on the market. The cloud has reached saturation point and the natural consequence is a precipitation of rain.

It is interesting, and not unilluminating, to hear that certain well-known houses are large lenders of stocks in the loan crowd. This would indicate a corresponding short interest. But it by no means follows that the people borrowing could not deliver the stock if they chose. Indeed, if they had more to sell from the same sources it would be to their manifest advantage to create the impression of a vulnerable bear account. Experienced Wall Street is skeptical of such indications. It remembers how stock was taken out of New York by the ream in 1919 by the investment of war profits. It wants to know whether this stock is coming back.

So far as the averages are concerned they are far from encouraging to the bull, but they do not yet jointly indicate a definite resumption of the main bear movement.

The Wall Street Journal: September 21, 1921

A STUDY IN THE PRICE MOVEMENT

When the price movement was last discussed in this place, on August 25, with the applied test of the average prices of the active railroad and industrial stocks recorded from day to day, it was pointed out that however bearish a new low point in the industrials might look it had not been confirmed by the railroad stocks, which were then (and are still) making a significant line within narrow limits which experience has proved must necessarily be either one of distribution or of accumulation.

On August 24 the industrials made a new low for the primary market operative since October-November, 1919, at 63.90. On the same day the railroads weakened their line of resistance, where in a succession of trading days sufficiently numerous for a test the price had not touched 74 or sold below 70. The figure of 69.87 then recorded was a caution and anything below 69 would have been positively bearish. It would not have recorded a new low for the main bear movement so far as the Rails are concerned, but it would have shown that the market was saturated with stocks.

No such confirmation was forthcoming, however, and the line was resumed with a rally above 70. Since that time, on September 13, considerable strength developed in the upper part of the line and the average closed at 74.30. This looked more bullish as the industrials had simultaneously rallied 8 points from the bottom to 71.92. Here again the bullish warning was taken back and the line of distribution or accumulation was resumed. The railroad averages are still well within that line and the industrials are showing a parallel movement at a range between 69 and 72.

This is highly significant, and within the next few days an indication might well be given of a developed movement of at least secondary and perhaps primary importance. It may be taken as a sound rule that we are in a bull market if in the fluctuations of the average the new high figures in both averages are even a little above those last recorded. Anything above 75.21 for the railroads would give such a bullish indication, especially as the industrials would reflect a like movement at 72 or over.

The reasoning is not at all abstruse nor is the conclusion far-fetched. It would be obvious that the floating supply in both industrial and railroad stocks had been absorbed, and that it had become necessary, therefore, to advance prices materially to attract new sellers. The bear market, which has now dominated for only a month short of two years, has shown an unusually long swing; and the change in market tendency, with new tops developing out of a line of accumulation would be radical.

It is beside the point to say that we are facing a hard winter. The stock market is meaningless if it does not look beyond such a contingency. It seems to be forecasting a solid foundation for better general business in the spring. It may well be that the stage for a primary bull market is being set.

The Wall Street Journal: October 4, 1921

A LOOK AHEAD

More than one correspondent has written to this paper to call attention to unsatisfactory conditions and to ask, therefore, why it should be said, in the study of the price movement, through the averages, published September 21, that the stock market seems to be setting the stage for a long upward swing in prices. All sorts of reasons are given for a pessimistic view—bankruptcy in Germany, railroad rates and wages, tariff and tax uncertainty, and the obtuseness of Congress in considering such matters with common sense. The answer is that the stock market has considered all these things, with sources of information far more exhaustive than any these critics can possibly possess.

By the well-tried methods of reading the stock market averages, only a decline of eight points in the industrials average, and nine points in the railroads, or below the low figures of the main bear movement recorded June 20, would indicate a resumption of that movement. On the other hand, the rail-road stocks alone at present figures would need to advance less than a point to record the repeated new high for both averages which would indicate a primary bull market. The industrials have already recorded that point, and both averages have shown a remarkably clear and distinct line of accumulation which is likely at any time to disclose a market bereft of its floating supply of stocks.

It cannot too often be said that the stock market reflects absolutely all everybody knows about the business of the country. The corporations which sell the farmer implements, motor trucks and fertilizers know his condition better than he knows it himself. There are corporations listed in the Stock Exchange, complying with its stringent listing requirements, dealing in practically everything the country makes and consumes—the coal, the coke, the iron ore, the pig iron, the steel billett, the manufactured watch spring—and all their knowledge is infallibly reflected in the price of securities. All the banks know about the exchange of those commodities and the financing of their production and marketing is reflected in stock prices adjusted to the value of each contribution to knowledge small or large.

Prices are low because all these bearish factors our critics adduce have been discounted in the prices. When the market is taken by surprise there is a panic, and history records how seldom it is taken by surprise. Today all the bear factors are known, serious as they admittedly are. But the stock market is not trading on what is common knowledge today but upon the sum of expert knowledge applied to conditions as they can be foreseen many months ahead.

The Wall Street Journal: December 30, 1921

THE PRICE MOVEMENT

It was pointed out in this column on August 25 that the stock-market averages, which were then far from encouraging to the bull, did not indicate a resumption of the main bear movement which had prevailed for eighteen months up to last June. On September 21 the inference was clearly drawn that the main swing of the market had changed, and that the stage was being set for a bull market in 1922. From August 24 the twenty industrials now show a net advance of nearly seventeen points. The advance in the railroads has been much less, extending to barely seven points on November 22. The closing figure is now four points above the low of August 24, but more than eight points above that of last June, at the end of the primary bear market.

On all previous experience of the stock-market barometer as set forth in the averages, we are in a major bull market which has seen, so far, two secondary reactions, neither of them of any great depth. In each case the market has become characteristically dull after the setback. On the well-tested rule of reading the averages, a major bull swing continues so long as the rally from a secondary reaction establishes new high points in both averages, not necessarily on the same day, or even in the same week, provided only that they confirm each other.

Confirmation of the resumption of the major bull market so clearly indicated and so confidently predicted in its initial stages in this column would be had if the industrials advanced less than a point, from present figures, and the railroads rather less than three points. One of Wall Street's old maxims was, "Never sell a dull market." Rallies in a bear market are sharp, but experienced traders wisely put out their shorts again when the market becomes dull after a recovery. Exactly the converse is true in a bull market, where traders buy stocks if the market becomes dull following a reaction.

As a standing rule, it may be taken that the stock market is always many months ahead of business conditions and is moved by the sum of everybody's real knowledge. Nothing is more childish than the use of such an epithet as "manipulation" to describe the market movements, especially when they run counter to popular fancy. Every movement has a good and satisfying reason. But the superficial financial newspaper reporter, too lazy to get at the facts, writes down "manipulation" as the simplest explanation. Any newspaper proprietor, even if he does not possess much personal knowledge of news gathering in Wall Street, should regard that reason for a stock-market movement with the gravest suspicion. It usually means that the reporter is shirking his work.

There is no reason to take back anything in previous forecasts published in this place. We are in a primary bull market tending to become dull on reactions, but slowly gathering strength for a more impressive advance.

The Wall Street Journal: February 11, 1922

THE PRICE MOVEMENT

Students of the stock market movement as recorded by the average closing price of twenty industrial and twenty railroad stocks, taken for comparison in the Dow, Jones news service, ask for some discussion of the market, on Dow's well-known theory of reading it. He showed clearly enough that there were three simultaneous movements—the major swing, lasting from a year to three years; the secondary reaction or rally in a bull or bear market, with a duration of a few days to a month or more; and the daily fluctuation. The market seems easy to read at present but people still write, presumably to have their opinions confirmed.

At present the major swing of the market is upwards. The low of the preceding bear movement, which had lasted a year and ten months, may be said to have occurred last June, although there was a subsequent new low for the industrials alone in August. This did not have the necessary confirmation of the other average, but it makes no difference if the turn in the market is calculated from last August. It was pointed out in these columns as early as last October that "the stage" was "being set for a bull market," and the subsequent movement has amply confirmed that inference.

Since the railroad low figure of June 20, 1921, the railroad stocks had recorded up to February 9 an advance of 11.30 points, at 76.81. From the low figure of August 24, 1921, the industrials on February 6 had recorded an advance of 19.80 points, at 83.70. This is an entirely consistent rise, with small but characteristic secondary reactions of a very few points, followed by a period of dullness and a subsequent resumption of the main movement, with new high figures in one of the averages, confirmed, at the time or soon after, by a similar new high point in the other. There has been nothing spectacular about the movement, but it would be hard to find one which more closely confirms Dow's tested theory. It does not even present any of those exceptions which are said to prove the rule.

It may once more be repeated that the stock market is acting not upon the known news of today but upon what conditions will be as far ahead as the combined intelligence and knowledge of Wall Street can foresee. There are plenty of bear arguments in the complicated conditions in Europe, the uncertainties of taxation and the interested aberrations of Congress. All these factors are known and, if possible, overdiscussed. The overwhelming bullish feature is the cheapness of money and the small speculative account open. Speculation is the barometer of general business, and the stock market is saying that there will be a real, if slow, improvement in the early spring and summer, the duration of which it cannot foresee.

The answer to these inquirers, therefore, is that we are still in a bull market and that it should run much further, possibly well into 1923, and certainly for a time well beyond the improvement in general business which it forecasts.

The Wall Street Journal: February 28, 1922

Having discounted all the depressing possibilities in business, the market, since last August, has shown that it sees the end of them and the return of better times. These are already indicated in several directions and the market is saying today that there will be a general recognition of better business in the coming spring and summer. Never did the stock market barometer more accurately vindicate its usefulness. On the average closing price there has already been an advance of about twenty points in the industrials and fifteen points in the railroads.

The Wall Street Journal: April 6, 1922

THE PRICE MOVEMENT

Second rate newspaper writers are fond of saying that "nobody reads editorials now." It may be true in their experience, at that. It depends on the editorial. But there seems to be an unfailing appetite for discussion of the stock market price movement in this column, even where fulfilled forecast seems to have made such discussion unnecessary. A newspaper should have something more useful to say than "I told you so." But students of the price movement, as shown in the averages, demand discussion of the stock market. They ask if the bull movement has run its course.

During last September and October, the present bull movement was recognized in these studies, when the people who could see no top in 1919 could see no bottom to a market which had been declining for more than two years. The previous study of the price movement was published here on Feb. 11. The last paragraph said, in response to inquiries of students of the price movement and others:

"The answer to these inquiries, therefore, is that we are still in a bull market and that it should run much further, possibly well into 1923, and certainly for a time well beyond the improvement in general business which it forecasts."

There has been a further substantial advance in both averages since those lines were written. The twenty industrials are now 26 points above the low of last August, and the twenty railroad stocks some 15 points above the low figure of the previous June. If there is a feature to a remarkably normal bull market it is that the secondary reactions have been rather shorter than they usually are. This has had the effect of encouraging a number of professionals to sell short, on the theory that a reaction is overdue. The technical result of this was, of course, to add further support to a market strong enough to absorb all they chose to sell.

There is no reason to suppose that the present bull market is within months of its culmination. It would probably be all the stronger for a sharp reaction, although it is doubtful if the present bears, who are merely sold-out bulls, would not be still more bearish on an average five-point decline and thereby miss their market once more. The market is much bigger than any manipulation could possibly be. It discounted the coal strike six months ago. The improvement which it then foreshadowed is increasingly in evidence, and will attract general attention in the next few weeks. Unless experience teaches nothing the business improvement and the stock market will run together until the latter is based no longer upon facts but upon prospects.

To those who apparently would feel happier if they were quite certain that nobody was making any money, in the stock market or out of it, it may be said that the market will ultimately turn when general business is still good, but not far from a turn. But these same people would be just as bullish then as they are bearish now.

The Wall Street Journal: May 8, 1922

A STUDY IN THE PRICE MOVEMENT

Many years' experience in the stock market, tested by Charles H. Dow's theory of its movement, has taught students the significance of a "line" in the averages. To be of real value the requirements are strict. The industrial and railroad averages should confirm each other. The period taken should be long enough to afford a real test, relative to the volume of trading. The fluctuations from day to day should be so narrow that they can be confined within a range of less than four points. Given these conditions an important deduction may be drawn.

In the stock market there has been a development of this kind, of both present and ultimate significance. From April 7, for twenty-four completed trading days, to May 5, inclusive, the twenty active railroad stocks have not sold below 83 or above 86. This is a remarkably close line particularly as the only time when the average went up to 85 was on April 25, closing at 85.09. During nearly the same period, or from April 10, for twenty-two days to May 5, inclusive, the twenty indus-

trials did not sell below 91 or touch 94. This is a period long enough to satisfy the requirements of experience. Such a line indicates either accumulation or distribution.

On the strength of this "line," a student of the averages, writing to the Boston News Bureau, takes a bearish view. He says that the "pools" and "insiders" seem to have been unloading on the public. This may be the case, but the conclusion does not follow from this premise. The market in both averages is nearer giving a bull point than a bear point. If, indeed, the twenty industrials sold at 94 or over, with a closely previous or subsequent confirmation by the railroads at 86, it would be good evidence that accumulation had exhausted the floating supply of stocks. A vigorous resumption of the bull movement would be as nearly certain as human probabilities admit.

If, on the other hand, the railroad stocks, with a decline more considerable from present figures than this supposed advance, sold below 83, while the industrials gave a nearly simultaneous bear point under 91, further reaction would certainly be indicated. The inference would be that the market had reached saturation point and that at least a secondary swing would be in order. This would not indicate the end of the bull market, and a subsequent recovery of the averages to 94 and 86 respectively would be strongly bullish. Of one thing our Boston friend may be sure. This is that the market itself is bigger than all the "pools" and "insiders" put together.

But the "line" is a most interesting one. There has not been one like it since the autumn of last year, before the present major bull swing set in.

The Wall Street Journal: May 22, 1922

A STUDY IN THE PRICE MOVEMENT

On Friday the stock market averages each confirmed the other's bull point on the same day. This followed one of the most interesting and even remarkable, "lines" ever made in the record of the price movement. Regarding the stock market as the invaluable business barometer it is, and using, after a quarter of a century's test, the averages in connection with Dow's theory of the market movement, some important indications for the future of general business may be drawn from the price movement as it stands today.

For thirty-four consecutive trading days of real activity the twenty railroad stocks in the average fluctuated within a range of barely three points. They sold on one occasion as high as 85.09, the only day when they crossed 85, and they never touched 83. On Friday the average emerged on the upper side of the line to 85.28, a new high for the year. Concurrently, and for thirty-two consecutive trading days, the twenty industrials had not been below 91 or touched 94. On Friday they also burst through the upper limit of the line, closing at 94.80, confirming the new high for the year shown by the railroads.

There is only one interpretation to be placed on a line like this, on all experience of the averages. If the break had been below the line the correct inference would have been that the market had reached saturation point and that precipitation must follow, or, in other words, that there would be a substantial decline until a more stable and attractive level had been reached. But the advance above the line is equally authoritative. It shows that the equilibrium maintained for more than a month represented a period of accumulation, and that the market is now bare of stocks. The inference is a resumption of the primary bull movement which set in last autumn, calculated to carry prices up to a figure again attractive to profit takers, or where the market will once more become overbought, as it probably was in the early part of April.

In one of these discussions published May 8, attempted bear prediction on the theory of the supposed distribution by "pools" and "syndicates" was deprecated. As a matter of fact, when a line is in process of formation it is the hardest thing in the world to tell either the nature of the selling or that of the buying. Both accumulation and distribution are at work, and no one can say which will ultimately exercise the greatest pressure. If it be permitted to criticize critics, it is submitted that stock market "pools"—the number of which is always exaggerated—do not

usually do their selling with a brass band.

It is clear from the averages that the stock market has resumed the major bull swing. Unless the present bull market is shorter than any of which we have record, it should run for many months, and possibly well into 1923. One thing which would be calculated to check it would be a serious return to dear money—not a mere temporary flurry, like that sometimes brought about by crop moving requirements. The tendency of money is rather the other way. It may be respectively submitted also even to the Comptroller of the Currency himself, that the market for money is an international affair and that its fundamental condition is not dictated by the Bank of England or the Federal Reserve Board.

There is no present or proximate danger of industry suffering from a diversion of capital to speculation in stocks. The speculation in stocks itself creates exactly the confidence which stimulates an expansion of general business. This is really only another way of saying that the stock market is a barometer, acting not upon the news of the day, but upon what the combined intelligence of the business world can anticipate. The prediction of better general business in sight is positive and trustworthy.

The Wall Street Journal: July 8, 1922

In the studies of the price movement, based upon Dow's theory, so successfully applied in The Wall Street Journal for the past twenty years or more, it has been repeatedly found that the two averages of twenty railroad stocks and twenty industrials must confirm each other to give an authoritative prediction. The railroads on July 6 gave a strong bull point, but it should be noted that an advance in the industrial average of nearly two and a half points would be necessary to confirm it.

Although the nature of the secondary decline in a primary bull market has been explained here time and again, and forms an illuminating part of the recently published "Stock Market Barometer," it still fails to make itself clearly understood and is frequently confused with a return to a primary bear market. With inconsiderable reactions the price of the industrial stocks advanced from 63.90, August 24, 1921 to 96.41 on May 29 of this year. The simultaneous movement of the railroads was from 65.52, June 20, 1921, to 86.83 recorded, like the last high of the industrials, on May 29, 1922.

Following the May high points, which were made after an interesting line of accumulation extending over a month, there was a typical, and therefore deceptive, secondary reaction. It carried the industrials down to 90.73, or a little short of six points, by June 12, 1922, while the railroads on the same date made a low for the reaction of 81.81, a recession of five points. Since then there has been the characteristic slow recovery of such a movement. The railroads may, therefore, be said to have partly established the fact of a resumption of the major bull movement by making a new high for themselves on July 6.

Secondary reactions result from technical conditions (like overbuying) and also from events which the market cannot possibly foresee. Major movements in the market precede and predict broad general changes in the business of the country. The secondary reaction, like a secondary rally in a major bear market, may be loosely called the stock market barometer's method of adjusting itself. Experience has proved that inferences drawn from a single group of stocks are easily deceptive, but become of the highest prediction value when the two averages confirm each other. If the twenty industrial stocks sold at 94.62 or better, it would be a positive indication, so far as all experience goes, that the bull market which set in in the latter part of last year was again in full swing and well calculated to advance much further.

With these provisos it may be said that the indication of the averages is distinctly bullish. The present bull market, dating from the low of the industrials in August, 1921, has not lasted a year, and the average length of the six bull markets in the past quarter of a century has been twenty-five months. The shortest of these was twenty-one months and the longest three years and three months. There is no good reason to suppose the market is not still predicting an expansion of general business, the extent of which we can hardly foresee.

The Wall Street Journal: July 22, 1922

THE PRICE INDEX

Expert readers of the stock market barometer see in it no evidence of a change in the move toward improvement. The price index also shows a healthy growth in business. It does not indicate anything like a boom, but instead a steady growth in improvement, notwithstanding the industrial disturbances.

More than two years ago, or about May, 1920, price deflation began in earnest. By June of the following year the general index of wholesale commodities, according to the Bureau of Labor, had fallen from its high point of 272 to 148. The greater part of this was at the expense of a few groups which bare the brunt of deflation, and business suffered because of the great inequality. But for months those groups have been approaching a common level. Some are still far out of line, yet they are being slowly adjusted, and now, after a year of fluctuation within a range of four points, the index for all commodities in June settled at 150, which is exactly the middle point between the two extremes since the first of June, 1921. A reasonable price stability is the conclusion.

The general index now ranges around 50% above the pre-war level. The steadiness with which it has held to within two points above or below that level justifies the reasoning that a return to pre-war prices is not to be thought of in the immediate future. Trade has been good, car loadings when the index was made were at the peak for the year, building active and a growing scarcity of all kinds of labor has been manifest. Even now optimism dominates the markets notwithstanding the coal and rail strikes, and this feeling is strengthened by a belief in foreign improvement.

There is concrete evidence of such an improvement abroad, and this means much in our price index. It means a market for all our surplus productions, especially farm products, foods and cotton. This group suffered the most seriously of any in the deflation process.

In consequence the purchasing power of a large percentage of the population was greatly reduced and in some instances destroyed. That group is slowly improving, with a June index at 131, compared with 114 the year before.

With the exception of cotton, farm production this year will be, not of record proportions, but large, and raised at comparatively low cost. The assurance of a good foreign market for the surplus is a strong argument in favor of good business and maintenance of price stability.

BARRON'S: July 24, 1922

THE PRICE MOVEMENT

On July 18 the action of the industrial averages in rising to 96.53 as against their previous high record of 96.41 established May 29 gave final confirmation to the correctness of the frequently expressed opinion that the action of the market for the past six weeks has been simply a normal and typical secondary reaction in a primary bull market.

The railroad averages had significantly pointed the way by registering a new high on July 6. A fortnight ago, it was declared in these columns:

"If the 20 industrial stocks sold at 96.42 or better, it would be a positive indication, so far as all experience goes, that the bull market which set in the latter part of last year was again in full swing and well calculated to advance much further."

In the discussions of the price movement based on Dow's theory of the averages that have appeared from time to time, it has been repeatedly noted that inferences drawn from the action of either one of the averages, while often significant, may easily be deceptive, but that the inferences become of the highest prediction value when the two averages confirm each other.

So it was that two weeks ago when the railroad averages alone had just gone to new high ground, it was possible to say that this was a strongly bullish indication which, if followed up, as it now has been, by a similar action on the part of the industrial averages, would amount to a positive indication of the continuance of the upward trend.

The average say that in spite of strikes and European unsettlements, the stock market found securities cheap on the June reaction and discounting all the well-known adverse factors now sees better business ahead.

The Wall Street Journal: August 1, 1922

A STUDY IN THE PRICE MOVEMENT

Whatever uncertainties may be created in the public mind by labor conditions and the shortage of coal, there is no question that the stock market has given and confirmed a highly consistent bull point. After a typical secondary reaction both the industrial and railroad averages have now recovered to figures above the points from which the reaction was made. On all experience this indicates a resumption of the major bull swing which has now been in operation since August of last year.

In the secondary reaction the industrials declined nearly six points and the railroads reacted a trifle more than five points. In the last study in these columns the railroads had recovered all their loss and made a new high in the major movement. This was, however, not at that time confirmed by the industrials although they were then well on the road to confirming the other average. It was said in that editorial of July 8 that:

"If the twenty industrial stocks sold at 96.42 or better it would be a positive indication, so far as all experience goes, that the bull market which set in the latter part of last year was again in full swing and well calculated to advance much further."

On July 18 the industrials confirmed the railroads at 96.53. It is true that there was a subsequent reaction in them of less than two points, but this is of small moment and does not, on any previous experience, take back the bull point. The action of the market in the past few days, so far as both averages are concerned, has amply justified the bullish inference. The market has run true to form in a way to convince any student of the price movement that all the bear influences were fully discounted in the typical secondary reaction and that the major bull market is again in full swing.

Broadly, it may be said that the

stock market automatically discounts everything it can foresee. It is saying as clearly as print can record it that the strike situation is reaching a settlement, that the damage to industry has been estimated and fully discounted and that a counterbalancing recovery in business is clearly foreseen. Secondary reactions are largely influenced by the element of surprise, but news once known is news discounted, so far as the stock market is concerned. Its business is to look ahead. It is not recording what business is now but what business will be in the coming year.

There is no pretense here to offer opinions on individual stocks. Active floor traders may still make occasional profits on reactions. But so far as the general market is concerned, the trader without that advantage seems certain to lose money on the short side.

BARRON'S: August 21, 1922

AN AUTHORITATIVE STOCK MARKET

Following its policy of more than twenty years, *The Wall Street Journal,* which has specialized in the study of the price movement as shown by the average of stock prices from day to day, refrains from discussing the market when there is nothing to say but "I told you so." On August 1 it pointed out that the industrial average had given an explicit bull point on the general market in confirming that previously disclosed by the railroad average. In spite of a downward fluctuation of over a point and a half in the railroads the bull movement since that date has been consistent, and the remarkable strength in the market in the face of obvious bear factors is worth more than passing comment. The key to its action was clearly set forth in the series of articles in *BARRON'S* on Dow's theory of the price movement, now published as "The Stock Market Barometer," in which Mr. Hamilton pointed out and reiterated from the example of past years that the market is never deeply influenced by passing events unless they are absolutely unexpected and, therefore, incalculable.

This is not to say that holders of railroad stocks did not sell in some cases where the railroad strike developments aroused distrust. This was probably the case in the downward fluctuation in the beginning of last week. But the much more important fact is that there were buyers ready to absorb the stock thus sold. The conclusion of "The Stock Market Barometer" holds good. Eliminating individual stocks and small groups only occasionally active for special reasons, the stock market moves not on considerations patent to everybody today—the railroad strike, the coal shortage, the complications in Europe the bewildered muddling of Congress, even the Congressional election in November—but upon what the combined intelligence and information of the whole country can see of conditions many months ahead. With the coal strike settled, production will rapidly catch up and the big crops must tell, even if such superficial bull arguments were not open to the same criticism as the bear arguments so frequently advanced during the course of a primary bull market.

But the stock market today is consistently justifying its unique position as a barometer of trade. Its interpreters might well say that the bear arguments were, as usual, discounted in the secondary reaction of over six points in the industrials and nearly eight points in the railroads, between June 12 and August 7, while the fundamental conditions making the primary bull market continue to rule. And with all its combined foresight it may be said that the market does not foresee the end of that great movement.

The Wall Street Journal: September 19, 1922

A STUDY IN THE PRICE MOVEMENT

Past experience has shown that the method of reading the stock market averages embodied in Dow's theory of the price movement, recently set forth in "The Stock Market Barometer" and used in these columns for twenty years or more, has attained a high degree of dependability and usefulness. The market barometer does not pretend to do the impossible. It forecasts, defines and confirms the major swings, like the bull market which has been in operation since August, 1921. It does not pretend to forecast the secondary reactions any more than it clearly foretells the corresponding rallies in a major bear market.

This is because the secondary reaction as distinguished from the major movement, is governed by the unexpected. The most important secondary reaction of which we have record, that in 1906, was mainly due to the San Francisco earthquake and fire. The most marked secondary reaction in the present bull market, that from May 29 to June 12, with a decline of nearly 6 points in the industrials and a little over 5 in the railroads, was accentuated by unexpected complications in the industrial and railroad labor situations. It will be noticed that the market was far ahead of events, as it always is where it can foresee them, because the rally was well established and the main advance well under way again before even the coal strike was settled.

On September 11 the industrials sold at 102.05 and the railroads at 93.99, since which time there has been a decline with a less settled feeling. There has also arisen, in the Near East, an uncertain factor, the efforts of which may or may not be far-reaching. For the present at least, no international banker can foresee what the Turks may do, and the possible action of the Russian Soviets is beyond the reach of all conjecture. These two elements may combine, and the result may well be disturbing in fanning anew the smouldering flames of war. It is strictly in character with the market's action that it should protect itself by a secondary reaction in a bull market to a point where the combined intelligence which influences all its movements can see its way to a resumption of a major movement which is certainly not over.

There is no use of disguising the seriousness of the situation in the Near East, but it has one important aspect of reassurance which may easily be overlooked. It must not be forgotten that the British Empire is far and away the greatest Mohammedan power in the world. There has been unrest in India and Egypt, and in other parts of the empire of which the average American never heard. But this unrest has unquestionably been allayed and brought under control, or the British Government would not have acted so decisively in the matter of Constantinople.

It is considerations like this which will ultimately govern the market, but the averages at present point rather in the direction of a secondary reaction. It may not carry far, or exceed that of the beginning of June. Technical conditions will decide, including the large underlying reservoir of credit available for conservative speculation, as the money now required for moving crops returns to the financial center.

BARRON'S: September 25, 1922

THE PRICE MOVEMENT

There is an aspect of the secondary movement of the stock market which might well be discussed more fully in the next edition of Mr. Hamilton's otherwise exhaustive analysis of the market movement, "The Stock Market Barometer." This may be described as a fundamental difference between the reaction in a bull market and the rally in a bear market. Each of these movements is secondary to the major swing, in Dow's theory of the market movement, but experience shows that they may occur for radically different reasons. The rally in a bear market is seldom or never dictated by external circumstances. It is almost invariably based upon an over-sold condition making the bear account vulnerable, aided by the courage of the most intelligent class of speculative investor, which grows (as it should grow) when the line of values is obviously below the line of prices.

But a secondary movement otherwise parallel, the reaction in a bull market like that at present operative in the Stock Exchange has almost invariably other things to consider than the mere circumstances of a top-heavy bull account. Such an account is of course a contributory cause, and its strength is tested by the occurrence of the unexpected—something which the combined intelligence of the stock market, having access to every source of information, could not foresee. It was remarked in Mr. Hamilton's book, and the analysis of the movement constituted the whole of one of his chapters when "The Stock Market Barometer" was published serially in these columns, that the San Francisco earthquake, coming on top of an over-extended bull account, was responsible for a secondary reaction in a bull market so serious that it almost amounted to a major swing.

This element of uncertainty was apparent in the previous secondary reaction of the present bull market, that which set in at the end of May and culminated in the middle of June. Unexpected complications arose in the labor situation, and a market which practically never goes down on a strike itself developed an uneasiness on these complications which was reflected in the average prices. This decline has been far more than recovered on September 11 when unsettlement again developed, becoming active, and almost menacing, on the war news from the Near East. This, at the close on September 21, had developed a recession of 3.68 points in the industrials and 2.63 points in the railroads, or a well-defined secondary reaction which might well carry further.

There is nothing in barometer reading to indicate how far a secondary rally may carry, but it clearly shows that the bull market is not over. The resumption of the primary movement will be shown when the averages pass the figures of September 11,—102.05 for the industrials and 93.99 for the railroads. It cannot be too often repeated that the stock market, while adjusting itself to the unexpected, as in the secondary reactions, is based not upon surrounding conditions but upon what may be expected as far ahead as the combined intelligence of the market can see. The present bull market has been in operation a little over a year, and the shortest bull market in a quarter of a century lasted for a year and eight months. It was not particularly strenuous, and above all it had not the present market's basis of an almost unlimited access to cheap money, even now despite seasonal crop-moving requirements.

The Wall Street Journal: October 18, 1922

A STUDY IN THE PRICE MOVEMENT

Any prophet may well feel nervous when his prediction comes off. It will be assumed that he knows what will happen next, and that is where prophets usually fall down. It may be said, therefore, that the study of the price movement of stocks, based upon a sufficient number of them to eliminate any possibility of manipulation, is not prophecy but deduction from reasoned premises. The principles upon which the stock market barometer is analyzed have been repeatedly set forth here. The stock market today, after a typical secondary reaction, is pointing nearly to the resumption of the major upward movement which developed in August, 1921.

To those not familiar with Dow's theory of the market movement it may be said that the closest analysis of the fluctuations day by day, year in and year out, over much more than a quarter of a century, shows well-defined primary and secondary movements giving meaning to the third or daily fluctuation of the average prices. A primary bull market has typical secondary reactions, exactly as a primary bear market is checked and steadied by rallies. The present bull market showed, last June, a reaction in both averages, giving each other the necessary confirmation, of from 5 to 6 points. When that reaction was recovered the major bull movement was resumed.

This was again interrupted, strictly according to precedent, by a secondary reaction from the high of September 11, 1922, of 5.75 points in the twenty industrials and of 4.39 points in the railroads. So far as the industrials are concerned, more than this decline had been recovered on October 14, At the time of writing the twenty railroad stocks are a fraction of less than half a point below the last high of September 11. On all previous experience the railroads would give the strongest possible bull point if the average rallied still further to 94 or better, thus confirming the tentative bull point given by the industrials on October 14.

It is unvarying experience that the two averages must confirm each other. The industrials may even react from the price of 103.43 of October 14, but if the railroads advance to 94 the bull point on the market will still be valid. There has never been a more consistent market movement among all those analyzed in Mr. Hamilton's now well-known and authoritative work on "The Stock Market Barometer" which shows how

The Wall Street Journal, for twenty years or more, has been able to foretell the broad stock market movement with astonishing fidelity.

There is no empiricism, to say nothing of quackery, about the method. The stock market would be meaningless to the point of chaos if it did not predict, some distance ahead, the course of the country's business. It is predicting now a consistent improvement lasting well into 1923, and it need hardly be said that Dow's theory is the simple but expert method of reading the barometer.

The Wall Street Journal: November 3, 1922

A STUDY IN THE PRICE MOVEMENT

A Boston student of the stock market price movement, as recorded in these columns by the averages of twenty industrial stocks for considerably over a quarter of a century, correctly points out the nature of the present secondary decline. He finds its true parallel in at least three of the seven bull markets analyzed in Mr. Hamilton's book on "The Stock Market Barometer." In each of those cases there was a moderate secondary reaction in a clearly defined major bull movement which was more than recovered, and later a more serious secondary reaction, more irregular, as represented pictorially on the chart, but also more than recovered before the primary bull market terminated. These movements can be seen in the bull markets of 1919, 1916 and 1906.

A number of students demand from the stock market barometer, which means the price movement read on Dow's theory of the triple market movement, a degree of mathematical and even pictorial accuracy which it neither possesses nor needs. Some of these have asked if the averages, which on Oct. 31 sold below the September 30 previous low point of the present secondary reaction, did not thereby indicate the termination of the major bull swing. The answer is, No. The Sept. price was made from an incomplete top on Oct. 14, when the industrials had made a new high but the railroads had failed to do so, once confirming the established rule

that the average indications are invariably deceptive when they do not corroborate each other.

There is a philosophy about the secondary reaction in a bull market which should not be overlooked in studying a system which is scientific, with no elements of empiricism or quackery. It has been remarked here before that such secondary reactions are started by developments which could by no possibility have been foreseen. These have their obvious effect upon an over-extended bull account. The market, therefore, proceeds to perform its most valuable service, that of insurance. It recedes to a safer level until it is entirely clear as to the nature of the unfavorable symptom which it cannot yet diagnose with certainty. Indeed, it may almost be said that a bear argument understood is a bear argument discounted. The present market has interrupted its primary direction upwards to protect its front from an attack, the nature of which it has not yet been able to estimate.

What that menace may be is any man's guess. There has been some disturbing selling of French holdings in Copper stocks lately, the cause of which is not entirely clear. Banks throughout the middle west have been carrying stock exchange securities in loans and there has been local calling of such loans in order to provide means to handle crops without calling money from New York. The collateral is liquidated in New York, however, and the stock market reflects it. More than one stock operator has been over-extended, and some connection has been traced between this fact and the way a projected steel merger still hangs fire. There may well be other points which have not been cleared up to the satisfaction of the market.

On all experience of the averages, however, the bull market which set in about August, 1921, is still the major and underlying influence. There is no evidence from the barometer that it has run its course and conjecture as to the length of that course would be valueless.

BARRON'S: January 8, 1923

"A PROPHET NOT WITHOUT HONOR—"

It is not true that, as a people, we are slow to recognize merit at home, although public opinion on what constitutes merit is apt to be erratic. Neither is it a good standing rule that a prophet is not without honor save in his own country. But readers of William Peter Hamilton's series of articles on The Stock Market Barometer, published in these columns and now attracting thoughtful attention in book form, will be interested to note that the first public recognition of what has been pronounced by good judges as the most illuminating ray of light yet cast upon speculation in stocks, its meaning and its teaching, comes not from the colleges here but from London. On the nomination of Sir William Acworth, K.C.S.I., seconded by Hartley Withers, one of the most distinguished of English economists, the editor of *The Wall Street Journal* has been nominated for a fellowship of the Royal Statistical Society and will be elected in due course, as nominations are not made to the British learned societies except on the assumption that the new Fellow will add lustre to the society.

This is the more remarkable as, both in method and conception, the reading of the stock market barometer, formulated in Mr. Hamilton's book, is essentially American and all its materials are American. It does not propound a theory and assume that the facts ought to corroborate it. It shows that the facts of the past twenty-five years have confirmed the theory and, also, how Charles H. Dow's theory of the price movement has been used by *The Wall Street Journal,* and is used today in these columns, logically and successfully to predict the course of the stock market, which in turn forecasts the course of business. These distinguished British economists found no difficulty in looking past what to them might seem a local set of facts to the principle involved, first clearly set forth in Mr. Hamilton's book. As the book itself says, the analysis of the stock market from the daily prices of one or more groups of stocks could be used as easily and as profitably in London as it is here, because the theory is sound of any great market.

Indeed, it is interesting to know that the Harvard Economic Service is adding a London service to its own in which twenty English industrial stocks are taken for the purpose of charting the indispensable line of speculation there. Whether the Harvard Service got the idea from Mr. Hamilton is of small moment, least of all, we may be sure, to that gentleman himself. England at any rate does not take without acknowledgment, and the Harvard Service used the line of speculation, presumably based, like the stock market barometer, on the Dow-Jones averages, from the time it was founded in 1919, while Mr. Hamilton's first article appeared in June, 1920.

The Wall Street Journal: January 16, 1923

A STUDY IN THE PRICE MOVEMENT

There is no reason to take back the opinion strongly expressed in this column that the stock market, as reflected by the averages of twenty industrial and twenty railroad stocks, is at present in an extended but by no means unprecedented secondary reaction in a bull market. The primary upward swing which set in for the industrials in August, 1921, from a low of 63.90 and in the railroads as early as June of that year with a low of 65.52, carried to 103.43 for the industrials in October last year and 93.99 for the railroads in the previous September. From those points the secondary reaction set in with a low of 92.03 for the industrials and 82.17 for the railroads, both made on November 27, 1922. At the beginning of the present month there had been a rally of over seven points in the industrials and about four points in the railroads.

What is particularly interesting, instructive and helpful about the study of the price movement on Dow's well-known theory, is the illuminating minor movement called the "line." At present this is beginning to make a most significant showing. A line may be said to have been started in the industrial stocks in the second week of last December, and for thirty consecutive trading days the industrial average has not been below 97 or above par. In the corresponding period the railroad stocks have shown equally significant limitations, within a point wider range, as for thirty-seven consecutive trading days the confirmatory railroad average has not been below 83 or above 87.

On deductions from Dow's theory, brought out in Mr. Hamilton's now well-known book on "The Stock Market Barometer," there is clearly indicated here a period of distribution or accumulation of stock, as the event may prove. Traders report what is called "good selling" and profess to see no equivalent buying, although long experience of the stock market would indicate that one of the indications of the best buying is the excellence of its disguise. Other things being equal, notorious "inside selling" is rather a bull argument. People with a lot of stock to distribute do not usually go about it with a brass band.

It is a question which may have an early solution, although the fear of a summer full of politics, with an intractable extra session of Congress, may make for an evenly-balanced opinion for some time yet. But if the industrial average touched par, with a simultaneous or near advance to 87 by the railroads, the showing would be positively bullish. A less positive inference might be drawn from an industrial average at 96 and a railroad average at 82. This would point to lower prices, but would by no means imply that the major bull movement had run its course. The impossibility of manipulating the entire average, so frequently pointed out in these columns and in Mr. Hamilton's book, should reassure the student of the market movement.

As it stands the position is highly interesting, with some unquestionably hopeful elements.

The Wall Street Journal: April 4, 1923

A STUDY IN THE PRICE MOVEMENT

On a volume of trading of less than a hundred thousand shares the average price of twenty active railroad stocks on Monday declined 1.31 points, giving something of an independent (and,

therefore, untrustworthy) bear point on the theory of a line of distribution. What is important to note in the market at present is that the averages have only confirmed each other in a deceptive way. The last consistent indication was when the industrials gave a bull point at 100 and confirmed it by an advance to 105, with a practically simultaneous bull point in the railroads at 87, confirmed at the same time by an advance above 90.

Since that time a new period of distribution or accumulation set in, but by no means so definite or clear. The fluctuations in the industrials between 105.38 and 101.51 and those in the railroads between 90.63, on March 3, and 85.84 on April 2, were wider than the three-point range of a line, and have not the same clear-cut inference of the early advance. That advance would have shown a resumption of the major bull market, which has now run for about a year and a half, if the railroad average had followed the industrial to a new high. But it failed to do so, and the only inference that can be drawn from the averages at present is that we are in another secondary reaction in a major bull market.

On previous experience it seems unlikely to be a prolonged or extended reaction. Like all secondary movements, it is influenced partly by the unexpected and partly by technical conditions, which include some temperamental critics of the market who will apparently be bitterly disappointed if the country does not go to smash in the near future. It has been pointed out in this column before that inflation talk is based entirely upon higher commodity prices. It is not confirmed by the conditions of currency, brokers' loans, inventories, buying by retailers, or even as yet, exorbitant labor demands and reduction in individual productive power. Discussion of the stock market, indeed, has taken a turn where the academic omniscience of the theorist from the classroom has had the usual effect of "a little learning." This country is not yet financed by gutta-percha dollars.

Every day brings its new experiences, but it is tolerably certain that we shall not have the record of a bull market in which the little speculators successfully liquidated at the top, getting their information from the comic strips in the newspapers. Criticism of the market seems to come mostly from those people who are nervously afraid of anybody making any money. Technically, the floating supply of stocks is small, and on a most moderate development of activity would probably be found inadequate.

The averages are giving no bear point such as would indicate a contraction of general business in the next six months. The professional is, in fact, more or less in charge and for the moment gets showy results on a small expenditure of brain matter with an almost nominal risk. The trader who looks further ahead would be inclined to think that the anti-inflationists make up in loquacity what they lack in knowledge.

The Wall Street Journal: April 27, 1923

WHY NOT LEAVE IT ALONE?

It has been demonstrated to the satisfaction of everybody not obsessed with what the French call the idee fixe, the irremovable false idea, that fears of stock market inflation are, to put it mildly, premature. In spite of the fact that ill-considered taxation drives floating capital out of its natural market, bankers are eager lenders of money and borrowers are indifferent. Retailers are buying from hand to mouth and production is limited by labor scarcity. In the meanwhile the stock market, which is just as sound a prophet when it is silent as when it is talkative, indicates steady business as far ahead as it can see.

Look at the figures of that barometer and remember that the market is always right, even though we cannot understand it at the time, for the reason that no power, not the U. S. Treasury and the Federal Reserve System combined could usefully manipulate forty active stocks or deflect their record to any but a negligible extent. During the present year there has been an extreme range of nine points in the industrials. They were above 96 in the middle of January, on the average of twenty active stocks and below 106 in the middle of March and are now rather above 101. In the same period, and at almost exactly the same dates, the railroads were above 84 in the middle of January, below 91 in the middle of March and now

above 86. Here is an extreme range of six points to nine in the industrials with a uniform movement or stability in both averages.

Tested over a quarter of a century, the Dow-Jones averages have shown that the stock market is six months or so ahead of the business of the country. The Harvard Economic Service, working back from the period of the war, shows a line of speculation in its reconstructed chart which exactly corroborates the evidence of the Dow-Jones Service, recorded at the time and used for barometrical inferences here for many years. Remember that this is a barometer and not a thermometer. People who are prematurely anxious to save a perfectly completed market from its head-off seem to think they are holding a lump of ice to the bulb of a thermometer. But an aneroid barometer is not responsive to an ice pick or a red hot poker. All they could do would be to put it out of kilter, and the school-room economics to which we have been asked to listen lately cannot even do that.

The stock market has been tested by all sorts of short selling and bear talk and its steadiness, as shown by the averages over a period of four months, is the answer. There is not the slightest indication that the major bull movement is over. Not only is there no danger of an "inflated" bull account, but in the strictest sense of the term there is never any such danger. The moment the market is really overbought, as it was in the autumn of 1919, there are plenty of people waiting for the opportunity to puncture it. It automatically deflates itself, months before the general business of the country realizes that there is something wrong.

No one need concern himself about preventing the stock market from going ahead too fast, although the Federal Reserve System is frequently asked to do that impossible thing. In the deflation of 1920 Wall Street had cleared its deck-load long before the rest of the country came to its senses and was therefore, as it always is, ready to help the rest of the country, as the comparative figures of The Federal Reserve Centers in the deflation year conclusively show.

The Wall Street Journal: June 13, 1923

A STUDY IN THE PRICE MOVEMENT

There is nothing at present to show that the stock market averages indicate that the major bull movement which developed from August, 1921, has spent its force. There has been a long, but by no means unprecedented secondary reaction in one of the slowest bull markets recorded, and it is to be remarked here that speed has a good deal to do with the question. Major bull and bear movements vary in length, but when they are violent they are usually relatively short, as all past experience shows. The present secondary reaction has been long and slow but is in neither respect unprecedented. There was a like secondary reaction in 1906, but what is there taken as the top of a long bull movement came at the end of that year, conspicuously in the case of the railroads.

Probably what has given rise to a number of uneasy letters from students of the averages is that the present secondary reaction in a way seems to have repeated itself. On May 21 both averages, after rallying to near the old high point, gave an indication of breaking through the last low point of November 27, 1922, when the industrials touched 92.03 and the railroads 82.17. Only one of the averages, in this case that of the twenty active railroads, went through the November low and a bear point by one not confirmed by the other has constantly proved misleading. In this case the inference was additionally doubtful from the fact that when the low point of the railroads was reached it was because the Louisville & Nashville stock dividend accounted for a loss in the railroad average of 2.68. Without this the figure would have been above the November low.

This is not to say that stock dividends or other large distributions affecting price value should not be remorselessly deducted, for the average would become meaningless unless it were established on a basis firm enough to meet any blow of fate. Obviously, if Louisville & Nashville distributes something of value, that something is no longer in the price of the stock or in the averages. It has been intelligently proposed that some equation should be devised to allow for extraordinary, and occasionally deceptive, influences such as this. The matter is extremely complicated and for the present, at least, is of somewhat academic interest.

As the averages stand now, the railroads are nearly two points above the November low and the industrials nearly four points better than that figure. To indicate definitely a resumption of the major bull movement, the latter would need to sell above the price of 103.43, the high of October 14, 1922, rather than 105.38, the high point of last March, unconfirmed by the railroad average. The railroads would need to cross 93.99, the high of September 11, 1922, and would at present prices have rather more than ten points to travel. Both movements are well within the scope of a market which seems to have been slowly gathering strength in the face of heavy realizing of a character seldom or never encountered at the top of a major bull swing.

It has often been said in this place, and is much emphasized in Hamilton's work on "The Stock Market Barometer," that the task of calling the exact top to a major movement is beyond the scope of any barometer. It is additionally difficult where there has been no inflated speculation. If the present bull movement terminates without such a development it will be for the first time in the history of the averages.

The Wall Street Journal: June 21, 1923

PSYCHOLOGY FOR THE MARKET

Probably there will never come a day when the layman will thoroughly understand a proposition so technical as the money market, its relation to a nation's business, its international implications and its sound barometer, the average of Stock Exchange prices as recorded from day to day. But unquestionably the general public is becoming more sophisticated, or at least better informed. It no longer believes, in any defective number, that it is possible for any individual or combination of interests to manipulate usefully forty active stocks.

Indeed, the barometer of the stock averages has proved so effective, thanks to a quarter of a century's interpretation in these columns, that it has come, in quarters which should know better, to be regarded not as a means but as an end in itself. There seems to be at present a campaign to influence the barometer in the direction of conservatism which can hardly be described as a product of far-seeing statesmanship. The weather cannot be affected by stirring up the aneroid with a red hot poker or swatting it with a chunk of ice. But there is a feeling that an active bull market at this time might have disagreeable consequences in the coming Presidential year. Intellectually it is about on a par with the idea that a more generous distribution to railroad stockholders should be avoided in order not to infuriate the forces of radicalism.

In every major bull market there are three well-known stages. The start of it is at a range of prices far below values. The second stage is an adjustment of present values involving those fluctuations called secondary reactions. The third and last stage of a major bull market is the discounting of possibilities which, human nature being what it is, tends inevitably to run to excess. It may be said of the stock market barometer, therefore, and of the major bull market which it has clearly indicated since August, 1921, that it has not yet begun to show signs of this third stage, while there never was a primary bull market which failed ultimately to do so.

BARRON'S: June 25, 1923

THREE STAGES OF A BULL MARKET

There is a substantial reason for a comment in Hamilton's "Stock Market Barometer" of which the present stock market is an excellent illustration. That accepted authority on the price movement frankly said that he did not attach great importance to "double tops" or "double bottoms." It had not been his experience, in the close analysis of the stock market movement for twenty-five years, that mere mathematical data, unsupported by psychological considerations and influenced to some extent by accidents, as, for instance, the deduction from the railroad averages of the Louisville & Nashville stock dividend, could or ought to be authoritative. It may be pointed out that the stock market as set forth by the averages offers a method of forecast which appeals to a higher type of reasoning and, indeed, discloses why the multitude of cranks who work out mechanical assumptions are so untrustworthy and so uniformly wrong.

Not only in the past quarter of a century but obviously in any great major bull market which existed anywhere, at any time, there were three well defined stages in its progress. The preceding bear market had driven securities far below their acknowledged worth, for the good reason that the Stock Exchange presented a market for them at some price where the market for other things had disappeared altogether. It is part of the barometrical effect of the stock market that it must necessarily be the first to feel the pressure of general liquidation.

In the first stage of a bull market, then, there is a return to known values. In the second stage, and often the longest stage, there is an adjustment to these values as they become more stable with improving general business, and it is this period which most frequently sees the longest and most deceptive secondary reactions in a major bull market. The third stage of the market is equally clear and is still to be anticipated in the present market, unless all records fail. This is the stage where general confidence is discounting not merely present values but future possibilities.

In the bull market which developed from August, 1921, we have seen completed the first stage, together with a part at least of the next stage, the adjustment to values, but we have yet to see the final stage when that judgment has engendered general confidence with a movement to buy stocks on the problematic developments of the future. It may also be said that each of these stages is subsequently reflected in the current of general business.

It is almost morally certain that no bear market has ever been generated by such a condition as exists at present. There must be some sort of eminence to fall from, and no one gets seriously hurt rolling back down a gentle slope.

BARRON'S: July 2, 1923

IN DEFENSE OF THE AVERAGES

In its Sunday edition of June 24 The Boston Herald indulges in a shallow criticism of the Dow-Jones averages, used for so many years by *The Wall Street Journal* and *BARRON'S*. Its obvious point of attack is the twenty active industrial stocks and its complaint is that these are of a higher quality than some which have been more active in the market. It claims that there are ten of this conservative sort in the average and if more of the comets of a season were included, a wider fluctuation in the average would be shown and, presumably, some of the critic's bearish views would be more adequately confirmed.

The point is not well taken. The twenty active industrial stocks average something else besides price. Obviously, as the years go on, they average quality. When one of them, through character and good management, becomes a completely investment security and automatically retires from the speculative market, a more active stock is substituted. The violent fluctuations to which this critic refers are made by stocks of the character of Stutz Motor, which, so far as the average is concerned, are meteors and not dependable and measurable stars.

So long as the twenty stocks are really active, every requirement of the average is fulfilled. They reflect the real market, the average market, and not its violent extremes, and this is exactly what the average is intended to do. Frequent changes, and particularly those of new and feverishly active issues used in substitution for stocks with a steady market, would throw the whole average out of kilter.

In matters much more serious we have too many citizens like our critic who must be forever tinkering with a competent machine. Our politicians are fond of pulling up their carrots to see how they are growing. The stability of the stocks in the Dow-Jones average is itself a testimonial to the wisdom with which they were chosen and a guarantee of the sound construction of the barometer of which they form a part.

BARRON'S: July 30, 1923

SOME BAROMETER READERS

If one point was more completely and constantly stressed than another in a series of articles in *BARRON'S* published during the latter part of 1921 on "The Stock Market Barometer," it was that Dow's theory of the price movement was not a system of beating the stock market or in any way a guide to speculators in individual stocks. The desire to get something for nothing is, however, so widespread that *BARRON'S* and *The Wall Street Journal,* the first exponent of Dow's theory of the price movement, were bombarded with letters from speculators during the recent decline in the stock market. They would generously be called investors here, on the slightest evidence, but for the fact that the moment the market turned and showed strength on the upward side the flow of critical, and even abusive, correspondence immediately ceased. There is an important inference to be drawn from this phenomenon. It is that the overwhelming majority of speculators are, or would like to be, on the bull side.

In Mr. Hamilton's book it was pointed out that the prediction of a declining market was a thankless task. It was certain that people of unequal mental development, unable to reason from cause to effect, would inevitably blame the prophet for the subsequent decline. The hope that springs eternal in the human breast is in its nature never a sentiment of pessimism. Neither *BARRON'S* nor *The Wall Street Journal* ever gave a tip on an individual stock in the market or did more than indicate present general tendencies with future possibilities and dangers.

But the man who picks the wrong stock for a speculative purchase, or, more rarely, the right stock at the wrong time, must always find someone else to blame for his defective judgment. He has no use for the stock market as a barometer of the country's business. He believes he can make money by reading the barometer first and reading the business afterwards, or not studying it at all. Is it still a hopeless task to tell him that he should exactly reverse the process? It has recently been demonstrated, at Wellesley Hills, that the attempt to do both things leads to inextricable confusion.

The Wall Street Journal: August 29, 1923

A NEW FACTOR IN THE AVERAGES

A noticeably large number of letters has been received from readers of The Wall Street Journal asking for an analysis of the averages and in interpretation of apparent eccentricities in the stock market barometer not explained in its history during the past twenty-five years. Studies in the price movement would be oftener published in this place if it were not that readers of such discussions forget that the average prices are analyzed as a barometer of business, but not as a guide to those speculating in stocks.

It was because such discussions had been placed, by people who should know better, on a footing with the forecasts of mere stock tipsters, whether calling themselves analysts or not, that it was felt that such discussion might be profitably suspended for a time. The Wall Street Journal is not competing in any such field. But there is a reason why the barometer in the past few months has been deflected by an influence not felt before in a major bull market. This influence undoubtedly is the cumulative effect of the income surtax.

Brokers can tell how steadily the dividend paying common stocks, representing thirty out of the forty taken in the two averages, have been sold by large holders on any development of comparative strength. It is correct to call this a new factor, although it has been germinating since the bull market started in the autumn of 1921. The whole theory of the stock market barometer is based upon the assumption that pressure on stocks can only forecast coming liquidation of general business. But here, for the first time in the history of the averages, is a pressure of stock for sale which bears no reference to coming events.

It is as though a hot coal or a lump of ice had been applied to the bulb of a thermometer. If it is too much to hope that Congress may see a return to sanity in taxation, this is a condition which will nevertheless cure itself, but only over a period of time beyond present calculation. That stage will be reached when every one of the twenty active railroad common stocks and the twenty industrials is as widely held as the stock of the Pennsylvania Railroad, where the average holding is round about fifty shares per stockholder.

A rich man cannot afford to hold a common stock returning him six per cent. on its cost. Not only is he liable to see more than half of the return deducted by the tax-gatherer. Such a holding pulls up the tax he must pay on all his other income. He, therefore, has been a steady seller for many months past, and this is "inside" selling with a vengeance. It is well-informed selling, in a way, but obviously it need not predict the general course of business. Congress, in imposing impossible taxes, has not merely laid a handicap on the country's business. It has falsified the very barometer of business.

Will our readers therefore take it that this is why the averages at present are unenlightening or even misleading? Mr. Hamilton's book on "The Stock Market Barometer" was written in the lowest depths of the last bear market, and published serially in *BARRON'S* in the last few months of 1921. It correctly forecast the ensuing bull market. It could not forecast the destructive effect of bad taxes, because at the time it was written such taxes were regarded as merely temporary and likely to be repealed in due course with other emergency measures which had survived the Great War.

BARRON'S: October 15, 1923

A LINE IN THE AVERAGES

Premising that the pressure of selling of dividend yielding railroad and industrial stocks, in order to exchange into tax-exempt bonds, may well have impaired the barometrical value of the Dow-Jones averages, it is still interesting to note that a line of accumulation or distribution has for some time past been in process of formation, particularly in the railroad average, and may have considerable bearing on the future course of the market, according to the way it ultimately works out.

For sixty trading days past, or since August 4, the average price of twenty active railroad stocks has not been below 77 or above 81. The upper limit extends considerably further back, indeed, as far as the beginning of July. The action of the twenty industrial stocks, while partly confirmatory, has not been quite so definite or so long. Since, however, that average broke from above 92 to below 90 on September 13 there has been a line with a range of about four points, once emerging above 90 but taking back the bull point, if any, and not at any time touching a figure below 87. A price of 81 for the rails confirmed by 91 for the industrials would be bullish.

This, judged by both averages, seems sufficiently definite and significant to justify the assumption that prices have reached a figure where a large class of comparatively small investors are willing to accumulate. In the case of stocks at least this demand implies a supply, and it may be assumed that larger holders have been selling irrespective of possible business developments, even of the most favorable kind, in order to get away from the tax-gatherer. If all these common stocks were held as the stocks of Pennsylvania, United States Steel or even Great Northern are held, the influence of tax-exempt bonds on the averages would cease to be as serious a factor as it undoubtedly is at present.

The politicians are denouncing tax-exempt bonds on the one hand and dishonestly encouraging their issue on the other, being unable to resist the temptation to squander. They cannot make this action square with their policy of maintaining a prohibitive income surtax, and it is to be remembered that the incoming Congress is in this respect more radical than the old one. Secretary Mellon correctly says that a reduction in the surtax would greatly increase revenue. The stimulus to business and prosperity would be enormous, and one of its effects would be, almost inevitably, the development of an aggressive bull market in stocks.

BARRON'S November 5, 1923

A LINE IN THE AVERAGES

In our issue of Oct. 15 the significant line in the stock market averages was discussed in these columns. In such a discussion the effect of the continual transfer of investment from dividend-paying stocks to tax-exempt bonds may be to some extent disregarded. Whatever the reason for the selling may be, whether induced by a faulty system of taxation or fears of the business outlook, the fact remains that the saturation point is reached and the indication is bearish if there is a break below the line, subject to the old and safe rule that the railroad average should confirm the industrial. When the technical condition was last discussed, for sixty trading days the average price of twenty active railroad stocks had not been below 77 or above 81 and, indeed, the upper limit extended as far back as the beginning of July. The industrial line was not so long as this, but from Sept. 13 the average price had fluctuated within a range of about four points and had not broken below 87.

It was then argued that a rally above 81 for the rails confirmed by 91 for the industrials would be bullish, while a price below 86 for the industrials would be bearish if it were confirmed by a price below 77 for the rails, which had not sold at that figure since Aug. 4. This price for the rails has been closely approached several times recently, while the industrials actually broke a trifle below 86 but took back the bear point in the rally following the declaration of the extra Steel common dividend.

Until and unless this rally develops sufficient momentum to carry the averages through the limits mentioned above, 81 for the rails and 91 for the industrials, it fails to have any important technical significance in settling the question whether the line has been one of accumulation or one of distribution.

Students of the averages will watch their course for the next few days with much interest. If the result of this new optimism is an important volume of constructive buying, the market may reasonably be expected to work out of its rut on the up side and head for higher prices, but if the buying that so sharply advanced prices on the unexpectedly favorable developments in Steel represented nothing more than the run to cover by timid shorts and no important purchasing for the long account is stimulated, the chances would favor the bearish view.

The Wall Street Journal: February 4, 1924

Stock tipping had become so prevalent up to the last top in the averages as

shown in March, 1923, that the use of
the stock market barometer was somewhat reluctantly dropped in this column, although its value to those who
have to consider the trend of general
business remains unimpaired except as
affected by tax-exempt bonds and the
income surtax. There was no desire here
to appear in competition with Mr. Babson and the less sanctified minor prophets. It was because discussions on the
price movement in *The Wall Street
Journal* were construed as stock tips
that they were abandoned.

On the method of reading the averages which is known as Dow's theory,
the stock market is in a major bull
movement, after the shortest bear movement of record, one barely lasting eight
months. So far as the low of the present movement is concerned, it would
presumably date from November 1; but
the bull point was given after both the
industrial and railroad averages had
made one of the most consistent lines of
accumulation on record, emerging on
the bull side last December. The railroad stocks lagged, probably indicating
a sufficiently well justified fear of Congress.

BARRON'S: March 10, 1924

AMENDING THE BAROMETER

A distinctly important amendment to
the accepted method of reading the
stock market barometer has been suggested and is well worth discussion. It
is based upon that condition of dullness
which supervened after the great upward movement of the beginning of the
century. From 1909 to 1914 it could be
held, with some show of reason, that the
larger fluctuations in the stock market
averages were not sufficient to indicate
either a major bear movement or a
major bull movement.

The period taken in Mr. Hamilton's
book, "The Stock Market Barometer,"
was one of twenty-five years to the end
of 1921, when a great bear movement
had terminated, as the book clearly and
correctly showed. It is to be admitted
that the movement in the five years here
instanced was not important either way.
But it is to be remembered that the
length and extent of major swings adds
a great deal to the prediction value of
the barometer. There is no rule to indicate exactly how many points constitutes a major swing, any more than
there is a rule to define the extent of
business expansion or depression which
the movement predicts.

What is to be gained by importing
such a refinement into the reading of
the averages? It suits a good many people, with what may be called a fifty-
fifty attitude of mind, to use phrases
like the following, taken from one of a
number of market letters by brokerage
houses—"All chance of a further general upward movement in stocks this
spring can be dismissed from consideration, although indications point to a
continuation for a time of the present
fair business activity." That is an impressive way of saying nothing. It is
true that in some latitudes a ship's
barometer hardly changes from day to
day for long periods of time. But in the
latitude of American business there
would be little use for a barometer commonly at "set fair," still less a barometer at set fair to middling.

The instance of inactivity cited is the
only one of record, and the barometer is
really vindicated because the narrow
and slow fluctuations in the averages
reflected in advance narrow and slow
changes in business. Only with years of
further experience would it seem necessary to add this balancing amendment
to the constitution of our barometer.

BARRON'S: April 7, 1924.

A "LINE" IN THE AVERAGES

Students of the stock market averages may very well have noticed that
when the twenty industrials and the
twenty railroads make what is technically called a line, a fluctuation for
a measurable period confined to a range
of three or at most four points, an unconfirmed bull or bear tip by one of
them sometimes gives the reverse of the
bearish or bullish indication when the
change for the better or worse is shown
by both averages. A "line" may be
roughly taken to indicate distribution or
accumulation. The advance above it
means that the floating supply of stock
in the market has been exhausted and
is dependably bullish if one average
confirms the other. On the downward
side the same indication marks what
might be called saturation point, and,

as in the weather, precipitation follows.

Between the middle of February and the middle of March, or for rather more than a month, the industrials did not touch 95 on the down side or 99 on the upper border and during that time the railroads never quite reached 83 or 79. But the two averages parted company. The industrials gave a bear point at 95 and since sold in the neighborhood of 92. They have, in fact, reacted about three-fifths of the distance from the top above 101 towards the low point of 85 in November.

This is a true secondary reaction and would be entirely consistent with a major bull market starting with last November, in spite of the inconsiderable fluctuation of the railroads. The line there has been quite remarkable, as the averages has not been so high as 83 or so low as 79 since January 15. This is an interesting condition and one where a line in one average may have a little more than its usual significance. If, for instance, the secondary reaction in the industrials has been arrested, 83 or better for the railroads might well be bullish on both stocks and could forecast a definite resumption of the major bull movement for the whole market.

It may be said that the enemy's fire has been concentrated on the industrial group while the railroads have been marking time and not under serious pressure, within a range of less than three points. There may well, therefore, have been accumulation of the latter, which are certainly below the line of value, while the industrials seem to have been sold to a standstill. The railroad average, particularly, will bear watching, and 83 or over would be a bull point, while sales below 80 would indicate that the secondary reaction was not over.

The Wall Street Journal: April 29, 1924

THE STOCK MARKET BAROMETER

A reader asks:

"Are we in a bull or a bear market, based on your interpretation of the stock market averages?"

It was the custom in these columns for many years to discuss the stock market barometer for its value in predicting the course of general business. After the publication of Mr. Hamilton's text-book on the subject, "The Stock Market Barometer," there was a popular disposition to take such discussions as being intended for speculative purposes, a sort of guide to margin trading.

Neither that book nor the articles published here had any such intention. There are plenty of such tipsters, sanctimonious or frankly mercenary, and *The Wall Street Journal* is not competing in their field. The Stock Market averages, however, make an interesting showing, although their prediction value for the moment is not great.

One of the first and most remarkable features is that the twenty active railroad stocks since the first week in August have not sold below 77 or as high as 84. Here is the most remarkable line either average has ever made, for there is an extreme fluctuation of less than seven points over a period of nearly nine months. While a "line" is in the making it is dangerous to predicate either accumulation or distribution. Both processes may be going forward at the same time; but there is some evidence of a broad distribution into the hands of the relatively small investor. The floating supply in the market seems small.

On the basis of Dow's theory of the price movement it would be possible to infer a bear market from the beginning of 1923, turning to a major bull movement about November 1, more particularly marked in the industrial average. Between the low point of 85 at the end of October and the high of 101 there was a range of 16 points, with what may well be a secondary reaction carrying the price below 90, followed by a rally which at least has not been contradicted by the railroad stocks. It has been truly said that the market is influenced by the sum of what it can foresee. It must be obvious, also, that it is influenced by what it cannot foresee, as, for instance, the vagaries of Congress.

In spite of reports of contracting general business in various directions the condition is not incompatible with a rather slow bull market showing narrower fluctuations than in earlier years. It is at least tolerably certain that neither average can be called high in relation to any line of values on yield of the stocks in the averages and surplus available for dividend. What the averages seem to say about general business is that it might be expected to improve with reassurance about taxation.

The Wall Street Journal: May 24, 1924

LOOKED AT FROM THE AVERAGES

From the point of view of the stock market averages, regarding them strictly as a barometer of business and not as a guide to margin trading, the business outlook is uncertain. There was a promise when the present session of Congress opened of early and intelligent tax legislation; that business generally would improve, and the stock market shared that hope. It may be laid down as a broad and sound principle that a barometer predicts just what a barometer can foresee, taking a longer view than the aneroid, because the trading in stocks represents everybody's knowledge of the future. No one could have foreseen what Congress would do to the business of the country in the six futile months of its present session.

But at least the averages do not say that business is going to smash. Following a rally from the first of November which carried the industrial stocks from a fraction below 86 to something above 101 there has been a steady and discouraging reaction since the middle of February, or rather over three months, which has lost all but two points of that gain. If there had been a corresponding secondary reaction in the railroad average the inference would be bearish. But the railroad average, so far from sharing this secondary decline, has recorded the most surprising line in its history. Since August 4 the extreme fluctuation has been less than seven points.

Since the middle of December, or for six months, the average price of twenty active railroad stocks has not been as low as 78 or as high as 84, a range of less than six points. For nearly three months past the range has been less than five points. Since early in April the line has still further narrowed within a range of about three points and the price is now nearer the high than the low point of this long period of accumulation or distribution than at any time since the beginning of April.

It seems a clear inference, in a movement where the averages do not confirm each other, that uncertainty still continues as concerns the business outlook, with an underlying confidence reflected in the railroad stocks, where the buying must necessarily have been largely for that most stable of all purchasers, the small investor. The line there is distinctly below any line of values which could be computed from dividend yield plus the undistributed surplus. The business outlook in a presidential year is normally uncertain, and pronounced market movements do not occur in such years. Congress has made the outlook more uncertain than ever, and the business barometer is saying exactly that.

Certainly the averages give no explicit bullish or bearish indications. They do not seem to indicate what might be called a safety level, and the much reduced brokers' loans sufficiently show that the market is not vulnerable so far as the speculative position is concerned. The bonus bear raid on the market seems significantly unfruitful.

BARRON'S: June 9, 1924

A STRONG BASIS IN THE AVERAGES

While the stock market averages at present throw little light on the Major movement, the extraordinary "line" made by the railroad stocks is well worth note. Since the middle of January that average has not been so low as 79 or so high as 84. This is a range of less than five points, and since May 1 the range has been contracted to less than three points. Indeed, since the beginning of November the range has been less than six points. Opinions may differ as to whether this line indicates accumulation or distribution, or both, but it is clear that from the small volume of brokers' loans the floating supply of stocks cannot be large. An average price of 84 or better would be distinctly bullish, as indicating that stocks had gone into hands so capable of carrying them that a substantial advance would be in order before an adequate floating supply would check the advance.

On a broad reading of the averages there could be no better basis for a bull market, and at least the industrials do not contradict. The average there is more than four points above the new low of the secondary movement which carried the price down from above 101 early in February to below 89 in May. Considering the distracting effect of congressional uncertainties upon the general business of the country, it may at least be said that an impartial reading of the stock market barometer would point to fair weather with a tendency to improvement. The barometer predicts all it can, but Congress itself could not predict what it would do next. Indeed, its unfailingly popular prediction is the announcement of its intention to adjourn. That announcement has certainly been accompanied by a development of stock market strength from what looks like one of the soundest foundations in the history of the averages.

The Wall Street Journal: June 13, 1924

AN INDICATION IN THE AVERAGES

It is a year since the average price of twenty railroad stocks recorded the figure of 84. It was, in fact, in the early part of June, 1923, that this point was reached with a rally from below 81 which did not hold. Since August 4 of last year, however, the railroad average had not been as low as 75 or as high as 84. Since the middle of January it has not touched 78 or crossed 84 until the advance of June 11. There has, in fact, been a "line" for six months past, within the narrow range of four points, and the average has now emerged on the upward side.

In discussing the stock market barometer in this place, not for tips on the stock market but for its forecasting value as regards to business of the country, it has always been pointed out that the averages should confirm each other. There has been no such corresponding line in the industrial stocks, although something of the kind has been forming since early in April, with a range of rather over five points, and the industrials are now close to the upper side of that line. What is significant in the barometer is what the railroad average has done, or, perhaps more exactly, has not done, without contradiction by the industrials.

A little thought will show no paradox in saying that accumulation and dis-

tribution mean nearly the same thing. With the present public investment interest in the market what looks like accumulation by the line in the averages has really been a wide distribution into the safe hands of the small investor. In the old days there was such a thing as buying for accumulation by a single interest or small group of interests. But the days of capturing the control of a railroad by purchase of the stock in the public market have gone by. The railroad stocks have been bought on their investment value, dividend or no dividend, and it is significant that any line of value calculated upon the actual dividends and the surplus available for distribution would, at present, be much above the average price of the railroad stocks.

This is a good sign because it shows that the vagaries of Congress in the past six months have not disturbed the confidence of the permanent investor and this argues an underlying confidence in the general business of country. It may even be that the tax bill as finally passed into law has stimulated the small investor, with a maximum income from all sources of not more than $10,000 a year and perhaps much less. This is not to say that the Mellon plan would not have been better for him, for it would have tended to give him a cost of living a thousand dollars lower as against a reduction in income tax of a tenth of that amount.

Whatever the varying causes may have been, the bull point in the railroad averages is an uncommonly cheerful sign. The course of the market after it was recorded seems to indicate that a higher level would have to be established in order to provide a floating supply of stock equal to growing investment requirements.

The Wall Street Journal: July 15, 1924

CHEAP MONEY AND THE BAROMETER

As quoted by the Cleveland Trust Co., its vice president, Leonard P. Ayres, has decided to scrap the Stock Market Barometer. He says:

"It now appears that stock prices, as well as bond prices, are determined by current interest rates, and not by the discounting of future business prospects, long regarded as the determining factor of stock market movements."

That is a plausible generalization and its only defect is that it is not true. If dearer money does not reach stringency rates stocks will advance when other factors are favorable. If money is as cheap as it was in the years between the panic of 1893 and the revival of 1896–7, stocks will not advance. In the past 25 years there have been bull markets with stiff money rates and low money rates. In 1894 the Bank of England rate went to the irreducible minimum of 2 per cent., and continued at that figure for nearly two years. Foreign money was easily obtainable here, but no bull market was stimulated, although London had a boom in Transvaal gold shares in 1895.

Colonel Ayres makes his narrow deduction no better by proposing to found a new barometer upon the record of pig iron furnace operations. The Stock Market Barometer takes account of dear money and pig iron furnace operations, together with crop prospects, grain prices, bank clearings, merchants' collections, political prospects, foreign trade, savings bank figures, wages, volume of railroad freight and a hundred and one other things. The average price of active stocks is the result of all this, impartially reflected in a market which no interest is big enough to influence. The Stock Market Barometer at present is predicting better business ahead.

It is able to do this because it reflects all that everybody knows about everything. When a large manufacturer sees bad times ahead he sells securities to put himself in a strong financial position and he is only one of thousands. The stock market declines long before the emergency develops which he and others foresaw. Cheap money is a good bull argument on stocks only if the price level is attractive and if the multitude of other influences are favorable.

In the stock market the thing everybody knows is not news, and ceases to influence business. Everybody knows that money is cheap. The market reflects a multitude of facts, each of which only a few people know, and each, like Colonel Ayres, knows about his own business, in his case banking. It is to the credit of this new prophet that even if it be only pig iron furnaces he can see something beyond the walls of his bank.

It would be for the benefit of himself and that institution if he devoted a little real study to the Stock Market Barometer before he does away with it.

BARRON'S: August 11, 1924

A STUDY IN THE AVERAGES

All students of the stock market averages will agree that a resumption of the major bull market, after a somewhat one-sided and prolonged secondary reaction, is now in operation. There was a major bear market with all the usual characteristics and marked only by its brief length, from the middle of March, 1923, to the beginning of the following November. Technically the railroads did not actually make their low on that date. It may be pointed out that, on the accepted theory of reading the barometer, a low or high point for both averages on the same day, or even in the same week, is merely a coincidence when it happens to occur. The early stages of the present bull market were sufficiently characteristic even if the industrials tended to recover faster than the railroads. Taken as the sum of all possible knowledge of future events, the stock market can forecast only what it can foresee. It was impossible for the united intelligence of everybody to say what the late Congress would do next, or what the effect of its dilatoriness and obstruction would be upon the business of the country.

In spite of its length, the secondary reaction of the industrials from above 101 in February, 1924, to below 89 in May, followed by a recovery which has carried the average above the last high, was a typical movement and by no stretch of the imagination could it have been divided into two major movements, even if it lasted nearly six months. What was unusual was that while the railroad stocks did not advance against the general current, they made a remarkable line, fluctuating within a range of less than five points, while the industrial average declined thirteen points. This further minimized the importance of the secondary reaction in the industrials and made the resumption of the major bull movement, beginning in May and becoming definitely marked by the middle of June, all the more convincing. It may be recollected, not with any futile "I told you so" implication, that on each of these occasions the true tendency of the market was correctly pointed out in these columns.

How far the primary bull movement will continue is anybody's guess. It is not worth scientific discussion in this place. There is no intention here of giving tips on the market or of treating the averages as anything else but a barometer of general business. That barometer is unquestionably forecasting better times before the end of the year and may well have a bearing on the result of the Presidential election.

The Wall Street Journal: August 28, 1924

INDUSTRIALS AND THE AVERAGES

A Baltimore reader, wisely skeptical about amateur interpretation of the stock market averages, puts his finger on a piece of false reasoning which has had some circulation in the financial pages of general newspapers. This is that the average price of twenty active industrial stocks having recorded a point of 105.57 on Aug. 20—this being the highest point since the inflation bull market of 1919, with two major bear markets and a completed major bull movement intervening—have necessarily reached the top and should accordingly be sold.

There can be little difficulty in shooting that kind of reasoning full of holes. The circumstances are not parallel. The bull market of 1919 is convincingly quoted in Hamilton's "Stock Market Barometer" as the exception that proves the rule. All the speculation in that market was in the industrial stocks. The railroad stocks were under government ownership, control and guarantee. It was not thought at that time that they would ever go back to private ownership. Railroad stocks were held for fixed income, the yield of the government's guarantee. They actually declined, with the bond market, while the industrials were soaring, because securities held for fixed income tend to decline when the cost of living is inflated and advancing.

In 1919, therefore, there was an inflation bull market in the industrial stocks which carried the industrial average to

118.92. This was followed by a precipitous decline in a major bear movement lasting nearly two years. Industrials in 1919 had so monopolized speculation, in an exceptional market not likely to recur, that they were selling far above the line of valuables. They were accordingly deflated in a way the farmer never was and, indeed, gave the unheeding farmer and his friends a barometrical warning of what was coming.

But it cannot be said that industrial business today is inflated or that, on consideration of earning available for dividend and actual yield, the present price is even above the line of value. It might much more truly be said that the average price of 85.76 in October, 1923, or of 88.33 last May had discounted any possible inflation and left a sound basis for the present bull market. Values of the industrial corporations today are not represented by bloated inventories but by positive value and productive power stripped to its true worth. How far the present bull movement may run, after the secondary reaction of the past few days has been recovered, the stock market barometer does not pretend to predict.

But the idea of selling the industrials short on a purely imaginary double top of this and the last bull market has its only basis in a fallacy.

The Wall Street Journal: September 11, 1924

A STUDY IN THE PRICE MOVEMENT

Students of the stock market averages, following the method of reading their indications which is known as Dow's theory, must have been struck by the way in which they are running true to form. Although Charles H. Dow died at the end of 1902, he could hardly have desired a clearer example to make his point than the present secondary reaction in a major bull market. From May 20 of this year to Aug. 20, almost exactly three months, the industrial average advanced from 88.33 to 105.57, or rather better than 17 points. In the same period, to within two days, the twenty active railroads advanced from 81.37 on May 20 to 92.65 on Aug. 18, or better than 11 points.

Since that time the twenty industrials

have reacted to 100.76, or not quite 5 points, and the railroads to 88.78, or rather under four points, or roughly about 30 per cent. of each average. Even the day before the result of the Maine election was known there was a rally in both averages. Technically, anything over 92.65 would be strongly bullish on the railroads as would also a corresponding recovery by the industrials, and the two together, or within a few days of each other re-establishing the high points of Aug. 18 and 20 for the railroads and industrials respectively, would indicate an authoritative resumption of the major bull movement.

More than twenty years' experience in discussion of this kind has taught that the secondary reaction in the market, superficial in itself, is not governed by the same laws as those which obtain in the major bull movement of which they are a characteristic part. The reaction in a bull market resembles only in direction and not in kind the true primary bear movement. As students know, the averages are by all odds the most impartial barometer of business. The present major bull market forecasts a resumption of commercial and industrial activity now well in sight. The reasons for a secondary reaction are largely technical.

To ascribe that minor movement to last week's uncertainty on the Maine election is a matter of market convenience. Anxiety on that account might have produced a little selling even in the face of the startling betting odds on Coolidge of four to one. Wall Street looks around for reasons when the market sells off and rather weakly concludes that a poor reason is better than none. In the course of any primary advance the bull account goes stale, and the professional element is testing it for weakness all the time.

What can safely be inferred is that the major bull movement is not over. The indications given by the three months advance are still in force, nor would they be called in question except by a severe reaction after failure to re-establish the high prices of both averages made in the third week of August.

The Wall Street Journal: November 12, 1924

A LEGITIMATE BULL MARKET

There is no such conservative as the man who has been wrong about an incipient bull market and sees all his pessimistic guessing falsified. Here is a comment which appears, most improperly, in the general news section of a New York daily:

"How long the present violent market will last is a matter of speculation. In many conservative banking quarters it is believed that the market has been traveling too fast and that, while in potential value most stocks are worth what they are selling for, there is danger of the markets getting out of hand.

"Should the 'boiling' markets continue, it is suggested that banking institutions and wealthy individuals will furnish a volume of sales that will serve as an actual brake to speculative enthusiasm. Another probability is that some sort of artificial brake, possibly through the money market, will be imposed."

There never was a more legitimate bull market than that which is foreshadowed in the Dow-Jones Averages, by the new high points on November 8 and November 10, in the railroads and industrials respectively. This critic assumes exactly the attitude of the professionals when McKinley was re-elected in 1900. The public vision was clearer. The outsider took all the stock the insider was willing to sell. A bull market set in which did not culminate until the autumn of 1902, in spite of the interruption of the Northern Pacific panic, which was a pure accident and not a result of overtrading.

Never was a bull market inaugurated under more satisfactory conditions. At this time of year money is ordinarily tight, and the call money rate is at 2½ per cent. Manufacturers' inventories are light and there is relatively small amount of unsold goods on retailers' shelves. Brokers' loans for customers in Wall Street are not ⅓ of what they might safely be. They could be increased to four billion dollars more usefully and without the slightest danger to anybody.

But in order that this inexperienced amateur shall have some sort of offset for his own bad guessing the Federal

Reserve System, or even Congress, is to meddle into an incipient bull market and say that people all over the country shall not be allowed to use their own money in fair speculation in securities. Because there have been a few days of trading of over two million shares, less than ⅔ of the record, with facilities for doing business infinitely better, the stock market is to be described as "violent," and anybody who can make a few intelligent dollars in it is to be rapped over the knuckles by the banks.

For goodness' sake, cannot we inaugurate a condition of real Americanism, where we are allowed to blow our own noses? There has scarcely been an occasion in its history when the New York stock market has not perceived dangers ahead long before anybody else and safely liquidated itself accordingly.

BARRON'S: November 17, 1924

A STUDY IN THE PRICE MOVEMENT

In the long and useful record of the Dow-Jones averages there has never been a more emphatic bull point than that given by the railroad stocks at the close of the trading on November 8, with a new high at 94.10, confirmed by the industrials two days afterward with a new high at 105.91. It may be said that there has been a sluggish major bull movement since May of last year, recently interrupted by a secondary reaction which set in about the middle of October and has now been more than recovered. It is trustworthy experience that the market is always well ahead of the development of the country's business. The averages have in the past indicated caution and a coming recession in general activity as far as ten months before the records of trade vindicated the sensitiveness of the barometer. It is probably saying today what conditions will be next spring after the demise of a Congress which has, upon the whole, done the business of the country a great deal more harm than good.

One of the features of the present advance is that the professionals of the stock market failed to see it coming and under-estimated its strength. There are few better judges of the relative force of daily buying and selling than the traders on the floor of the Stock Ex-

change. Their judgment on a major movement is as amateur as that of anybody else. The excellent reason is that they cannot see the wood for the trees. They are in no position to take that detached view which is necessary to interpret barometrical indications. When the Republican victory at the polls was recorded the professionals, as a whole, took profits and sold stocks on the theory that all the good news was known. The theory was unsound, because the good news could not possibly be known until its effect upon feeling all over the United States had been reflected in the market. It is curious and perhaps a little humiliating, that the professionals made exactly the same mistake on the re-election of McKinley in 1900.

So far as the mechanical movement of the market is concerned, it is clear from the movement of the averages that Wall Street is carrying no large quantity of stocks, and that prices will have to advance to a substantially higher level before the floating supply is replenished.

The Wall Street Journal: November 24, 1924

A STUDY IN THE PRICE MOVEMENT

Almost immediately after the election, in spite of a volume of short-sighted professional and semi-professional selling of stocks, on the theory that "the good news was out," the market developed a vigorous upward movement. It was then pointed out in these columns that the new high point for the average price of 20 railroad stocks made on November 8 at 94.10, confirmed by the 20 industrials two days afterwards with a new high of 105.91, indicated a resumption of the major bull swing. Subsequent market movements have only confirmed the confident inference there drawn.

To keep the record straight it may be said the present major upward movement in stocks developed in the middle of May. It was most deliberate so far as the railroads were concerned, although the trend in both averages was identical. In each there was a secondary reaction from the last high points made in August, with the half-hearted rally and a technically bearish low point in the middle of October. As major bull movements have a minimum duration of much more than a year and have extended to considerably over two years, the secondary reaction was of small consequence.

There is a word of caution necessary for students of the averages who expect from Dow's theory of the price movement, as discussed in Hamilton's "Stock Market Barometer," a degree of mathematical accuracy which nothing so human can usefully attain. The subject is discussed here for its barometrical value on the future of general business. The indications of either average or both taken together are surprisingly sound on the general trend of the market but utterly deceptive in a given stock. People, therefore, who propose to base a system of speculation on these market indications do so at their own risk.

Given sufficient capital and a gambling house which makes no limits, there are mathematical formulae which might break the bank of Monte Carlo. In actual practice, and certainly in Wall Street practice, the speculator with such a "martingale" will not beat the bank. The broker, for his own protection, will see that the speculator does not carry any dangerous number of eggs in one basket. The banks, and even the Stock Exchange itself, will compel the broker to exercise a supervision of that kind.

Much twaddle is being written about the "gambling" in stocks, especially by people who missed the market or predicted a reaction. The financial center was never in a better condition to handle a broad and thoroughly justified advance. Unless all signs fail the time for that sort of worrying is many months away.

BARRON'S: December 29, 1924

THE PRICE MOVEMENT

More than six weeks ago it was pointed out in these columns that the Dow-Jones averages of twenty active railroad stocks and a like number of industrials had never given a more emphatic bull point than when the railroad stocks, at the close of trading on November 8, made a new high at 94.10, which was confirmed by the industrials

two days afterwards with a new high at 105.91. This inference—and it would be contrary to the policy and purpose of these discussions to call it a prediction—was a result of analysis by the method known as "Dow's theory," exhaustively interpreted and explained in Hamilton's "Stock Market Barometer." Since that bullish indication was given the market has amply justified it with an average advance of more than five points in the railroads and ten points in the industrials. This is a continuation of the major bull swing, which may be said to have set in last May, gathering impetus in the usual way as it went along. It was characteristically interrupted by a considerable secondary reaction setting in about the middle of October, and it may be said that the secondary movement is as much an essential part of the theory of the price movement as the main direction.

It cannot be said too often that the stock market is a barometer and not merely a needless daily record. It represents everything that anybody knows, and certainly many times more than the knowledge of the most experienced and well informed individual in Wall Street. It says that a broad development in business was visible as far away as last May and that the certainty of that development has been made more sure throughout the autumn and the early winter. It clearly foresaw the result of the Presidential election. It foreshadowed record car loadings for the railroads, and improvement becoming more marked in every branch of industry. It predicted the success of the Dawes plan and the broad expansion of business throughout the British Empire. The barometer is easily many months ahead of the events it predicts, and it is fair to infer that the coming year will see an expansion of sound business, safe-guarded by low inventories and cheap money without, so far as can be seen, any sign of inflation anywhere.

It is sometimes asked how the culmination of a major bull movement can be recognized. The average life of a major bull movement, on the experience of the past quarter of a century, is not less than twenty months, and there is no reason to suppose that the present bull movement will culminate until far into 1925. The occasion of a break in the market at the top might well be accidental, but the causes would be due to overtrading, giving clear evidence that the slack in the world's capital had been taken up. Technically, the stock market would then rally, but would fail to carry the averages through the old top. We may well cross that bridge when we come to it. In the meantime the indications are a clear track and full speed ahead.

The Wall Street Journal: February 23, 1925

A SECONDARY REACTION?

Comment here made on the stock market, with its price movement analyzed on the lines laid down in Hamilton's "Stock Market Barometer," is something of an experiment which should provide its own test of usefulness. It is written four trading days before publication, following the signs of a sharp setback in a major bull movement, and all manner of things may happen before the inference sees the light of cold print. On Monday, February 16, the averages in a single day's trading showed a decline of 2.90 in twenty industrials and 1.05 in the twenty railroad stocks. They did more than this because they broke through a line which had been in process of formation since the beginning of January. In that time the industrials had not been below 120 or as high as 124, while the railroad stocks had not sold below 98 or as high as 101. This is a range of three points in the latter and less than four points in the former. On Monday of last week the industrials broke below 118 and the railroads below 98.

It is clear that at that date the market had become too full of stocks and could be forced lower before finding support in new buying at a more attractive level. There is nothing extraordinary in the reaction of a bull market which has not had a substantial secondary swing since the development of its post-election activity. What seems sufficiently indicated is not the termination of the major bull market but a pending secondary movement, a thing so easy to describe and so hard to predict with any degree of accurracy. It begins or ends with a line— or it does not. If the major movement is sluggish but well-defined, the secondary

reaction is apt to be sharp with a correspondingly slow recovery. Dow was not afraid to give it a duration as long as three months, although our experience and analysis of the averages over a quarter of a century has mostly shown shorter periods before the resumption of the major movement.

What can be said on the accepted reading of the averages is that a secondary reaction seems due, but that the major movement has not yet reached its top, unless the Coolidge bull market has been one of unprecedentedly short duration, counting its genesis, as we do, from the end of October, 1923.

BARRON'S: March 9, 1925

HAMILTON ON THE MARKET

Well Known Market Analyst Says Stocks Have Not Seen Best Prices—New High Marks for Averages Very Significant

In an interview Editor W. P. Hamilton of The Wall Street Journal, author of The Stock Market Barometer, says:

"There is always an element in Wall Street which runs counter to the general tendency, based upon the somewhat cynical view that the crowd is likely to be wrong and that what everybody knows is not worth knowing.

"Some professional traders are bearish, but they admit that they are not making money. The major premise of their argument is wrong, because it is not true that the public is always wrong, at least so far as concerns the general tendency of the market.

"The very fact that major bull markets last on an average twice as long as major bear markets shows that public opinion is not at fault to anything like the extent the cynical professional assumes.

TOP PRICES NOT YET IN SIGHT

"It will at least be admitted that we are in a major bull market which has now been running for less than a year and a half showing its greatest strength in the two months following the election of President Coolidge. On any reading of the stock market barometer I cannot see that the bull market is over or even within sight of dangerously high levels.

"Secondary reactions in a bull market are hard to guess and even the indications are sometimes deceptive. On February 16 both the railroad and industrial averages gave a bearish point after making something of a line, although it is to be remembered that the rights on General Electric had been subtracted. This may fairly be said to have made a bearish indication—breaking through the lower limit of a line less convincing than it might ordinarily be. At any rate, the bearish indication was taken back.

"On Monday, March 1, the industrial average by advancing above the previous high point and above the line which the averages had been making within a four-point range, gave a bullish indication which was partly confirmed on the following day by the railroad stocks.

STOCK DISTRIBUTED ALL OVER THE COUNTRY

"The technical condition of the market should always be kept in mind. Stocks are better distributed than they ever were in previous bull markets. The Stock Exchange itself restricts the quantity of stock a brokerage house can carry to its capital capacity and the consequence has been that people who are holding stock for a long pull are financing it themselves. They are carrying it in boxes or on loans in their home towns and these are distributed all over the country. I have had letters from as far away as Seattle, San Diego, Houston, Texas, and Tampa, Florida, asking for advice on stocks bought at much lower figures.

"There are two consequences from this condition. One is that a professional raid on the market does not shake out a great deal of stock, because of the limitations on what the brokers in Wall Street can carry. If there is no thoroughly bad news to justify the raid, the raiders are in the position of having to cover their shorts.

"The second consequence is more remote. Should something arise of an unexpected character to disturb public confidence there would be a large volume of selling from all over the country, such as Wall Street could not calculate with anything like the degree of certainty possible in the past, when it knew that the bulk of the bull account was being carried in New York.

"I do not see any such development threatening.

GENERAL BUSINESS STEADILY IMPROVING

"My advices are that while business is not booming, it is distinctly improving from week to week. If the stock market barometer is what I think it is, even supposing that the barometer has reached its top or somewhere near it— a fact of which there is no present indication—then the improvement of business has many months still to run. Unless all precedents fail, the stock market will turn long before business does and we shall have the usual experience of being told that Wall Street is the only blue spot in the country.

"So far as the barometrical indication for the immediate future of the market is concerned, both averages—on Monday in the industrials and on Tuesday in the railroads—gave one of the strongest bull points by advancing above the line which they have established in the recent past. The point is made all the stronger in the fact that the previous bear indication of three weeks ago was taken back."

BARRON'S: March 16, 1925

MODIFYING THE BAROMETER

An interview with the author of "The Stock Market Barometer" published in these columns last week did not, perhaps because it was not necessary at the moment, emphasize how the change in technical conditions in the stock market has modified that important movement shown in the record of the averages, the secondary swing—the reaction in a major bull market, if not the rally in a major bear movement. It must be fairly obvious that with the brokerage houses limited to a bull account for customers measured by their capital resources (the measuring to be done by the highly conservative Stock Exchange governing committee), the surface supply of stocks in a bull market which could be forced out to precipitate a reaction is smaller than it was and therefore less vulnerable. There is little question that the American public has plenty of money to play with, and if the brokerage houses cannot carry the stock the customer can take it up even if he has to borrow elsewhere.

One of the safeguards of a bull market is the secondary reaction. It is the most effective check on excessive speculation. It is said that something of the kind was occasionally brought about when bucket-shops were flourishing, in order to fleece customers who were making profits in spite of earnest efforts to see that they did nothing of the kind. Any bull market tended to get top-heavy, and with most of the bull account well in sight and reach, a substantial reaction really brought itself about. But with much of the bull account carried all over the country, in customers' boxes or in loans with out-of-town banks, it is by no means so easy to shake out the bulls as it was. As Mr. Hamilton points out, this is a source of potential weakness in the rare event of the market being taken by surprise. The market foresaw the World War, as the action of the barometer in the early part of 1914 clearly showed. It could not foresee the San Francisco earthquake or the Baring failure at the end of 1890.

The principles governing the action of the stock market barometer are unchanged, but it is reasonably clear that their action is modified by new conditions. Perhaps it might fairly be said that the market is not so free as it was, with its usefulness as a barometer, therefore, slightly impaired.

BARRON'S: March 23, 1925

A TRUE SECONDARY MOVEMENT

After a somewhat prolonged hesitation the stock market averages have shown what may be fairly called a typical secondary reaction in a bull market. In the space of nine trading days this carried the industrial stocks down seven points from the top, while the railroads declined five points. It is a movement that might logically run further, and it is rather due to the technical condition of trading that such a shaking-out has not happened before. With a large amount of stock held for the rise, locked in private boxes or carried in out-of-town bank loans, it has been clear that some influences other

than a mere local bear raid, based upon the assumed over-bought condition of the market, would be necessary to start a secondary reaction At this point it is easy to err in ascribing causes. It is manifest, however, that the causes for the secondary reaction, other than the vulnerable condition of the bull account and the absence of new buying, must be made sufficiently obvious, in a nation-wide sense, to produce outside pressure.

There is always a danger of the old fallacy of post hoc ergo propter hoc, but at least there are two influences conspicuous enough to have attracted attention all over the country and to have disturbed the confidence of bulls on stocks. One of these is the weakness of Chicago, Milwaukee & St. Paul stocks and bonds culminating in a receivership which many had hoped might be avoided, but which every well informed authority felt to be a necessity. There is also the turn for the worse in politics at Washington. It should not be overlooked that the new Senate is now in session and that it is obviously not on good terms with the President. Part of the confidence generated by the election of President Coolidge and reflected in the bull market in stocks was due to the anticipation that the Capitol and the White House would work in harmony as soon as the new Congress was called together. The Senate of the United States has shown itself almost as little-minded as its predecessor. It has inflicted a humiliating defeat upon the President in a nomination for his own Cabinet, the first rebuke of the kind in something like sixty years. This may well have disturbed public confidence sufficiently to bring about the necessary outside pressure of stocks which would produce, so far as the stock market barometer is concerned, the well known secondary movement, a reaction in a major bull market.

That this is anything more than a secondary movement is not indicated by any sign of the barometer. The termination of the somewhat violent but entirely typical reaction may easily be shown in dullness, followed by a slow recovery reaching new high points in the major movement. There is no method of gauging how far the secondary reaction may carry or what its duration may be. The fact remains that the major bull market has not completed its swing on any fair analysis of the relation of the averages to the rising line of values.

The Wall Street Journal: April 1, 1925

A SECONDARY REACTION

It has been pointed out in these columns before, in discussing the stock market averages on the Dow theory of the price movement as set forth in Hamilton's "Stock Market Barometer," that a secondary reaction in a bull market which is long delayed is apt to be severe. There is no evidence in the movement of the averages that the reaction which has been in force since the early part of March marks the inception of a primary bear movement.

It has also been pointed out that a change in technical conditions made it practically certain that the secondary reaction following a continuous advance since the election of President Coolidge, or more correctly since October 14, 1924, would be especially sharp when it came. The governing committee of the Stock Exchange exercises a close censorship on the operations of its members. Their commitments for customers, therefore, are limited to what that committee considers safe for the capital they employ.

As a consequence a large quantity of stock had been carried in boxes of customers or in loans made by customers with their own bankers all over the country. This set up a new condition, because in times past Wall Street had a fair idea of about how much stock could come to market under the stress of a severe shake-out. It was all, or nearly all, practically in sight. It is now impossible to estimate the quantity with any real accuracy. The traders consequently mark down prices, where they can, in order to protect themselves and maintain a free market. One of the features of the secondary decline has been the extent of the fluctuation in the third movement of the averages, that which occurs from day to day.

Reasons for a secondary reaction are usually technical and have far more to do with the overbought condition of the market than with bear arguments brought out by newspaper commentators after the events. Much has been made of dearer money, merely because the Federal Reserve rate was advanced

and the Bank of England also protected itself in the same way. The demand for money is purely seasonal and will have spent its force within a few days, if it has not already done so.

Weak spots like St. Paul do not make a major bear market any more than one swallow makes a summer. Such incidents, however, unquestionably influence the judgment of people who are carrying stocks out of town and of the country or provincial bankers who have made loans on them. So far as the price movement is concerned, it is impossible to call the bottom of the secondary reaction; but the bull market should ultimately be resumed with a higher level of prices in the course of the summer for both averages than has so far been attained.

BARRON'S: April 20, 1925.

THE PRICE MOVEMENT

Dow's theory of the stock market averages, the triple movement including the primary bull or bear swing, the secondary reaction or recovery, and the daily fluctuation, while not professing to be anything more than a theory, has stood the test of experience remarkably well. Over a period of more than a quarter of a century it has been tested, in The Wall Street Journal and in these columns, as a method of forecasting the general movement with a view to its barometrical indication of the course of business. There has seldom been a more typical condition than that which has developed in the recent past. A major bull market emerged slowly from about the end of October, 1923, gradually gaining strength and authority and developing great vigor from about a fortnight before the Presidential election. The bull market saw its top for the time being at the beginning of March, when a sharp and typical secondary reaction set in which carried the industrials down 10.68 points of an advance of forty points, while the railroads declined eight points out of a total advance of rather over twenty-two points.

For this secondary movement the low point was made on March 30 in both averages at 115 and 92.98 respectively. Since that date there has been a recovery of over six points in industrials and nearly four in rails with a less active market and a more leisurely price movement. The action of the market after the low point of the secondary reaction was reached is most characteristic and has been paralleled many times in the past, practically always indicating a resumption of the interrupted major movement.

The alternative was fairly submitted in these columns last week. The stock averages form a barometer of business, and if the reaction which set in at the beginning of March were to be regarded as the beginning of a major bear market conditions of general business in the United States would be far different. Unless all information fails and the exceptions to general prosperity are to be regarded as establishing a new rule, there is clearly not the material on which to found a bear market. There is the suggestion that we might have neither—that the stock market might back and fill for an indefinite period, forecasting a like uncertainty in general business. But, on values, the major bull market had by no means over-discounted dividends, earnings, and prospective developments fairly in sight. If for other reasons, mainly technical, the market had lost a third to a fourth of its main advance, the tendency would still be to return to the high level of the end of February and to establish new high points before the major movement culminated. The present action of the market, on all previous experience, is a clear evidence of its inherent strength.

BARRON'S: May 25, 1925

THE PRICE MOVEMENT

Any student of the stock market averages following the rules undogmatically set forth in Hamilton's "Stock Market Barometer" will recognize that they have been running true to form. As the studies in the market movements published in these columns have from time to time pointed out, the top of the major bull movement had not been reached when the twenty industrials recorded 125.68 on March 6 and the twenty railroads 100.96 on March 3d. A number of writers on the market, with a much more pretentious system of indices and tabulations, announced at that time that the bull market was over.

It was correctly pointed out here that the long-delayed secondary reaction, itself characteristic of a major bull market, had developed. That reaction culminated on March 30, with a decline of more than ten points in the industrials and rather less than eight points in the railroads.

Not only have the industrials recovered that decline; they have made a new high point for a major bull movement which has now been running since October, 1923, or substantially less than the average duration of a bull market, which works out at a little under two years, if that kind of average were of any real value with only seven bull markets to compare. The railroad stocks have not yet made a new high, and, at the time of writing, are still two points below the last top of March 3. It has been the safe experience that these averages must confirm each other, and that has been the reason why two dissimilar groups of twenty stocks each have been chosen for purposes of record instead of a miscellaneous group of forty stocks. The indications in the matter of major swings, recoveries in a bear market and reactions in a bull market, seem to be definitely more dependable.

It might fairly be said that there is some uncertainty about the general business outlook, which in places is broad but not expanding and in other places tending to hesitate. The action of the stock market now would seem to predict some continuance of that uncertainty for a distance ahead, but not to indicate anything which could, for a moment, justify the early inauguration of a major movement on the bear side.

BARRONS: July 6, 1925

A STOCK MARKET TEST

On Monday, June 29, the stock market had an interesting test. The Santa Barbara earthquake was a bolt out of the blue, something that even the aggregate knowledge of the stock market could not foresee, and a number of people sold the market short, succeeding in establishing a decline of .50 of a point in the 20 industrials and .77 of a point in the 20 railroad stocks. It is astonishing how people will risk good money on the most superficial examination and on apparent resemblances which do not bear analysis. Subconsciously at least, these operators were banking on a repetition of the severe market decline which which followed the San Francisco earthquake in 1906 and helped to make the longest and most severe secondary reaction in a major bull market which the Dow-Jones averages have ever recorded. The result of the short selling on the present occasion was anything but encouraging to the militant bear, for the industrials recovered 1.78 on the following day and the railroads .61, the latter nearly as much and the former much more than had been lost in the bear raid.

It need hardly be said that there is no real analogy between Santa Barbara and San Francisco. In 1906 the market was on the down grade. A substantial secondary reaction had been established and there was a weak and therefore vulnerable bull account. But the raid of last Monday was a first-class testimonial to the market's technical strength. Some few weeks ago it was estimated in these columns that more than half the business in the Stock Exchange was virtually swapping contracts on the floor, with pool operations in specialties perhaps 30% and the balance representing the general public interest. It is obvious that without any bear pressure a bull account like that could liquidate itself in a couple of trading days. It is impossible to have a bear market unless there is an over-extended bull market.

Although the present major upward movement in the Stock Exchange has been in operation since October, 1923, it is still based on values rather than prospects. It will be up to be shot at when fairy tales of rapid fortunes are current and the popular following is really large.

The Wall Street Journal: August 14, 1925

A STUDY IN THE PRICE MOVEMENT

When the twenty active railroad stocks crossed the old high point at 100.96 they definitely confirmed a bullish indication only partly implied when the industrials sold at 131.76 on July 1. In these studies in the price movement, as based on the Dow-Jones averages of twenty industrials and twenty railroad

stocks, it has always been found safe and wise to consider indications only when the averages confirm each other.

Early in June the industrials made a new high, but took it back. They have not taken back the subsequent still higher point reached on July 1, so that it can be taken in conjunction with the new high for the railroad stocks. It has always been a legitimate inference on the completion of such a bull point that the floating supply of stocks had been absorbed and that a new high level will be in order to attract new sellers. So far as the railroad stocks are concerned, the present bull market may be said to have started from the low (rails) of August 4, 1923, at 76.78, confirmed by the advance of the industrials from the low of the following October 27 or 85.76.

It will be seen that in this bull market of no unprecedented length the industrials have advanced over 51 points and the railroads more than 24 points. This is by no means a new record, as the high point of 1906 followed an advance of over 60 points in the industrials and nearly 50 points in the railroad stocks. By analogy the newly confirmed indication of a further advance would seem to be specially bullish on the railroads, which have certainly not been conspicuous for activity in the present bull market.

A number of commentators on the market have assumed that the danger point of a long advance has been reached because of the spectacular fluctuations in a limited group, chiefly industrials. That phenomenon is more spectacular than convincing. On the general market trend, and on the quality of the averages as a barometer of trade, that part of the trading has probably not much more significance than an unforgotten display of pyrotechnics in Stutz Motor. Brokers are demanding almost prohibitive margin in such stocks as Mack Trucks, and if the speculation in a few of them collapsed the bearish effect would probably be momentary, while the ultimate general influence might well be good.

After a bull market which has lasted nearly two years the third stage, the discounting of hopes rather than values, cannot be relatively far away and may have even been reached in a few individual instances. The fact, nevertheless, remains that the averages proclaim a further upward movement of the market.

BARRON'S: October 5, 1925

THE PRICE MOVEMENT

A study of the stock market, always strictly considered here as a guide to the broad tendency of business and on the lines set forth in Hamilton's "Stock Market Barometer," discloses a highly interesting position. The twenty industrial stocks attained an average price of 147.73 on September 19, since which time they have reacted nearly four points and rallied again, encountering more resistance to the all-conquering bull movement than the market has experienced hitherto. The net advance in the industrials has been great, compared with any bull market of record. The yield in dividend of these twenty stocks is appreciably below 40% and the market, so far as the industrials are concerned, may therefore be said to have reached its third stage, where people are buying on hopes and potentialities rather than on demonstrated values.

By comparison the twenty active railroads make a more conservative showing. Their high point was made on September 23 at 103.78. There has been no reaction so considerable as that in the industrials, and a week after this figure was reached the average price was within less than a point of the top. It is worth saying, also, that the dividend yield is still close to 5%, or, in other words, that the railroad stocks can more nearly carry themselves on any averaging of call money at a time of the year when rates are likely to be stiff. The railroads, therefore, have not so obviously extended above the line of values or beyond the secondary stage of a bull market. They tend, of course, to work upward as their merits for the small speculator become apparent in comparison with the industrials.

On any reading of the averages based upon sound principles it is clear that the major bull market is still in force, but will bear watching. It has reached a stage when it presents a shining mark, and it is noteworthy, even if in a way reassuring to the bull, that professionals are, for the most part, bearish. They say, not untruly, that profits in the industrials now are being snatched off the hot coals. They claim that the higher value disclosed in the price of the railroads only makes that group more vulnerable, because in a bear market people sell what they can get at some price, or even at a concession, where they cannot sell something else at any price. All this is sound and well worth considering, although it should also be said that if the industrials alone sold above 147.73, as they may well do before this appears in print, the indications would be for a further advance. The point is that the time for caution has arrived in a bull market which has been running for something more than twenty-three months, dating from October, 1923.

That large volume of general trade and tangible prosperity which the bull market forecast has materialized and seems likely to continue. Indeed, it is so well established that one of the most probable predictions in the near future, so far as the stock averages are concerned, would be a period of adjustment and stabilization at a high level. This is a time when the old theory of double tops might prove useful, as, for instance, any close approach to the high points of September 19 and September 23 respectively, followed by a reaction in both averages.

It can only be repeated that the market will bear watching.

The Wall Street Journal: November 3, 1925

So far as any inference from the Dow-Jones stock averages is concerned, the major bull market in stocks is still ruling, with some secondary reaction due, but no bear market in sight.

BARRON'S: November 9, 1925

A LOOK AHEAD

With a bull market in stocks which has carried on, with ever-increasing momentum, over a period of more than two years, it is natural that conservative folk should be asking themselves and each other what will finally check the upward movement, bringing about what is technically known as a primary bear market. It is not to be denied that the great strength in the stock market has been vindicated by remarkable prosperity, plentiful and easy money, good crops and a condition of the railroads better than it has ever been in their history.

It may also be taken that the coal strike has been justly disregarded by the stock market and by general business, except where production may be locally embarrassed. It has been pointed out, also, in this place that even if there is a sum of $2,000,000,000 tied up in purchases under installment plans, not including houses, that amount is spread out so thinly that it could not hurt business except in the event of an improbable number of simultaneous defaults in payment. But this condition does indicate something which should give us a clear view of the next reaction in business.

Never in our history has there been so tremendous a conversion of floating capital into fixed capital as that now in progress. Real estate development is beyond all belief, and it is far more costly than it ever was before. A "sub-division" in a suburb is not opened, for selling lots, nowadays, until concrete roads are laid out and finished, at a cost of $30,000 a mile and upward. Within a radius of twenty miles of Asheville, N. C., two projects out of many each involve seven miles of road at $44,000 a mile. And this is going on round every city in the United States. Florida is merely the froth on this flood, although it need hardly be said that when lots in Miami fetch better prices than lots on Fifth avenue, New York, the ultimate purchaser is bound to get hurt.

Although the tendency of money, together with wages, rents and the cost of living, will in all probability be downward throughout the next twenty years, there will be occasional interludes of tighter money. Sometimes, and probably next year, we shall experience a marked shortage of capital for investment and speculation, and the stock market will know it first. It will develop a major downward movement, when the whole country is bubbling with prosperity and ever-expanding hope. We shall, as usual, be told that "Wall Street is the only blue spot in the country."

No doubt Wall Street will be able to stand it, for its skin has been toughened by much beating in the past. So far as any inference from the Dow-Jones stock averages is concerned, the major bull market in stocks is still ruling, with some secondary reaction due, but no bear market in sight.

The Wall Street Journal: November 12, 1925

A STUDY IN THE PRICE MOVEMENT

In a study in the price movement, based on "Dow's theory" as set forth in Hamilton's Stock Market Barometer, published in these columns August 14, it was pointed out that in spite of an advance at that time of 51 points in the Industrials, since October, 1923, a further upward movement was to be expected. The major bull market accordingly carried on and, after a reaction of a trifle over 3 points in the Industrials in the latter part of September, a new high point for both averages was recorded on October 20.

As readers of these studies know, such a new high point was a clear prediction of a further advance which continued up to and including November 6, when the highest point on record for the Industrials at 159.39 was reached, the high for the Railroads being 105.19. On November 7 a secondary reaction, described as already over-due in The Wall Street Journal leader of November 3, set in. It will be observed that the Railroad stocks have made a most conservative advance in view of the pyrotechnics in the Industrials. Their reaction on the average was less than a point on November 10, when the Industrials showed the violent decline of 5.83.

Such a decline is spectacular, even as the rise has been. Newspapers like the New York World, suffering from what may be called the anti-Wall Street complex, described it, in the question-begging terminology of thirty years ago, as "shearing the lambs." Other papers, with their usual helpfulness, content themselves with talking in terms of a first class panic, like that of 1873. What has happened has been a secondary reaction in a bull market, no more, and certainly no less.

Secondary reactions are usually sharp and the recovery is leisurely. This has been the case throughout the present upward movement. They are a note of warning especially in a bull market which has now run over two years. If, for instance, the Railroads recovered to the near neighborhood of 105.19, but did not quite reach it, while the Industrials rallied from the break to the old high figure of 159.39 without crossing it and then both averages developed a new decline, there would be a strong reason for suspecting that the major upward movement was over, although it might take weeks of trading before a major bear market could be confidently diagnosed.

As the last study in the price movement said, we have reached the stage where the bull market requires careful watching. The averages continue, as they have done for the past quarter of a century, incomparably the most trustworthy barometer.

The Wall Street Journal: December 17, 1925

A STUDY IN THE PRICE MOVEMENT

While the Dow-Jones averages used for more than a quarter of a century in these studies in the price movement broadly foretell the course of future business, and even their own direction, they have a discretion not shared by all prophets. They are not talking all the time. Discussions on the subject are immensely popular, to judge from the correspondence they excite, although students are learning generally to use the text book on the subject, Hamilton's "Stock Market Barometer." In view of the high level of the bull market, which the averages correctly foresaw, some thoughts on the present position are in order.

In the past few days the Railroad average has been making new high points, but the twenty Industrials at the close on December 15 were more than five points below the high figure of 159.39 recorded on November 6. It is clear that the averages are giving no signal of any kind of a change in the general direction. The major bull movement in operation since October, 1923, is still in force with a typical secondary reaction in the Industrial stocks uncompleted. An advance in the Industrial group above the level of November 6,

or to 159.40, would be strongly bullish on the whole market.

Indeed, to give a bearish indication, a reaction in the Railroad stocks something like the eleven-point recession shown between November 6 and November 24 in the Industrials, but not necessarily of such extent, would be required. If after that reaction, which might still be merely secondary in a continuing upward movement, the Railroads failed to recover the decline completely while the Industrials approached the old high, but did not cross it, the general indications would be for a change in the broad movement. The inauguration of a major bear market would not be far away. On the balance of probabilities a resumption of the present major bull movement is by far the more likely. In any case, it would take a considerable period of time to establish a condition of the barometer showing bad weather ahead.

It has often been said in these studies that experience fully justifies the keeping the averages of two separate groups, with the refusal of indications given by one of them but not confirmed by the other. For the moment the two averages are not acting together in any significant way. One of the most dependable of the indications given by the averages was again exemplified in the Railroad stocks, where a long "line" within a narrow range not below 101, or above 105, gave a most dependable bull point when the latter figure was crossed.

This, of course, indicated a large absorption of stock, finally restricting the market supply and forcing an advance to bring out new sellers at a more attractive level. Subject to the hesitation in the Industrials, the indications of the averages are still strongly bullish, but will, of course, bear watching.

The Wall Street Journal: December 22, 1925

TO TEST THE AVERAGES

So much importance is attached to the Dow-Jones stock market averages, not merely in these columns, where that barometer of business has been usefully applied for more than a quarter of a century, but by students all over the country that a test of their representative quality should be welcomed. Do the 20 Industrial stocks in the Dow-Jones average correctly reflect the movement of the entire Industrial market, so greatly enlarged in the past few years?

Here is an independent test, and it comes from one of nation-wide authority, Colonel Leonard P. Ayres, of the Cleveland Trust Company. In a recent comparison of furnaces in blast with the price of over 200 Industrial stocks, he drew some inferences which made it possible to get from him an independent opinion. He says:

"The 201 Industrial stocks making up the index line reproduced in my current Business Bulletin are those entering into the tabulation of the Standard Statistics Company. They base their figures on the closing prices each Monday. The figures are not direct means or averages but are in relatives. For this group of 201 Industrial stocks the mean of the 1917–1921 stock market was taken as equal to 100, and all the subsequent figures are reduced to that basis.

"I think the results reinforce one's faith in index numbers and the method of sampling. Here are two indexes constructed on radically diverse principles. One is based on ten times as many cases as the other, and more than that, the Standard Statistics figures are weighted according to the volume of the outstanding stock. Nevertheless, your Dow-Jones averages run just below the original data, and show almost every minor variation as well as the major swings of the first series. There is some difference in 1921, but otherwise the lines are in surprisingly close agreement."

There is an interesting confirmation of this reassuring test from what may be called the other end. Another real friend of *The Wall Street Journal*, who also shows his affection by not writing to the Editor unless he has something to say, recalled that before the Stock Exchange reopened after the outbreak of war there were only 12 stocks in the Industrial average. No more were needed at that time, and during part of the Roosevelt administration it was necessary to include Western Union in the group to get sufficient activity.

This analyst's idea was to continue the 12 stocks used in 1914, in order to see how they would compare with the Dow-Jones 20. The result was an agreement certainly as close, if not closer,

than that which Colonel Ayres so industriously and usefully obtained from 201 stocks. Of course, reduction in the number could be carried too far. It would be absurd to expect three stocks to show the same degree of dependability.

It seems fair to infer that given a free market, with a careful substitution of active issues for those which have lost or discarded their speculative market, a relatively small number of stocks is entirely trustworthy to constitute the Industrial half—or, indeed, the Railroad half—of the stock market barometer.

The Wall Street Journal: January 26, 1926

THE PRICE MOVEMENT

A study of the stock market price movement, as reflected by the Dow-Jones averages and interpreted by Dow's theory, is enlightening at this time. The conclusions possible are somewhat tentative, but are full of interest after a bull market which has been running since October, 1923. The 20 industrial stocks have displayed the phenomenon of a clearly marked double top. On November 6, 1925, they made the high of the movement, and the highest point on record, at 159.39. From this there was a well marked secondary reaction, with all the characteristic features of such a movement, carrying the price down over 11 points, to 148.18 on November 24. The subsequent rally was to 159.00 and from that the market, on January 21, had reacted to 153.20.

This would be highly significant if the confirmation from the 20 railroad stocks were more nearly parallel. But the railroads did not share the 11-point reaction in the industrials. They eased off a point or so, but made the high of the present movement on January 7 at 113.12. From that figure there was a reaction of less than 5 points to 108.26 on January 21.

To indicate a resumption of the major bull market, which would be thoroughly dependable on all previous experience, it would be necessary for the industrials to sell above the November high and the railroads to sell above the high of January 7. But as the industrials have already made a significant double top, a recovery of the railroad average to a figure close to, but less than, 113.12 followed by a subsequent reaction, would come near to indicating that the long bull movement had seen its close.

The example of 1906 shows us that an immediate major bear market need not necessarily be assumed, although it would be dated from the time when the high points of the averages confirmed each other. As the stock market barometer is usually six months or more ahead of the general business of the country, the inference would, of course, be a check in the expansion of trade in the second half of 1926.

The Wall Street Journal: February 15, 1926

THE PRICE MOVEMENT

Never were the Dow-Jones averages harder to read than they are at present, and never was the temptation so strong to say nothing about them. The industrials made a high point in November, but the railroad stocks did not respond. The railroads made a high point on January 7 at 113.12, but in the meantime the industrials had reacted substantially and then advanced again, but without making a new high. A new high, had it been made then, would have been bullish on the whole market, and have indicated a resumption of the major bull movement, which has been in progress since October, 1923. The railroads reacted from 113.12 to 108.26 on January 21 and rallied to 111.36 on January 30, selling off subsequently. Here was another case of double tops, and the advance of the industrials to a new high of 160.53 did not confirm the bullish indication in the railroads on January 7 as might be superficially assumed. It required, and at the time of writing still requires, another confirmation by the railroad averages taking back the bearish indication given in their "double top."

It has been the experience, in writing these studies for something like 25 years, that it is much harder to call the turn at the top than at the bottom. After a long bear market the discrepancy between the average price and what may be assumed as the line of values on real earnings, dividend yield and the value of money, is easily apparent. But after a long advance, many stocks are selling on the hopes and possibilities but some are selling well within proved value. Any may have possibilities by no means discounted. The market, moreover, perhaps because of the complexity of the situation and more truly because of the stability of the general prosperity predicted by the barometer, may hold within a relatively small distance from the top for an indefinite time. It might indeed be said that there are instances of nearly a year with a range not far from the top, before an aggressive bear market has been established.

It can hardly be said that the averages at the moment look convincingly bullish, and a relatively small change in both of them would make them look decidedly bearish. The fluctuations at present are at least strikingly like those which have occurred in the past at the top of a long bull movement.

The Wall Street Journal: February 22, 1926

THEORETICAL PRICE CYCLES

Students of the Dow-Jones averages sometimes ask why longer periods would not be equally deducible from the price record? They suggest that a bear market from 1909 to 1917 could be inferred from the chart of the twenty active Railroad stocks. If we are to ignore obviously major movements in that way it would be possible to describe a bull movement in the Industrials lasting from 1897 to 1919. None of the low points made in those years reached the 1897 level, and the 1919 level was the top up to the present bull movement of the Industrials.

To that criticism the answer is that such long periods would be useless for any purpose of forecast. It might almost be said that a bull movement on the United States set in more than a hundred years ago, and that it is still in progress with secondary reactions, like that in the hungry nineties, or between the panic of 1873 and the resumption of specie payments (1879). This is only to say that a country with great natural advantages and an active citizenship has been able to grow under the assured safety of life and property.

There would be no barometrical inference to be drawn, although if there had been a stock market barometer for the full length of our nation's story it would in all human probability have consistently predicted the country's growth. It is of the essence of the stock-market barometer, constructed from the Dow-Jones averages, that it predicts the useful variations in business, the three-year advance, the twelve months' re-action and the two-year recovery. There is no sense in using a telescope for the things which are right under our feet. Over long periods of years the averages will precede, with an irregular certainty, the upward trend of the line of values.

Of these long movements, one of the most significant is the great decline in the Railroad average from 1909, right through the independent bull movement in the Industrials following the peace, to 1921. There we had the crippling influence of unintelligent legislation and overregulation. It was a warning that the richest country might not go on prospering forever, if fool politicians had their way. There has been a recovery, largely stimulated by the plain lesson of our great experiment in government management of the railroads. For the past four years our transportation system has been coming back, but it is still true that railroad credit is not what it should be, or what it would be if the railroads were not the target for the demagogue.

Our major movements, reflected in the averages, with a mean of over two years for a bull market and of something over one year for bear markets, are long enough to be representative and short enough to be helpful. The function of the averages is not to record history but to reflect coming events when, as the poet says, they cast their shadows before.

The Wall Street Journal: March 4, 1926

TESTING THE STOCK MARKET

When the average decline of twenty Industrial stocks in two trading days amounts to over seven points, a condition is established which rather accurately tests not merely the strength of the bull account but the sincerity and conviction of the investment demand. A decline so severe on the average is caused by exceptional weakness in part

digested pool stocks, and in such a slump holders on margin sell issues for which there is a certain market at some price in order to protect themselves in issues where the market has practically disappeared.

There is a fairly uniform rally from such a market depression. The decline tends to overrun itself, and there is usually a recovery which, as history over the past quarter of a century shows, frequently runs to as much as 60 per cent. of the decline. During this recovery strong interests who supported the market to help out weak holders distribute the stock they were compelled to purchase. The future course of the market turns on its ability to absorb this stock.

After this almost automatic recovery, following a semi-panic break, the market usually sells off again, slowly, day by day, and not uncommonly approaches the old low level which the first fever of selling had established. It is not true that such breaks necessarily mark the end of major movements, although they have occurred at such times. The most serious on record was that which arose out of the Northern Pacific corner in May, 1901.

In that case there was a recovery such as it here described, followed by some belated liquidation. After that the major bull movement which set in with the second election of McKinley continued; it did not culminate until eighteen months afterward in September, 1902.

Relative to the total advance in the stock market, the decline of Monday and Tuesday does not establish an attractive low level like that of 1901. Buyers on the present reaction might well have the feeling that although Industrial stocks had sold more than fourteen points below the high figure of the averages, that figure was still above all records. The assumption of a further major advance in a bull market which has been running for nearly two and a half years would indicate a degree of optimism which the general business of the country might not ultimately justify.

There is an old fallacy in logic, that of "post hoc ergo propter hoc," which will associate the Nickel Plate decision with the recent break in the stock market. It is more intelligent to say that the bull market had been carried too fast and too far, that amateur pools had become too venturesome, that bank resources tended to restriction and that the structure of speculation was resting upon a shaky base. Any concentrated pressure was capable of upsetting it. The real test is not now, but will come when the stock which was taken over to support the market is liquidated during the next recovery.

The Wall Street Journal: March 5, 1926

SOME STOCK MARKET PSYCHOLOGY

It was pointed out in this column on March 3 that the Nickel Plate decision could not possibly be the cause for an eighteen-point decline in the Industrial stocks, or even the eight-point decline in the Railroads, extending over eight consecutive days. Six days of decline had taken place before the decision was published. About the only news concerning that decision was the flatfooted statement in the New York American on February 27 that the decision would be favorable. There was like unfortunate guessing elsewhere, reprehensively offered as "news."

When the stock market gets itself on the front page, managing editors call for spectacular reasons. Their caption writers would not know what to do with psychological and mathematical causes, even if the proprietors of such newspapers, a curiously ignorant class, could understand the psychology of a bull market which has outrun its reason. As the readers of this column are of a different order, it will be simple enough to explain what happens.

Suppose a speculator correctly realizes the major upward trend and buys 100 shares at 90. When the stock reaches 100 he has $1,000 profit and buys 100 more. He buys on his paper profits on each 10-point advance, until his last purchase at 140, when he has a balance of $15,000 while he is long of 600 shares. If the market then reacts to 120 he has lost $12,000 of his profits, not counting his commissions or the cost of carrying the stock. It will be observed that a 20-point recession from the 50-point advance practically wipes him out.

This correctly describes the essential weakness of a bull market after an advance which has reached the third and final stage, when buying is based upon hopes and possibilities rather than values, even if some stocks are still worth the price at which they are selling on their true earning power and dividend yield. Any little thing will break such a market, and in the precipitous decline which follows the good stocks will suffer with the bad ones because people sell that for which there is an assured market at some price, in order to protect what they cannot sell at any price.

It cannot be complained that the barometer did not give a warning. In the "Study in the Price Movement," reprinted from *BARRON'S* in these columns February 15, the end of the bull movement was plainly shown as it has been in such studies for the past twenty-five years. The record is clearly set forth in Hamilton's "Stock Market Barometer," where the forecast of *The Wall Street Journal* is quoted for the fifteen major movements since about the beginning of the century.

In the decline here discussed one evidence of inherent strength is that the market never got out of hand. That favorite word of the fool newspaper, "panic," did not apply.

The Wall Street Journal: March 8, 1926

THE PRICE MOVEMENT

In a study in the price movement published in these columns February 15, the beginning of a week in which both the railroad and the industrial averages came within less than two points of the highest figures in the recent bull market, this paragraph occurs:

"It can hardly be said that the averages at the moment look convincingly bullish and a relatively small change in both of them would make them look decidedly bearish. The fluctuations at present are at least strikingly like those which have occurred in the past at the top of a long bull movement."

That unpretentious analysis may be said to have called the turn of the market at the top, or sufficiently near it for all practical purposes. Both industrials and railroads have made the significant "double top." The former at 161.09 and the latter at 111.22 recorded two days afterwards, February 22, made the unconvincing demonstration to which the previous study had referred. The setback from that point was convincing enough. The break of March 1 and 2 was notably severe, but in these studies time is not the most essential factor. In reading the averages and the well-defined major and secondary movements, one of the latter is equally convincing if it takes two weeks or ten.

What seems sufficiently clear is that the major tendency of the market for an indefinite time to come will be downwards, with the typical secondary rallies always observable in a bear market, and usually highly deceptive in its earlier stages. There is no rule about it, but such movements have completed themselves in a period as short as eight months, while there is at least one bear market on record, that which preceded the Great War, where considerably over two years was consumed in the decline. Like many of the events arising out of the war that was an exception, for we are not likely to see again a market which has to stand the liquidation of practically all the Euopean holdings of American stocks.

On the present indications of the averages, 1926 will be a bear year, while the immediate outlook is for a secondary rally in a bear market. It would be beyond the scope of these studies in the price movement to consider reasons why the stock market should decline. It is sufficient to say that eventually every decline of the past was fully explained by subsequent developments in the businesses of the country.

of the stock price movement has once more come successfully through a stringent test of its usefulness and dependability. It called the turn of the stock market exactly at the top of a completed bull market, and the inauguration of a major bear movement. Reasoning on the basis of that theory in these columns even indicated the extent of the rally from the continuous eight-day break in prices and correctly predicted the sag toward the low prices of the break which would automatically follow that rally.

It will be remembered that Mr. Hamilton's "The Stock Market Barometer" declines to adopt such supplements to the barometer as pig-iron prices, the blast furnaces in operation, or even the money rate in any of its forms. He says that if the price movement does not already include all these things, together with every other possible influence on the stock market, then Dow's theory and his own interpretation of it cannot be defended. The passionless barometer is disinterested because every sale and purchase which goes to make up its findings, is interested. Its verdict is the balance of all the desires, compulsions and hopes of those who buy and sell stocks. The whole business of the country must necessarily be reflected correctly in the meeting of all these minds, not as an irresponsible debating society but as a listening jury whose members, together, bring more than the counsel or the judge can ever tell them in finding what has been called the bloodless verdict of the marketplace.

BARRON'S: March 29, 1926

A TEST OF DOW'S THEORY

When sensible people discuss methods of reading the stock market, either as a guide to its own future course or as a barometer of general business, they do not ask whether such methods conform to the strictest rule of formal logic. They take a view decidedly in line with the pragmatism of William James. They ask if the method will work. They do not expect impossibilities, and they are, like the late Professor James, entirely prepared to discard any hypothesis when it is proved fallacious or been replaced by a better one. There can be no question that Dow's theory

BARRON'S: April 12, 1926

MARKET FORECASTS

All of us can be wise after the event: some of us can see trouble coming, and those who do are not thanked. They may be thanked ultimately, as, for instance, in the past when BARRON'S has recorded that the Dow-Jones averages were showing the end of the major bull movement with an impending recessi. Those who were unfortunately caught long at the top, being entirely human, are apt to say that the prophet was responsible for the reaction he foresaw because he had disturbed public confidence. This is a superficial effect which soon wears off. When BARRON'S says some time in the future that the market has turned for a major upward movement the man who resented its correctness on the decline needs only to make one or two fortunate purchases to tell all his friends how right the publication has been. It is all in the day's work; no publication should fail in its duty of interpreting the meaning of news, merely because the results of its reasoning will dash the sanguine anticipations of some of its readers.

It is relatively easy for a newspaper to buy circulation if it is willing to put up the price. The real difficulty comes in keeping the subscriber, and nothing will do that except a policy which commands his confidence. It was not difficult to see, before the stock market turned in the middle of February, that a relatively large number of pools were grossly over-exploiting the "holding company" idea, calculating upon unloading to an uninformed public at extravagant prices which could only be justified, if ever, by a phenomenal development of sustained prosperity. Some sympathy is expressed for the members of such pools when the market subjects them to heavy losses. At least a part of the sympathy might be reserved for the investor who has taken all their statements in good faith, to his own serious loss. This is no defence of the professional speculator who suspects such weakness and hammers the market with short sales. The bear can make money only when somebody else loses, and his action is, to that extent, unsocial, valuable as short selling may well be in deflating a market at danger point and reducing the volume of brokers' loans.

So far as the stock market is at present concerned, its violent oscillations are over. The arc of the pendulum is contracted to a reasonable daily movement, not at present giving special indications and certainly not taking back the inferences which were drawn in these columns when the price movement was studied seven weeks ago.

BARRON'S: April 26, 1926

DOW'S BAROMETER

Dow's theory of the stock price movement, with its major bull or bear swing,

its secondary reaction or rally and its third of daily fluctuation, has an unfailing attraction for intelligent speculators who want something to guide them other than mere judgment. It is true also that Charles H. Dow scarcely advanced, if he advanced at all, beyond devising a trustworthy guide, within limits, to the movements of the market itself. It was Hamilton's "Stock Market Barometer" which pointed out its larger reference to the general business of the country, and its high barometrical value in that respect. Many students of the averages write to *BARRON'S* and *The Wall Street Journal* with intelligent criticism or inquiry, and it is not difficult to see the entirely human fact that they are more interested in the forecasts of market movements than of general business. A result of this is that they almost invariably expect too much of the barometer.

They seem to read into it or attempt to extract from it a particularity of detail which it not only cannot possess but should not possess, in the public interest. While it is strictly true that when the market embarks upon a primary downward swing good stocks will suffer with bad, it by no means follows that the average of either group of twenty stocks, industrial or railroad, will afford a dependable guide to the tendency of any given stock. The course of that stock may be against the general current, especially in dull or featureless markets where the severity of the primary movement has abated. These inquirers also are unwise when they attempt, by a theory of double tops or double bottoms, to call the turn for reactions or rallies.

It is at least debatable if Dow's theory provides anything useful of that kind, and it should not be forgotten that it stipulates for a confirmation of one average by the other. This constantly occurs at the inception of a primary movement, but is anything but consistently present when the market turns for a secondary swing. This is the plain reason for the consistent conservatism of the "Stock Market Barometer," which makes good its title by claiming too little rather than too much. Its value as a barometer of business is thereby enhanced.

BARRON'S: September 20, 1926

AVERAGES AND ORPHANITIS

On September 13 the Dow-Jones averages of twenty industrial stocks showed a decline of 3.19, but the fact that General Motors sold "ex" the stock dividend accounted for a deduction of 3.55 points in the average. This is admittedly something different from an equivalent break in the market, for no part of the apparent decline is traceable to any lack of confidence in these securities. The question is therefore asked why some distinction is not made? The answer lies in the unaffected simplicity of the averages. Something of value, measured by that figure has been taken forever out of the twenty industrial stocks. For whatever cause, the average price of them has depreciated. Why make a distinction when there is no real difference? The investor cannot eat his cake and have it. Indeed, one of the consequences of a long advance in proved values and speculative anticipations ought to be just such a distribution of accumulated wealth.

C. W. Barron has written recently with enlightenment and understanding of what he calls "Orphanitis" as a disease attacking securities of high and established character. Stock becomes so well distributed among widows and orphans and small holders generally that the management develops conservatism to the point of a vice. It may think that it is strengthening its reasonable dividend by putting back earnings into the property, only to find that it has really been competing with itself, and that the new capital sunk does not begin to yield the old return. The stimulus to aggressive and forward-looking management is removed. The officers have a safe job and are taking no chances. They regard themselves as assured for life, forgetting that the stockholders may some day wake up to find that for any real earning purpose, the apparently impregnable reinvested surplus is no longer there.

The General Motors deduction from the average is a good thing, and it would be better for the business of the country if such distributions occurred oftener.

BARRON'S: September, 27, 1926

AVERAGES AND THE UNEXPECTED

How does the stock market take the unexpected? Its movements are overwhelmingly based upon the sum of all that can be foreseen and estimated. There are some things, however, which obviously do not come within that category, as, for instance, the earthquake and fire at San Francisco in 1906 or last week's disaster which laid waste some of the newest and most promising developments of Florida. It may be said that the stock market's attitude to the unexpected is precautionary. The average price of twenty industrial stocks, on the Monday following the news of the Caribbean tornado, declined 1.60 and the twenty railroad stocks declined .51. On the extreme estimates the hurricane damage was about one-fourth of the $600,000,000 which might be taken as the total cost of San Francisco's earthquake and fire. If the latter sum, as no one will doubt, was a much more serious matter twenty years ago than it is now, a sum which may not exceed $100,000,-000, calling for a replacement which will be spread over many months, is not calculated to change the broad trend of the stock market.

This is the unimpassioned estimate of the market place and it is worth noting that while the San Francisco calamity came towards what might well have been the end of a fairly extended secondary reaction in a major bull market, the hurricane interrupted for a day or so a market which, in its major aspect, may be said to have been definitely on the up-grade. The small reaction, therefore, may be taken as the market's premium of insurance. It takes newspaper hysterics and estimates with something more than a grain of salt. As *The Wall Street Journal* editorially pointed out, destruction could not be absolute. Serious as it is, that destruction is superficial. The essential part of what has been put into real estate developments in Florida remains. The repair of the sewer systems, streets and other essentials of young communities is a matter of a few days. The loss is in the buildings destroyed, and those are obviously not the most costly type of building, the large steel-framed structures. It is an unquestionable tribute to the strength of the stock market that it kept itself so well in hand.

BARRON'S: October 18, 1926

THE PRICE MOVEMENT

While the average prices of twenty industrials and twenty railroads by no means indicate the inauguration of a major bear movement, or more than the secondary reaction common in a primary bull market, there has clearly been a change in the showing of the averages sufficiently serious to require some reading of the stock market barometer. In a major bull movement which has now lasted for three years, or from October, 1923, the high of that movement of the industrials was 166.64, made August 14, while the high point of the railroad stocks, 123.33, was recorded on September 3. Since that time there has been a somewhat wide but consistent line of distribution, within a range of approximately seven points for the industrials and a somewhat closer range for the railroads. Each average may be said to have broken through the low figures of this line, which, it should be remembered, was established on a heavy volume of trading; large enough, indeed, to eliminate accidental influences like sensational advances in a very few stocks in one group, or the somewhat technical reduction in the industrials caused by the deduction of the valuable rights on General Motors.

It should also be said here that we may allow ourselves more latitude in the limits of such a "line" in view of the high figure of the average, especially in the industrial group. Obviously a decline of seven points in a stock standing at 166 is a much less serious fluctuation than a like decline in a stock standing at 83. If the figure were in the 40's, it would have the proportions of a devastating break.

This is in accord with the attitude necessarily adopted in regarding the severe break and recovery between the middle of February and the middle of June. So far as the industrials are concerned, they achieved a decline of twenty-seven points. If we could ignore the factor of time, this, in former days, has almost always constituted a major bear market in itself. Neither in the

spring break, regarded as a secondary reaction in a primary bull market, nor in the recovery was the fluctuation of the railroad stocks nearly so considerable. The range from the low of March 30 to the passing of the January high in June and the establishment of a new bull market level was only a conservative total fluctuation as compared with the much severer movement in the industrials.

As the averages stand today it is evident that there has been a large distribution of stock, not only in the flamboyant industrial group but in the much more sober railroad stocks. The apparent investment buying of the latter has, for the present, not proved sufficient to absorb the substantial offerings and maintain the old high level. For any forecast value a considerable movement either way would be required for a logical reading of the barometer.

Re-establishment of the major bull market would call for a recovery of over eight points in the railroads and more than seventeen points in the industrials. Against this a further decline, carrying the railroads down more than twelve points, and the industrials to a figure in the neighborhood of 135, below the point of the March break, calling for a further recession of fourteen points, would make an undeniable bear signal.

On previous experience of the averages a rally which failed to reach the old high, followed by a substantial decline like that which has taken place in the recent past, would be rather definitely bearish even before the old low points in both averages at the end of March were re-established.

For the present the steam is out of the big bull market, and the speculator who followed that market up for three years, or even for five years, if we ignore the shortest major bear movement recorded in the averages, cannot complain that he has not had a long run for his money.

BARRON'S: November 8, 1926

A CONTRAST IN THE AVERAGES

Students of the Dow-Jones averages do not seem to have noticed a strikingly contradictory movement in the twenty industrials and the twenty active railroad stocks. This is in spite of the fact that, with the single exception of the bull market which culminated in 1919, where the railroads through government ownership were taken out of the speculative class, the averages have always confirmed each other in the respect that their major movements up or down have been simultaneous. The contradiction is in the comparison of the movement over a much longer period than that comprised within the range of a bear or a bull market, however extended. In 1903 the railroads made a low point. The low of 1907 showed a further recession; that of 1917 was still lower, and this was true of 1920 and 1921. It would have been true in taking the high points from the 136 of 1906, which has never since been attained. In those same eighteen years the industrial low of 1907 was not down to the figure of 1903. It was lower than that of 1917, which again was under the figure shown in 1920.

Here we see over a period of eighteen years a recession of the railroads with an advance in the industrials, which has continued for the past three years. The other day Senator Norris of Nebraska said that the railroads would always be in politics, and the remedy was government ownership. Is it not clear that the railroads have been dragged into politics, while the industrials have had comparative freedom from interference? In no other way can so startling a comparison of earning capacity and value be explained. If Congress attempts to override the Interstate Commerce Commission in its quasi-judicial function of fixing rates or valuations, the railroads are compelled to protect their stockholders. The industrial corporations, placed under a like disability, would necessarily adopt the same policy. But could anything more clearly show the tremendously damaging effect upon what might be called the key industry of the country, of perpetual political persecution, day in and day out, without rhyme or reason? What other country in the world could carry on its transportation business with any such handicap?

BARRON'S: January 17, 1927

DIAGNOSING THE MARKET

To those students of the stock market averages who follow the well known Dow Theory and attach importance to the somewhat technical, but often useful, idea of "double tops," the present position should be interesting. The high points of a bull market which may be said to date from October, 1923, were made on August 14 at 166.64 for the industrials and on September 3 at 123.33 for the railroads. On September 7 the industrials had reached and rallied again to 166.10, making a double top, while the railroads did something like that as late as December 18, reaching 122.48, a price from which they have since reacted. The decline in the industrials from September 7 to October 19 was more than twenty points, followed by a rally of over sixteen points and a subsequent recession to the present level, which, at the time of writing, is substantially below the December high. As usual, the fluctuations in the railroad stocks has been much less than that in the industrials. But, roughly speaking, both averages have shown a similar trend, and each has failed to recover the old high points.

This would be a signal for caution, especially after a major bull market of three years' duration distinguished for at least two spectacular reactions. Conditions are peculiar, and some strength of the railroad stocks may fairly be ascribed to the fact that the average dividend yield of twenty stocks more than carries the bull position in a money market notably easy for the time of year. That is always a good bull argument, although it has been out-weighed often enough in the past for the good old reason that easy money, in itself, proves nothing. Expanding industrial demand might stiffen the money market, and yet be a strong bull argument on stocks, even where they did not carry themselves on the dividend yield. Bankers might have more money to lend than they cared about at a time when public confidence was shaken, and industrial activity was contracting. There is no great amount of security in a proposition which so obviously cuts both ways. There is clearly a large bull account open, financed with no difficulty at all, which nevertheless may be suspected of desiring distribution. Such bear arguments as exist may be described as latent. What the market seems to need is more light, and the averages rather distinctly indicate caution on the imperfect diagnosis.

The Wall Street Journal: April 23, 1927

A STUDY IN THE PRICE MOVEMENT

At the close of the stock market on April 21 the Industrial average made a new high point for the present bull market, and for all time, at 166.66, just passing the high of 166.64 made August 14, 1926. On well tested methods of reading the Dow-Jones averages this confirmation of the new high points which have been made right along by the twenty Railroad stocks is aggressively bullish in spite of the unusual duration of the upward Major movement.

The bull market, in fact, may be said to have started in October, 1923, after one of the shortest major bear movements of record. Exactly as figures that would have sounded impossible, for the Industrials at least, before the war have been reached, so the reactions, the secondary movement of the Dow theory, have been severe, notably that one which developed in the spring of 1926. The idea that because prices are high they cannot go higher is a false assumption which has been disproved repeatedly, to the discomfiture of speculators who sold short, really because they were not in sympathy with the bullish sentiment prevailing at the time. Prices are high, although the Railroads are still some points below the figure recorded as far back as 1902.

A strong case might be made for assuming that the Industrials had already given the bullish signal more than a month ago, because there had been two large deductions for stock adjustments, by General Motors and Woolworth, and but for the coincidence of these special distributions coming off at a critical moment the Industrial average would then have confirmed that of the Railroads. Nevertheless the custom has been, in more than a quarter of a centruy's reading of the averages on Dow's well-known theory, to regard such deductions as identical with a decline in the market. The reasoning is good and seems compelling.

After all, we cannot eat our cake and have it. We cannot take value off one or more of the stocks in the averages to distribute it among stockholders, in one form or another, without leaving the stock worth that much less. This matter has been found to adjust itself over a long period of years, and if once we start making exceptions we impugn the veracity of our barometer. Nevertheless the point is worth considering in a discussion like this, even if it now becomes automatically more academic than it was.

There is an inference to be drawn from the re-emphasized bullish condition. The barometer is saying that there is fair weather ahead for the business of the country. It is long experience that the market, representing the aggregate of all that everybody knows, is months ahead of any possible business tabulation or chart. The averages will register the top in good time, and when they turn downward we shall be informed, as usual, that Wall Street is "the only blue spot in the country." In the meantime the averages are saying that business is likely to maintain its volume and character for as many months ahead as the most efficient trade telescopes can see.

BARRON'S: May 30, 1927

A GLANCE AT THE AVERAGES

It is worth noting that the Dow-Jones averages have run true to form, almost continuously, since *The Wall Street Journal* published its "Study in the Price Movement" April 23, reprinted in these columns. The industrials average was then read as confirming the bull point given by the railroad stocks, and the assumption, on all precedents, was that the market was due for further advance. At the time of writing this has extended to over five points in the industrial group. There is no method by which the stock market barometer can be made to indicate the extent of such an advance. Minor reactions from day to day are of no value. A secondary reaction followed by a recovery, not extending to the old high, has significance, essentially when the two averages confirm each other, and the cautious observer would be on the watch for the useful and usually dependable warning of a double top. Some general considerations are worth a moment's notice in a time of easy money. That condition is sometimes deceptive, if only for the reason that all signs fail in dry weather.

It was assumed in the price-movement discussion here alluded to that much of the buying on the advance had actually been for investment, if only because stocks may still be said to carry themselves on their dividend yield at the low rate for money. In this connection it may be roughly said that there are two kinds of investment, permanent and tentative.

If stock is taken out of Wall Street, as it undoubtedly has been, thereby lightening the volume of Stock Exchange brokers' loans and modifying their importance, they may easily be carried in bank loans all over the country, forming good liquid collateral to any banker with more money than he knows how to use profitably. The danger of this is that if an accumulation of unfavorable conditions caused a check in public confidence, the first place where it would be felt would be the stock market. The stock held out of town would come back on the market in a hurry and the protective break in prices might well be severe, even if some of the selling looked as if it might be for a bear account. When the holder of stock on which he has been borrowing in San Francisco gives an order to sell over the wire, he cannot make his delivery good for four days, during which time the broker must borrow the stock. This gives a deceptive impression of a vulnerable bear account. The technical position is becoming interesting and may be much more so in the next few months.

The Wall Street Journal: July 15, 1927

A STUDY IN THE PRICE MOVEMENT

Discussing the Dow-Jones averages of stock market prices as the barometer of the market movement, and also, on past experience, an admirable guide to the general business of the country, it was pointed out on April 23 that the Railroad and Industrial averages had foretold a further advance in the long bull market, initiated in October, 1923. The averages ran true to form, and both groups advanced a further six points or so.

There was a subsequent decline of five points in twenty Industrials and about the same in the twenty Railroad stocks, culminating June 27th. This was a typical reaction, the secondary movement in a major bull market, and was equally true to form with the previous advance. After that decline the market was inclined to mark time for a few days but soon developed strength and not merely recovered the secondary reaction but made new high points in both averages, within a day of each other. The indication, therefore, is strongly bullish on all previous experience.

If the averages had recovered most of the secondary decline from May 31 and June 1 respectively, but had not reached the old high figures and had developed another reaction, the familiar indication of "double tops" would have been clearly given and might, upon previous experience, have marked the end of one of the longest bull markets on record, with a duration now not far short of four years.

As both averages went through the old tops, it seems clear that the floating supply of stocks has been absorbed at these levels, that realizing for holders who have been carrying their stock elsewhere has been sucessfully handled by a new set of buyers and that the technical position, therefore, is bullish with a prospect of higher levels before realizing, in any quantity, is stimulated. What the market is saying is that, as far ahead as everybody can see and the stock market can reflect, the prospect for business is good. The market would seem to have discounted unfavorable conditions like that produced by the floods, some congestion in new bond issues and a disappointing outlook for one of the most important crops, corn.

Of course no tree ever grows to the sky, but it is nevertheless, true that the market discounts everything but the completely unexpected. It does not profess to be able to foresee the San Francisco earthquake, or an incident like the Northern Pacific corner, and opinions differ as to whether the Great War was foreseen, and to some extent discounted, in the long bear market before its actual outbreak.

At any rate the barometer is now pointing to fair weather ahead.

BARRON'S: August 15, 1927

INFERENCES ON THE AVERAGES

It is noteworthy that when the stock market makes a sharp reaction from a very high level during a long advance there is always some specific reason to appeal to the popular imagination, not unusually a front-page newspaper reason. Since recording the spectacular advance, which was foreshadowed in these columns in the last "Study in the Price Movement," the stock market has experienced a typical and almost violent secondary reaction, based ostensibly on the uncertain political outlook. It is good experience that a change of direction, or an interruption of the major movement, has usually other explanations, to supplement at least the one which appeals to the popular fancy. To put it in another way, the advance in stocks had grown somewhat reckless, and any one of several things might have constituted the last straw. Against this it is true, as *The Wall Street Journal* pointed out the other day, that the market in a broad advance protects itself by a reaction to what might be called safety levels when it cannot see its way.

Just as the Mississippi floods and other specific unfavorable developments were ignored in a rising market, so it might very well be that Wall Street would have paid small attention to Mr. Coolidge's qualified withdrawal from the Presidential race if the condition disclosed by the stock averages had been on a sounder basis. The public tends to jump at conclusions, and frequent inquiries are received as to whether the present reaction marks the inauguration of a bear market or is merely a secondary movement. The answer is that on the well-known method of reading the stock market barometer nothing but a typical secondary movement in a major bull market has yet been indicated. It has been seen that a higher levels secondary movements are more severe than they were in the earlier history of the averages, with the two exceptions of the breaks which occurred on the Northern Pacific corner in 1901 and the San Francisco earthquake in 1906.

The market, therefore, might develop various familiar movements. The secondary reaction might carry much further, even on the precedent of last year. The market might make a line of accumulation or distribution, as the case might be, the averages might recover to a point near the old high and break again. This last movement would have considerable significance, as it would involve "double tops" in a bull market where stocks held for the rise have been financed all over the country.

The Wall Street Journal: October 4, 1927

A STUDY IN THE PRICE MOVEMENT

Reading the Dow-Jones averages in the manner formulated a quarter of a century ago by the late Charles H. Dow, the indication is plainly bullish. It has been demonstrated by long experience that when the twenty Industrials and the twenty Railroads, after a secondary reaction, make new high points for the major movement a further advance of the whole market is indicated. This by no means involves simultaneous action by the two averages, but each must confirm the other.

It is several weeks since the Industrials made a new high point after a secondary reaction. It was not until last Saturday that the Railroad stocks confirmed the other average. Indeed, if they had failed to confirm it and a new secondary reaction had set in, the indication would have been definitely bearish and rather pointing to a change in the major movement. It would have amounted, in effect and practice, to what is known to students of the price movement as a double top.

Such an indication can occur at the end of a bear market as well as at the top of a great bull market. In the autumn of 1921 one of the averages, after an unusually prolonged market decline which had lasted for approximately two years, made a new low point which was not confirmed by the other average. It really marked the turn of the market and an upward movement set in which has only been interrupted by the unusually brief major bear movement of 1923. There is no such complexity in the market now. The confirmatory action of the twenty Railroads, in crossing the old high point of August 2, may be said to regularize the stock market barometer.

All this is irrespective of the fact that stock prices are relatively very high and have now been advancing for a full four years. Beyond offering the somewhat trite reflection that no tree grows to the sky, there is no need to moralize about it. The stock market is saying, in so many words, that the business outlook is good and likely to continue so for as far ahead as general information can calculate, assuming that Wall Street is the reservoir of all that everybody knows about everything connected with business. The assumption is fully justified and that is why the stock market averages reflect so much more than any individual can possibly know or the wealthiest combination can manipulate.

What is worth bearing in mind is that at these high levels, secondary reactions tend to be much more severe than they were when the average prices were at half the present figure. In the present major bull movement there have been at least two reactions, of a true secondary character, which in extent were almost as considerable as actual major bear movements.

BARRON'S March 5, 1928

THE PRICE MOVEMENT

Speaking with considerable caution, it may be said that the stock market averages look rather bearish so far as the major movement is concerned. On January 3 the industrials made a new high of 203.35. Instead of receiving confirmation from a new high by the 20 railroads, the double top in the latter case has bearish implications. The October high of 144.82 was not regained after a ten-point rally to 143.44, and the indication therefore became adverse, suggesting that the major movement, which has lasted appreciably more than four years, one of the longest major movements recorded in the Dow-Jones averages, may have culminated.

While the failure of one of the groups to follow the other to a new high or low is strongly suggestive of a change of major trend, as has been pointed out in these studies, it is not until both averages fail to make new highs or lows that the forecast of a change of trend can be made with full confidence.

Although there has been some action at times on the downward side, the reaction has been gradual but distinct and well marked, representing at the time of writing some ten points, more or less, in both averages. It has often been said in discussions of the price movement that duration is never indicated by the

stock market barometer. Bear markets, even of a mild and humane character as the present movement promises to be, are much shorter than major upward movements. There is not the material in general business conditions for a smashing decline like that which set in late in 1919.

What seems to be indicated is a season of uncertainty marked by protective selling, mostly of a profit-taking character, by those who bought their stocks far below the present level, or by disappointed traders finding a failure to respond to aggressive action on the bull side. The condition is somewhat characteristic of a Presidential year, following at least a reduction in business profits and an uncertainty, partly political and partly industrial. Fundamental values are not affected, nor is there the slightest idea of intimating here that people should sell sound investments merely because of superficial price changes not dictated by any real decline in earning power, or deterioration in management. Such a market might well mark time at a level not tremendously below the old high points, waiting at least for the Presidential nominations, and perhaps also for the effect of such nominations on public sentiment. Wall Street is surprisingly sound in its political forecast. About the only time it has been wrong in thirty years was when it believed that Hughes would be elected in 1916. Everybody remembers how close the result was and that on pluralities Woodrow Wilson remained a minority President.

There is no need for a general discussion of business conditions here, and it need only be said that the averages reflect an uncertainty which business might increasingly show for the next few months.

BARRON'S: May 14, 1928

THE PRICE MOVEMENT

On April 27 the twenty railroad stocks in the Dow-Jones average at last confirmed a spectacular advance in the twenty industrials by recording a higher figure at 145.16 than the 144.82 which constituted the previous high of October 1927. On the Dow theory of reading the averages this is a strong and definite bull point indicating that the bull market, which has now been in operation for more than four and a half years, has not finished its course. The parallel to October, 1927, is clear, as anyone who files his copies of Barron's can see in the study of "The Price Movement" published in these notes on Oct. 10, 1927, when the high of the year and the movement in the railroad averages had been recorded.

Since that high figure the railroads have sold as low as 132.60 less than three months ago, rallying substantially but not to the old high. In fact, it looked as if that average would have made double tops, indicating a denial of the industrial advance and constituting at least a warning, if not a bearish indication. Not long ago it was necessary to point out this evidence of caution, particularly as prices are higher than they were ever before, and these notes are of course not committed to either side of the market. The barometer is running true to form, as many inquirers may now feel themselves assured. The bull point of April 27 was confirmed in subsequent action of the market, both in the railroads and in the industrials.

All sorts of reasons are offered for the great strength of the stock market, the outstanding one being the enormous supply of credit as evidenced in the brokers' loans and the relatively easy rates in the call money market. One indication of the stock market barometer may well be kept in mind, because in the past it has proved a dependable guide to the business of the country. If the stock market is strong today, it is a justifiable inference, on all past experience, that the business of the country will show marked expansion in a few months' time, after some contraction and even some unemployment. It may fairly be said that money is plentiful in Wall Street because resources are not fully taken up elsewhere. A larger use for floating capital in the early fall seems probable, even if the speculation in stocks simultaneously tends to contract. It need hardly be said that the barometer does not pretend to forecast the duration of that period of expansion.

BARRON'S: June 25, 1928

THE PRICE MOVEMENT

If Charles H. Dow were alive today—he died in November, 1902—the condition of the stock market as shown in the Dow-Jones averages, and as read by his own method, would make him decidedly thoughtful after a bull market which may be said to have been inaugurated in October, 1923, and showed its high points in May-June, 1928. When the industrials on May 14 sold at 220.88 they made a new high, following a corresponding figure of 147.65 for the railroads on May 9. By May 22 the industrials reacted nine points to 211.73 and the railroads 5.63 points to 142.02. This was a typical secondary reaction in a major bull market.

But on June 2 the industrials had made a new high of 220.96, which was, however, not confirmed by a corresponding recovery in the railroads. Dow always ignored a movement of one average which was not confirmed by the other, and experience since his death has shown the wisdom of that method of checking the reading of the averages. His theory was that a downward movement of secondary, and perhaps ultimately primary, importance was established when the new lows for both averages were under the low points of the preceding reaction. It is important to observe what has happened during the current month.

On June 12 the railroads were nearly thirteen points below their high of May 9 and the industrials at 202.65 had lost more than eighteen points from the unconfirmed high of June 2. There was a short and sharp rally, where, in two days, on June 14 the industrials had recovered eight points of their decline and the railroads less than three points. Observe again the poor support the railroads gave the industrials on the recovery. In the subsequent reaction both averages made a new low as of June 18 of 134.15 and 201.96, respectively. Dow would have called this distinctly bearish.

Early in 1926 the market had a substantial secondary reaction. It was said in these studies at that time that if this developed into a major bear movement it would be the mildest and most humane on record. It proved to be no more than a secondary reaction, and the great advance in the market has been since that time, including the greatest activity stocks have ever shown. But counting from June 18 the industrials would need to recover more than 19 points and the railroads 13½ points in order to re-establish the old bull market. The student of the averages may draw his own conclusions.

BARRON'S: July 30, 1928

MANIPULATING THE AVERAGES

A reader of *BARRON'S* and *The Wall Street Journal,* himself the manager of the Richmond branch office of an important brokerage house, suggests that the Dow, Jones averages have been misleading since the beginning of the year by reason of pool manipulation. He says that the pool managers know the great importance which is attached to the indications given by the averages and that they have been able to manipulate advances, especially in the industrial group, sufficient to make the record misleading. The theory sounds plausible, but will not hold water.

It is no light matter to manipulate both averages, and the indications of one without the other are generally disregarded. But in order to concentrate financial strength on so large an operation, the manipulator must relinquish his hold upon other stocks in a market where over seven hundred have been active at different times. He cannot hold up the whole list. The selling of stocks outside the twenty in the industrial average, or a sufficient number of the twenty to affect the average price materially, would bring selling all round, and the first stocks affected would be those which the pool was trying to manipulate for higher prices.

Again, it could hardly be charged that the averages have really been misleading. The high of the averages for the year was reported June 2 for the industrials and May 9 for the railroads. On the June date the rails made a substantial recovery, but failed to reach the May high. The warning was then given at least to the extent of casting doubt on the strength shown in the industrials. An analysis of the price movement was made in these columns on June 25 after both averages had shown significant secondary reactions with only partial rallies, and it was there pointed out that on Dow's theory a distinct warning was given which no one could afford to ignore after a major bull market which had then lasted more than four and a half years. Indeed, the indication was so clear that it may fairly be said to have justified the growing confidence in the stock market barometer. Its indications are most closely followed, and the temptations to manipulate are obviously great. It is only necessary to point out that this would be just possible if one of the averages was close to a critical point and could be pushed over to confirm an indication already given by the other.

BARRON'S: August 27, 1928

STUDY IN THE PRICE MOVEMENT

After the twenty industrial stocks in the Dow-Jones averages had touched what was then the high of the year on June 2 at 220.96, they had a serious reaction which carried them down to 201.96 or 19 points. There was a simultaneous decline in the railroad stocks. Since then the railroads have made something of a line midway between the last high and the low point of that secondary recession. The industrials made what can only be called a spectacular recovery, establishing a new high for the year and for all time. Readers, therefore, ask what are the present indications of the averages in the light of the discussion of them in these columns on June 25?

There is one fairly safe rule about reading the averages, even if it is a negative one. This is that half an indication is not necessarily better than no indication at all. The two averages must confirm each other to carry the authority which has been found so dependable in the barometer since its practical study was developed from Charles H. Dow's theories, set out in editorials of The Wall Street Journal twenty-seven years ago. Taken alone, the new high of the industrials is not a bull point on the market. The indication would become strongly bullish if the railroads advanced from their present level to a figure above the old high of 147.65, which, at the time of writing, would mean an average advance of some six points or so.

Such a change would show that the market had experienced a strong secondary reaction in what would still be a major bull market which has been in active force since October, 1923. If, on the other hand, the railroad stocks failed to respond to the strength of the industrials and the latter reacted only moderately, the half indication would be canceled and the secondary reaction would still be in force. At no time since the June high points were recorded has there been a condition where it could be definitely said that a major bear market was indicated. Warnings were given in June, and the bear point preceding the secondary reaction was a strong one. Such fluctuations were to be expected in the uncertainties of a Presidential year and perhaps in a money market which had not been allowed to take its natural course. The next definite indication in the averages should be given by the railroad stocks. An increase in the volume of trading might have considerable significance at this time.

The Wall Street Journal: September 11, 1928

DOW-JONES AVERAGES FIGURED ON NEW BASIS

CHANGE IN METHOD OF COMPILATION ELIMINATES DISTORTIONS RESULTING FROM MULTIPLICATION OF INDIVIDUAL STOCKS.

Beginning with Monday, September 10, the Dow-Jones average of 20 industrial stocks is being computed upon a new basis which eliminates the occasional distortions resulting from multiplying individual stocks, and at the same time preserves the 31-year sequence of the averages.

In the past it has been the practice to compensate for stock split-ups and stock dividends of 100% or greater, by multiplying the split-up stocks. American Can, for example, was multiplied by six after the split-up in 1926, while General Electric and Sears, Roebuck were both multiplied by four after their respective split-ups. Although this method reflected the relative fluctuations of the averages accurately for a short time, and at the same time preserved the sequence of the averages, it eventually caused distortions, as, for example, when one of the multiplied stocks moved counter to the general market trend. On the other hand, the old practice of making no compensation for stock dividends of less than 100% sometimes caused a serious break in the sequence, as, for example, after the 40% General Motors stock dividend.

The new method of compilation is based upon a simple mathematical expedient. Instead of dividing the total of the 20 stocks and their multiples by 20, the total of the 20 stocks without any multiples will be divided by 12.7. This constant divisor is arrived at on the basis of last Saturday's closing prices, and is merely a figure which gives the same average on the new basis as on the old basis on the day before the new method is put into effect. The total of the 20 stocks on the old basis (including American Can multiplied by 6, American Car & Foundry by 2, American Tobacco A by 2, General Electric by 4 and Sears-Roebuck by 4) was 4,-822.375 on Saturday, which total, divided by 20, gave the Dow-Jones average of 241.11. The total of the 20 stocks without any multiples was 3,060.5. Dividing the latter total by 12.7 gives an average of 240.98, or approximately the same as on the old basis.

The constant divisor, 12.7, will be used daily and indefinitely until some stock in the list of 20 is split or reduced materially in price by a stock dividend. The constant divisor would also be changed if at any time it were decided to make a substitution on the list of 20 stocks now used in the averages.

For a week or two the averages will be computed on the old basis, as well as the new, in order to demonstrate that the new basis, does not destroy the historical sequence of the averages nor result in any marked change in their significance or interpretation.

The Wall Street Journal: October 2, 1928

WHAT IS THE MARKET SAYING?

There is always a meaning in what the stock market says even if human limitations make it difficult, and for a time impossible, to tabulate all the evidence of which it is the expression. The market is significant both for what it says and for its silences. Great general interest is being taken in the presidential election but the market says nothing about it, or, what really amounts to the same thing, takes the election of Hoover for granted. There has been curiously little betting this year, but the odds have been steady at more than two to one against Smith.

Not every market sign is favorable as students will readily recognize. For two years past the stock market has tended to contract in the activity of stocks following secondary reactions and to expand in the number of popular issues when those reactions are recovered and new high in a long bull market are made. In the Industrial group, which monopolizes so much of the trading, it might be said that the front of advance is more widespread and therefore conceivably vulnerable.

But representing all that everybody knows about the business of the United States and possible foreign inferences, the confidence shown is undeniable. The market is saying that the results of the crop year are known and are highly satisfactory from the point of view of values, if not in some cases of prices. There is a reflection of a decrease in unemployment and a better extension of industrial activity in spite of the somewhat mixed money situation. It may have been noticed that there has been a reduction in commercial failures indicating an absence of soft spots.

No one expects that every concern in the country will be equally prosperous at the same time. For the broad purposes of the country's business it is sufficient that the textile industry, for instance, shall show a sounder condition. Perhaps the country does not quite know where it stands in the matter of building and Wall Street is watching that condition closely. Easy money stimulated speculative building, financed by so-called building bonds which were really to a large extent debentures on hoped-for earnings.

That was not altogether a wholesome condition and it seems to have caused some rather unprofitable production of building materials with a scaling of profits leading to unsatisfactory results. Here again the credit situation has manifestly been able to take care of itself and it may well be that the market is looking to that large release of credit which follows the moving of the crops.

Altogether the barometrical indications are fair. Indeed if it were the intention of certain of the Democratic stump speakers to get Wall Street rattled, the campaign has been amusingly barren of results.

The Wall Street Journal: October 29, 1928

CONTINGENCIES

In a rising stock market the advance on the average may be a point or more for days together and the move is taken for granted. No one telephones The Wall Street Journal to ask why the Industrial stocks have advanced two points. But in a major bull market which has now lasted for five years, with notably few secondary reactions, a five point decline in a single day from a price above 250 will keep the telephones busy with startled inquiries for explanations.

There is something not without a glimmer of humor in Friday's reaction because it synchronized the relating on the part of the Federal Reserve Board which is now permitting, and encouraging, banks to carry on the business of banking by lending money. An experienced trader would draw a curious inference from this by a sort of parallel. He would infer that some pool had unloaded and that stocks were relatively in weaker hands. Government institutions like the Federal Reserve Bank are usually wise after the event.

All kinds of reasons, bullish and bearish, might be drawn from the general business situation. If the stock market has any barometrical value it has been saying that we may expect a brisk and even booming condition of general business for some months to come. How long that improvement would continue cannot be inferred but a major bull market tends to react some months before general business contracts. Unless it be in the stock market there is no important sign of inflation anywhere. Probably the holding company device for public utilities has been much overworked and perhaps the speculative builder is beginning to have troubles of his own. These are not dangerous items and are sufficiently well known.

Certainly the prices of grain and cotton are not inflated while commodity prices do not indicate that any large inventories are being carried unless by the manufacturer himself. Retail trade is good and distress from unemployment is virtually absent. Railroad gross revenue shows improvement, as it should at this time of year in view of the crop movement. Searching the situation through it seems difficult to find anything more bearish than the tight money market, which however has had a damaging influence at this time of year on more than one occasion in times past. Perhaps a source of uneasiness is that the money market can be so stiff in face of the wonderful stabilizer we believed we had created in the Federal Reserve System. It was really assumed, almost throughout the long stock market rise, that money had ceased to be a factor and that even the moving of the crops did not stiffen credit as it so frequently had in times past.

Probably the stock market itself is its own best explanation.

BARRON'S: November 19, 1928

THE PRICE MOVEMENT

The vitality of the Hoover bull market received an interesting endorsement on November 10 when the Dow-Jones railroad average reached a new high record at 148.29, surpassing by .64 of a point the previous high mark of 147.65 established on May 9, 1928.

As the Dow-Jones industrial average had already vigorously entered new high ground on November 5, this confirmation from the action of the rails under the well known theory formulated by Charles H. Dow indicates that the fundamental bullish character of the present record-breaking stock market may be expected to continue for an indefinite further period.

During the past six months the industrial average has several times gone into new high ground without the railroad average following suit. This prolonged hesitation on the part of the rails naturally suggested the possibility that the broadest bull movement of history might be approaching the distribution stage.

Now, with the railroad average in new high ground, the stock market barometer has indicated emphatically that the fundamental character of the market is still bullish.

This indication in no way controverts the ever-present possibility of a substantial technical reaction whose severity might well have relation to the rapidity of the recent advance.

The Wall Street Journal: December 8, 1928

A SENSE OF PROPORTION

When the stock market has advanced to heights undreamed, over a period of more than four years, showing individual advances measurable in the hundreds with an average advance of over two hundred points in the Industrials of the Dow-Jones average and seventy points in the Railroads, a decline, on a weighted average of ten points in a single day may not be so formidable as it looks. Such a decline is equivalent to no more than two points at an average price of 60 although the weighting of the Industrial average makes a difference.

With this premise it can still be said that Thursday's break in the stock market conveyed a warning. It says much for its intrinsic strength that the market did not get out of hand even with a large public margin account open. Traders have grown used to wide fluctuations even if for a time they have all been one way. For the sensible observer the comment would be not that the decline was severe but rather that it should have been so long delayed. Everybody speculates nowadays and it is matter of many years' experience that everybody's judgment is not so good as somebody's.

There is obviously, and has been for some time past, an enormous amount of money in the country available for speculation, even irrespective of the New York call money market. We are still in a period of high prosperity, perhaps somewhat unevenly distributed, and with high wages considerably more general. It is sometimes claimed, on entirely insufficient evidence, that this represents what the worker would in the old unregenerate days have spent upon liquor. But high wages must have been greatly influenced by immigration restriction, keeping down the supply of labor, and mass production largely based upon individual efficiency. In an economic sense wages are not high relatively to per capita production.

It may be that the rich are growing richer, as the Socialists say, but it is certain that they are not growing richer at the expense of the poor, or of those with relatively modest means. The average income compares favorably with the true cost of living. This is highly important as a factor in manufacturing prosperity because our domestic markets are largely based upon the consumer of moderate means. The Wall Street millionaire does not buy radio sets, furniture or even motor cars on the instalment plan.

But admitting all this latent strength in the general situation it was time to call a halt in speculative activities because of their unsettling effect when they have extended out of Wall Street into every considerable town or city in the country. The people who have been active in the stock market, pyramiding their speculative position in the usual way, are for the most part those with affairs of their own which should not be neglected or minimized. It is not everybody who is built for successful speculation but it takes a check in a great bull market to disclose that important fact.

There is nothing said here on the barometrical indication of the averages because it is altogether too soon to draw useful inferences.

The Wall Street Journal: December 12, 1928

AVERAGE PRICES

Subscribers recently, and not improperly, have asked to be satisfied of the validity of the Dow-Jones average. Are the thirty Industrial stocks sufficient to reflect the character of the entire market? It is a fair question because there are nowadays many active stocks and the advance in the average should be reflected in the general list. It is encouraging to say that in the recent sensational advance, and also in the precipitous decline of Thursday, Friday and Saturday of last week, the general list confirmed the average.

From 238.14 on October 2 to 290.80 on December 1 the Industrial average advanced 52.66 points or 22 per cent. During that time the aggregate money value of three hundred stocks advanced 21 per cent. There is a striking confirmation here which can hardly be called fortuitous. The answer to students of the averages, therefore, is that they demonstrably constitute a dependable barometer. The change to a weighted average instead of the older and simpler method of dividing the total of 20 stocks by exactly that number seems to have worked well, showing a valuable gain in the matter of accuracy.

If the old method had been pursued the parallel with the whole market would not have been so close. The top of the average would not have been as high as it proved under the modern method and the decline would not have looked so formidable. The drop of December 6, 7 and 8 would have been 8½ per cent. under the old method while it was 11½ per cent. under the new. The latter more closely represented the whole market. The decline was most severe but it must be remembered that the averages had advanced to figures which would have seemed wildly impossible even as late as last year when a major bull market had been in operation for three years.

For many years, as the records show, such a price as 60 for the Industrials might constitute the top of a bull market. A decline of 10 points from a figure close on thirty would be therefore equivalent to a decline of 2 points at 60. Even a decline of 7 points from that figure in three days trading, the equivalent of last week's break, would be nothing to panic about.

Nevertheless to the trader who is pyramiding at the top the recorded reaction is a serious matter. Every experienced Wall Street trader knows that the operator who has been on the right side of the market, getting in and out but increasing his commitments from his profits over an advance of 100 points, does not need a decline of anything like that extent to leave him worse off than when he started. He is usually found pyramiding at the top and a relatively small decline wipes him out. Many conservative authorities have said that the break in the market was overdue and that a sharp check to public speculation would have considerable moral and material advantages.

Perhaps the best lesson to be drawn from the market movement is that it disclosed nothing in the business situation which could be truthfully called unsound.

BARRON'S: December 31, 1928

THE PRICE MOVEMENT

After a three-day decline of unusual severity, the Dow-Jones averages rallied and have now established a condition which is both suggestive and instructive. The first recovery from what can still be called only a secondary reaction in a major bull market was about 40% of the drop, notably so in the industrials. This is strictly according to precedent, and there is a practical reason why such a recovery occurs.

In a severe break there are some accounts which cannot be liquidated, for one reason or another, and these are protected. Such stock is usually sold on the ensuing rally, and a valuable test of the market is so provided. If the returning appetite of the speculator is equal to taking this stock and asking for more, a condition of considerable underlying strength is clearly indicated.

In the present illustration the prices backed and filled for a few days after the break and then developed definite further strength. This is decidedly bullish, as indicating new speculators for the rise to replace those who were shaken out. Moreover, the industrial average has already advanced 1⅝ points beyond the previous high of 295.62, and the railroad average has recovered to within 2½ points of the previous high of 152.70. If the rails follow the industrials into new high ground, this would give a definite bull point of assurance against a change in the major trend. There have been other declines as sudden and extensive as the recent break, as for instance, the Northern Pacific panic of 1901, which, however, only checked the main current of a bull market. That particular major movement continued for eighteen months after the panic, and did not culminate until towards the end of 1902.

The Wall Street Journal: January 1, 1929

HOPE

How many of the reviews of 1928 and the forecasts of 1929, or how much of any of them does a newspaper subscriber read? They constitute our hardy annual, a supplement to the daily newspaper well padded with advertising. As a rule the reviews are better than the forecasts and before the new year is a week old the forecasts are forgotten. They remain in the minds of the people who make them perhaps setting up a bias in the direction of making them come true, willy nilly.

What is the basis of all these forecasts, conceding that the ordinary means of information can be usefully tabulated? The acting principle behind the tabulations is hope. Everybody desires that prosperity should continue and increase. A note of caution is the invariable anchor to windward but the forecasts are virtually unanimous. Pessimism is not good for circulation. The advertiser desires to see expanding business with an increased purchasing power. We are a childish people; we like to be told what we want to believe.

But are these forecasts really as searching as they sound? After laboring over a number of them one curious thought emerges and perhaps only in one case it is recognized distinctly by the forecaster. This is that nobody takes a long view. Colonel Leonard Ayres of Cleveland, speaking in November, definitely declined to commit himself to more than the first quarter of the new year. The unprecedented stock market has plainly upset the calculations of conservative people. Probably it has not changed in principle, but modern practice is bewildering.

In October, 1902, the late John W. Gates and his flamboyant following said that 25 per cent. call money and even 100 per cent. call money, were matters of no consequence; that "the game was being played with blue chips" and that people who could not stand the pace or the price were not obliged to sit in. Gates and his son Charlie, and Drake and Leeds and the rest of them thought they had the market by the tail and could swing it accordingly. They had it by the tail but they could not let go. The facts proved too much for them and by the first week in December they had all been shaken out. Trading was re-established, so to speak, on a white chip basis.

There could be no better evidence that the stock market is really a barometer of business than the great bull market, which has now lasted over five years. The very extension of the speculation to cities all over the continent is evidence of the enormous increase in purchasing power. Developments on such an extraordinary scale has been unequal in the very nature of things, exactly as some stocks have advanced more than others and some have scarcely advanced at all. The stock market is saying that business will be better before it is worse. It is not indicating dates. Its longest view in forecast is seldom more than six months but is sometimes much shorter as students of conditions in 1907 probably know.

Lord Beaconsfield once described remarriage as the triumph of hope over experience. Perhaps that term might be applied to the stock market.

BARRON'S: January 7, 1929

THE PRICE MOVEMENT

In a study of the price movement published in these notes no longer ago than December 31 it was said that the industrial averages had made a new high and that confirmation by the railroad stocks would give clear evidence of complete resumption of the major bull market. The twenty active railroads in the Dow-Jones average established the new high point on the first trading day of the new year. It is seldom that an inference from the stock market barometer is so quickly verified. The intrinsic strength of the market is most remarkable.

Less than a month ago the averages, and especially the industrials, suffered a startling break, completed in three days. The normal recovery following the completion of urgent liquidation was about 40% of the decline, which, curiously enough, is exactly the ratio observed by the late Charles H. Dow thirty years ago. That was the test of what could still be called merely a secondary reaction in a major bull market, but still one with threatening possibilities. The check, for it was no more than that,

was caused by the distribution of stock which had been held over the break but still remained to be liquidated.

Everything turned upon the appetite of new purchasers. If this had been insufficient and the averages had advanced to somewhere near the old highs, but had not crossed them and then had begun to work downwards, the indication would have been bearish, and might have foreshadowed even a definite change in the major trend. Nothing of the kind occurred, however. There was surprisingly little hesitation, and the strength over the end of the year was most noticeable. Here was another test, as some of this stock was no doubt carried over in order to avoid establishing realized profits which would be subject to income tax and surtax in the returns for 1928.

But the realizing after the turn of the new year, which would have been entirely normal and had probably been expected by the professional traders, did not materialize. The clear inference now is that there is still large buying power behind the market. The barometer predicts fair weather and further advances.

The Wall Street Journal: April 5, 1929

A TEST OF VALUES

A reader suggests that a chart, consisting of the Dow-Jones averages of 30 Industrials and 20 Railroads, together with a line of dividend return for a representative number of years back and also a line based upon earning capacity, should be presented in these pages. No doubt something of the kind would be useful, although its construction is by no means so simple as this student seems to suppose. The real earnings would be modified and confused by the splitting of stock and the declaration of stock dividends, to name only two difficulties which would arise.

So far as the line of dividends is concerned there would be no great difficulty, allowing that the fiscal year is not the same in every case. About all that could be shown would be the annual change and the result would be a line on the chart notably different from that caused by the daily fluctuation in the average prices. Nevertheless the dividend line might well be more useful than the weighted average of estimated earnings.

It would seem as if a reader could construct it for himself with no great difficulty, especially if he had the chart of the Dow-Jones averages, occasionally published in The Wall Street Journal, on his desk. He could make a rough calculation of the prices at the beginning or end of such a month as March in this and preceding years. He could divide the dividend total for the stocks in the average into the added prices of the stocks themselves. If, for instance, he found that stocks on the average were selling at 22 times their dividend return in 1929, 17 times in 1928, 11 times in 1927 and barely six times in 1924, when the great bull market had been under way for only six months, he could at least infer that prices today tended to outrun values.

That is about what he would find and it recalls a simple explanation offered in Hamilton's "Stock-Market Barometer," It was there said that at the beginning of a major bull movement stocks are clearly selling well below the line of values as a consequence of the forced liquidation in a previous bear market. The tendency with returning confidence is to advance towards the line of values which is also rising, as a general rule. This is the secondary stage of a major bull movement and the last stage is that in which stocks are selling above the line of values and people are buying not on present yields but on future possibilities.

Here then is a sensible and conservative way of approaching the study of the present bull market, in spite of short but sharp recessions, has prevailed since October, 1923, following a major decline of rather over eight months. The student should ask himself if stocks are not selling well above the line of values, if people are not buying upon hope which may be at least deferred long enough to make both the heart and the pocketbook sick.

No opinion on the market is here advanced. The design is to let the reader form his own opinion in a sensible way.

BARRON'S: May 20, 1929

THE PRICE MOVEMENT

While it has not been the custom in these notes to discuss the price move-ment, as shown by the old barometer, the Dow-Jones stock market averages, unless there had been a definite change in trend of special significance, the demand for enlightenment on that point is so general that some discussion of the present position is in order. It may be said at once that there has been no indisputable reversal of a major upward trend, which has been in force since October, 1923. Indeed, in the recent past, on May 4, the thirty industrial stocks made a new high point for all time.

It is also conservative to say that a fluctuation of even ten points in a day in an average price of over 300 is not equivalent to more than a third of that fluctuation if the average price were 100. To put it in another way, we may fairly expect wider fluctuations at the higher levels, and we should not give them any exaggerated significance, but rather regard them in terms of a percentage of price. From January 22 there were thirteen fluctuations, four noteworthy ones in February, with an average extent of sixteen points.

This may well be a most significant series, coming as it does at the top of so long a movement, one of considerably more than five years, and it is worth noting in this connection that while the industrials made their new high on May 4, the railroads on May 14 were nearly eleven points below the high of February 2, when the railroads confirmed the bull point given by the industrials. There is no need to dogmatize about the position now set up, nor is it possible to say anything positive beyond recalling that neither singly nor taken together have the averages predicted a change in major direction.

What the industrials have shown is an increasing vulnerability for a secondary movement, and, as secondary movements sometimes develop into major swings, there is a suggestion of caution which students of the averages should not ignore. An advance of eleven points in the railroads would be definitely bullish as a barometrical indication, even if the industrials only marked time while it was in progress, because they have not taken back the high of 327.08 recorded on May 4.

The Wall Street Journal: May 21, 1929

SELF REGULATING

In a study of the price movement in the current number of Barron's, as registered by the Dow-Jones averages, it is pointed out that in a period of less than four months the 30 Industrial stocks have had thirteen fluctuations up and down, averaging 16 points. It may be pointed out that at a price well over 300 a ten-point fluctuation, even in a single day, is about as important as the fluctuation of a single point with an average price of 30. Nevertheless the fluctuation itself is absolute and at any price means the same thing to a trader on margin.

Here it will be seen by anybody, except certain people in Washington who are willing to regulate even what they do not understand, that the stock market is self-regulating. The volume of trading is not nearly so heavy as it was before the short swings of the pendulum developed. The market itself has thinned out the mob of speculators who imagined that Wall Street was the Tom Tiddler's ground of the children's story, where everybody was picking up gold and silver. A 16-point fluctuation has an astonishingly sobering effect upon such people.

It will be noticed also that coincidentally with this the more spectacular fluctuations of the call money market tend to subside. Money can hardly be called cheap, but the call money market is obviously in a more normal condition. It would be a thoroughly wholesome thing, and one tending to steady the barometer of business, if the Federal Reserve Board conceded an advance in the rate of the second Reserve district. The Board itself will have to expand credits some time not later than August, if only to take care of the crop movement. If only the members of the Board were also bankers, in the real sense of the word, the wisdom of taking time by the forelock would be too obvious to need suggestion.

This is not to say that the great bull market in stocks, which definitely started in October, 1923, is over. The sharp and frequent fluctuations seem rather to indicate that speculators are groping for direction and are by no means all of one mind. Everything that everybody knows about anything with even a remote bearing on finance finds its way into Wall Street, in the form of information; the stock market itself, in its fluctuations, represents the sifted value of all this knowledge. What the market is saying may sound like a platitude, but it amounts to the statement that much can be said on both sides.

There is no attempt to forecast in this discussion, but it is necessary once more to emphasize what amateurs in finance, including many prominent politicians, fail to understand, namely that the stock market, even in its wildest moments, is a great deal safer than it looks. Whatever the call money rate may be for twenty-four hours, the call loan itself is easily the safest a bank can make. There is an absolute choice of collateral and the margin is anything a lender chooses to ask.

Nobody who is paying rent and other office expenses desires a dull market. But a short spell of dullness might be an excellent thing if it persuaded people to talk about something else than stocks.

BARRON'S: July 1, 1929

THE PRICE MOVEMENT

When the Dow-Jones averages were last discussed in these columns, in the issue of May 20, it was pointed out that thirteen fluctuations since the beginning of the year to that date, averaging sixteen points, did not convey any necessarily bearish implication, although the unusual development inspired caution in the study of the price movement. At that time the railroad average was eleven points below the last high, and it failed to confirm, therefore, the new high point in the industrials.

Both averages have now made the highest recorded figures in their history, the railroads having recovered all their leeway. It need hardly be said that on accepted and well established rules of reading the stock market barometer this is a definitely bullish indication, carrying the implication that the great bull market which has now ruled for four months short of six years had resumed its upward movement, with each average confirming the other. The position indeed is technically one of peculiar strength, as a little analysis shows.

It will be clearly seen that the sharp

and extended fluctuations, especially in the industrial average, have amounted in effect to a distributive period not at all dissimilar to that which has occurred at lower levels when the averages have made a "line." Such a line indicated either accumulation or distribution, and the movement out of it in either direction has historically carried marked significance. At these high levels a much wider range of fluctuation in a distribution period is only to be expected. The advance of both averages above that area is a clear indication that a large quantity of stock has not only been distributed but effectively absorbed, presumably by investors or those who can finance their purchases by taking the stock off the market.

It only remains to be said, therefore, that the new high points are definitely and strongly bullish, indicating a clear resumption of the major movement.

eight months, is almost necessarily in the third or latest stage of such a movement, where stocks do not carry themselves on the dividend return, for the most part, and where sanguine expectations of the future exercise a greater influence than immediate results. All that the averages say when they give such a bull point as that of June 29 is that stocks are due for a further advance. They do not predict the extent of the advance.

One feature of the long major movement upwards has been that the business of the country has built up under the strength in the stock market and justified the advances. It has been uniform experience that strength in stocks has forecast improvement in business, and it may fairly be said that the market throughout has offered innumerable illustrations of hopeful anticipations fulfilled.

BARRON'S: July 8, 1929

A CONSISTENT STOCK MARKET

A better instance of a stock market running true to fundamental principles than that of Monday, July 1, could hardly be offered. On the previous Saturday the Dow-Jones averages had confirmed each other in new high points, giving the well-tested barometrical indication of a resumption of the major bull movement. Call money went to 15% on Monday, but, in spite of this, the 30 industrial stocks in the Dow-Jones averages advanced 1.43 and the twenty railroads 1.95, each making new high records.

It would seem that with the adjournment of Congress the agitation about the call-money market in New York has subsided. It was a useful point for politicians of a sort, but, like all issues which are either artificial or popularly misunderstood, it lost its driving power. This is not to say that with the crop-moving period well in sight we are to run into an era of easy money. It is merely evidence that the call-money market is relative to the general business of the country, and that the public, which really matters, has recovered its sense of proportion.

It goes without saying that the stock market, which has advanced with merely secondary reactions for five years and

BARRON'S: July 29, 1929

A LOGICAL BAROMETER

It is all very well to say that the stock market is not logical in its movements from day to day, but over any considerable period of time it respects the logic of events in a way the business of the country does not, except when it is too late. When the price of wheat at Chicago was making a further spectacular advance of 7½ cents a bushel, the stock market on the same day had a strong reaction, the industrials declining 4.50 points and the railroads 2.00 points.

It was argued by people who had bought on the strength of the previous Saturday that the market for wheat was speculative, and the interest of bulls of wheat was easily comparable to that of the bulls of stocks. Nothing could be further from the truth, because wheat has been advancing on a probable crop shortage, both here and in Canada, which would more than wipe out the embarrassing surplus which caused panic prices when Congress was in session. A short crop of wheat may mean money in the pocket of the speculator in that grain, but it means serious loss to business in important connections.

A short wheat crop means lower earnings for the railroads and a disappointing year for those farmers whose crops have been a comparative or absolute failure. Consumptive power and buying power is reduced in many directions, and is not compensated by the mere advance in the price of wheat. Something is added to the cost of living, while nothing is produced, to compensate for the advance, in some other direction. A total crop failure might be a wonderful thing for the few farmers with exceptional luck, but would be anything but a bull argument on the business of the country.

This is what the stock market calls the logic of events. It is true that the strong bull point given by the barometer of the averages has not been taken back. But the stock market demonstrates once more that it looks ahead, and that only its surface is ruffled by temporary influences.

THE PRICE MOVEMENT

Those who follow the stock market barometer as shown in the Dow-Jones averages frequently err in expecting too much. The barometer does not give indications every day and all the time; according to Charles H. Dow's theory, an indication remains in force until it is canceled by another, or re-enforced in some way, as, for instance, when the industrial average confirms the railroad average or vice versa.

Dow never contemplated an average which would have been much above par, and even when he died in November, 1902, there were scarcely a dozen industrial stocks sufficiently active every day to make a first-rate indicator. For a time Western Union was actually included in that imperfect and almost tentative list. As everybody knows, the number of industrials has been expanded to 30 with no real difficulty in selection.

It follows that with an industrial average above 300 a wider flexibility is to be expected, although the principles upon which Dow reasoned are undisturbed. In his time an average would make what he called a "line," with a fluctuation up or down confined for weeks at a time within a three-point range. It was good experience, although not invariable, that when the average advanced above the line or declined below it the supply of stocks in the market, or the scarcity of them as the case

might be, indicated a change of level to a more attractive or a more conservative point.

But at the present high level of the industrials a wider range for this area of distribution or accumulation may be safely assumed. The last point given by the barometer was strongly bullish. It was confirmed by the subsequent action of the market. But since the last high, made Sept. 3, there have been fluctuations of two, three, five and even 10 points, which are, of course, less than a third as significant as they would have seemed 25 years ago. In both averages at present the market seems to be "finding itself." Conceivably, its next move may be dictated by the floating supply of undistributed investment trust stock.

THE PRICE MOVEMENT

There is an interesting development in the price movement as shown by the two Dow-Jones averages since the industrial high of 381.17 on September 3, and the railroad high of 189.11 on the same date. In a month, or down to October 4, the industrials had declined 56 points, and the railroads, which have normally a much smaller range of fluctuation, had lost over 20 points from the high of the year.

Of course, 56 points represents a severe secondary decline in what has been a bull market for six years, remembering always that we are dealing in very high figures. Even then, with the industrial average in the neighborhood of 80, the equivalent would be an 11-point decline. Does the movement of the market indicate a little more than this? In the successive rallies it will be noticed that the first brought the industrials back to 372.39, the second to 355.95 and the third, on October 10, to 352.86, or each one lower than the last.

On Charles H. Dow's method of construing the barometrical indication, that would be a distinctly bearish warning, not indicating necessarily a change in the main market trend, but calling particular attention to the importance of future movements. If, for instance, the next rally carried the industrials above 352.86 and the railroads above 178.53, the bearish indication would have been to some extent taken back.

If, however, the market broke again, after a failure to pass the old highs, and the decline carried the price of the industrials below 325.17 and the railroads below 168.26, the bearish indication would be strong, and might well represent something more than a secondary reaction, however severe. It has often been said in these studies of the price movement that the barometer never indicates duration. There was a genuine major bear market in 1923, but it lasted only eight months. One good reason for not taking the present indications too seriously is that they have all been recorded in a most unusually short space of time. The severest reaction from the high point of the year had just one month's duration. In view of the nationwide character of the speculation, this seems a dangerously short period to infer anything like complete reversal in public sentiment.

The Wall Street Journal: October 25, 1929

A TURN IN THE TIDE

On the late Charles H. Dow's well known method of reading the stock market movement from the Dow-Jones averages, the twenty railroad stocks on Wednesday, October 23 confirmed a bearish indication given by the industrials two days before. Together the averages gave the signal for a bear market in stocks after a major bull market with the unprecedented duration of almost six years. It is noteworthy that Barron's and the Dow-Jones NEWS service on October 21 pointed out the significance of the industrial signal, given subsequent confirmation by the railroad average. The comment was as follows:

"If, however, the market broke again, after a failure to pass the old highs, and the decline carried the price of the industrials below 325.17 and the railroads below 168.26, the bearish indication would be strong, and might well represent something more than a secondary reaction, however severe. It has often been said in these studies of the price movement that the barometer never indicates duration. There was a genuine major bear market in 1923, but it lasted only eight months. One good reason for not taking the present indications too

seriously is that they have all been recorded in a most unusually short space of time. The severest reaction from the high point of the year had just one month's duration. In view of the nationwide character of the speculation, this seems a dangerously short period to infer anything like complete reversal in public sentiment."

There was a striking consistency about the market movement since the high figure of September 3. There were at least four rallies in the course of the decline in the industrials before the definite new low point was established and each of these was weaker than the last. Dow always considered this a danger signal, but for the past thirty years it has been the custom in discussing the stock market as a barometer of business to require that one average should confirm the other. Failure to agree has been found deceptive.

There are people trading in Wall Street, and many all over the country who have never seen a real bear market, as for instance, that which began in October, 1919, and lasted for two years, or that from 1912 to 1914 which predicted the Great War if the world had then been able to interpret the signs. What is more material is that the stock market does forecast the general business of the country. The big bull market was confirmed by six years of prosperity and if the stock market takes the other direction there will be contraction in business later, although on present indications only in moderate volume.

Some time ago it was said in a *Wall Street Journal* editorial that if the stock market was compelled to deflate, as politicians seemed so earnestly to wish they would shortly after experience a deflation elsewhere which would be much less to their liking.

The Wall Street Journal: October 26, 1929

So far as the barometer of the Dow-Jones average is concerned it has been clear since last Wednesday (October 23) that the major movement of the market has turned downwards. The market will find itself, for Wall Street does its own liquidation and always with a remarkable absence of anything like financial catastrophe. Beyond indicating the trend there is no idea here of prediction.

Conditions do not seem to foreshadow anything more formidable than an arrest of stock activity and business prosperity like that in 1923.

Suggestions that the wiping out of paper profits will reduce the country's real purchasing power seem rather far-fetched.

BARRON'S: November 18, 1929

THE PRICE MOVEMENT

A Canadian reader who is a student of the averages of stock market prices and the method of reading them as devised by Charles H. Dow has compiled some data to show from the figures of the original 20 industrial stocks that a bear market checks at about 42% of the previous high of the bull market. It was one of those nice appreciative letters which any editorial writer loves to receive, and might have made fairly good copy but for the fact that the break in the industrial stocks of Monday, November 11, knocked the theory over the fence.

In making a new low of 220.39, on November 11 the industrials confirmed the new low of the railroads made November 6, of 145.49. It did not need a further decline in the railroads on November 13 to 128.07 to emphasize the bearish indication of the averages. When that indication was first noted in these columns, in an editorial reprinted from *The Wall Street Journal,* the industrials had given a bear point more than 100 points higher than the average price at the time this is written.

It might well be thought that a decline from 381.17 to 148.69 in the industrials and from 189.11 to 128.07 in the railroads would represent all the deflation the most over-confident bull market could ever need. But the market is a law to itself, establishing its own precedents and accepting no others. It is saying that the liquidation is not completed; that it will carry further with the daily movements probably of decreasing range, as the pendulum comes to rest after the violent oscillations of the recent past. At least those who look for a resumption of the old bull market may be assured that there is not a single indication in the averages that the decline is over.

It should never be forgotten, however, that the averages do not predict the duration of a movement or the possibilities of any given stock. If the market is no longer in the condition that stocks with a good market have to be sold to protect those with no market, a stock with special qualities may easily advance against the general current. It need hardly be said that nothing of that kind is discussed here.

The Wall Street Journal: December 3, 1929

COMING TO REST

After the violent price movements in the Stock Exchange it is altogether in the nature of things, and in accord with past experience, that the swings of the pendulum should become shorter, with a resting and waiting market for such length of time as becomes necessary to measure the various influences which govern future movements. Some line on such possibilities may be had from a glance at what really happened.

On the first break in the market, which carried the industrial stocks in the average down some fifty points from the high of over 381, general newspapers found that "bankers were buying in support"; but after a half-hearted rally the industrial average declined another 130 points, reaching a figure well under 200.

It can be said now, and it was said in these columns at the time, that the topheavy market broke of its own accord. It was not smashed by foreign selling, for all the possible foreign stock to come out could hardly have amounted to two per cent. of the fifty million shares which came upon the market in four trading days. The Governing Committee of the Stock Exchange has not discovered any malicious short selling directed to breaking the great bull market.

Such short selling as there was could be easily explained by the orders of out-of-town holders of stock in boxes on the Pacific Coast and elsewhere, or pledged in local banks, which, of course, involved borrowing in the loan crowd for the two to five days interval until actual delivery could be made. A bear position would have been a support to the market, but these apparent short sales certainly were not. Floor traders, no doubt, sold short and it is equally certain that none of them went home without evening up his book on the day.

There is some uniformity about the extent of the decline in a major bear market and this one, at the worst, measured approximately 44 per cent. of the industrial average. This is fairly constant in the past thirty-three years and would indicate a thorough liquidation, although people assuming that the old bull market is to be resumed at once merely demonstrate that the wish is father to the thought.

Technically the position is sound and reassuring, and that should content those who have the best interests of Wall Street at heart.

The Wall Street Journal: December 10, 1929

WILLIAM PETER HAMILTON

The passing of Willam Peter Hamilton, for more than a score of years editor of *The Wall Street Journal,* leaves a wide vacancy in the journalism of a continent. It leaves a painful void in the hearts of those whose good fortune it had been to work with or under him, to know and feel the man's rare courage and singleness of purpose. Too few men are able as he was to hold a serene and vital confidence in right courses through the strain of the working day, or to turn a keenly and justly critical mind to the uses of warm personal friendship.

Few among American newspaper men have brought to their reportorial or editorial tasks an experience so ripe and varied, superimposed upon a mind so well fitted by natural gifts for accurate observation. Mr. Hamilton, however, was never content to be only a recorder of what he saw. For him there was always the hidden meaning, more valuable to the world than the bare fact;

always the logical relation of the event to what had gone before; always the background of human aspiration and human failing to illuminate what might otherwise be obscure or meaningless. His literary style derived both color and authority from the richness of his mental and spiritual resources.

Mr. Hamilton's editorials were widely read and there is abundant evidence that time and again they exerted a positive and practical influence. Their appeals to thinking men and women may perhaps be attributed in large part to the facility with which he brushed nonessentials aside and went straight to the heart of a question. This power accounted also for his mastery of condensation; he could say so much in so little space. But this was no mere trick of the pen—it was part of his innate character to think with directness and to speak with candor, wasting no time upon trivial compromises with passing modes of thought. His unusual intellectual vigor, moreover, was suffused and softened by a delicately appreciative humor which frequently gave unexpected and delightful turns to his spoken and written thought.

Born an Englishman, Mr. Hamilton retained through his life the love of England and the English ways his countrymen always have, but he possessed an understanding of the American scene that often surprised and enlightened his associates of American birth. To New Yorkers his speech was that of one who might have just left Whitehall or Downing Street, but he related with enjoyment that his mother, on the occasion of his last visit to her, had said to him: "I hope, Will, that you will refrain from using that atrocious Yankee accent in my house."

His associates will remember of Mr. Hamilton, in addition to the influence of his genuineness and his gallant spirit, a cordial helpfulness in which he never spared himself.